Faithful to Fenway

FENWAY PARK
P 1 2 3 4 5 6 7 8 9 10 R H E
56 NY 0 0 0
61 BOSTON 0 0 0
AT BAT - BALL - STRIKE OUT - H - E

FAITHFUL TO FENWAY

Believing in Boston, Baseball, and America's Most Beloved Ballpark

Michael Ian Borer

New York University Press

New York and London

NEW YORK UNIVERSITY PRESS
New York and London
www.nyupress.org

LIBRARY OF CONGRESS CATALOGING-IN-PUBLICATION DATA

Borer, Michael Ian.
Faithful to Fenway : believing in Boston, baseball, and America's most
beloved ballpark / Michael Ian Borer.
    p. cm.
Includes bibliographical references and index.
ISBN-13: 978-0-8147-9976-5 (cloth : alk. paper)
ISBN-10: 0-8147-9976-0 (cloth : alk. paper)
ISBN-13: 978-0-8147-9977-2 (pbk. : alk. paper)
ISBN-10: 0-8147-9977-9 (pbk. : alk. paper)
1. Fenway Park (Boston, Mass.) 2. Baseball—Social aspects—Massachusetts—Boston.
3. Boston Red Sox (Baseball team) I. Title.
GV867.64.B67   2008
796.357'640974461—dc22
          2007043282

New York University Press books are printed on acid-free paper,
and their binding materials are chosen for strength and durability.

Manufactured in the United States of America
c 10 9 8 7 6 5 4 3 2 1
p 10 9 8 7 6 5 4 3 2 1

CONTENTS

This Book
Donated by

ACKNOWLEDGMENTS

Studying the ways that people make sense of the world is impossible to do alone. We might assume that writing is a solitary act that we do sitting alone in our offices late at night, staring at our computers, spending too much time scratching our heads. But no one ever writes alone. We are social beings, even when we're by ourselves. Not only are the words we use somebody else's; most of our thoughts are too. Regardless of whether we're writing a novel, a poem, or a sociological study, there's always an audience. And when you're writing your first book, which is how this project was conceived, that audience holds a particular and somewhat daunting level of importance. My academic mentors provided a complicated mixture of leadership and evaluation, guidance and judgment. They are certainly a rare mix of academics who are not only challenging and tough, but kind as well.

This project would not have been possible without the guidance and red ink from my adviser, Daniel Monti. He pushed me to ask the question behind the question (and answer it) and not be afraid to take myself less seriously and draw outside the lines. Though John Stone spent a good deal of time trying to convince me that I should give up this baseball thing and study a real sport like cricket, he also spent a lot of time talking to me about this project. Our talks about sociological theory provided me with a strong base to compare and judge my interpretations and theories about civic culture and urban life. Nancy Ammerman's willingness to approach Fenway Park as a sacred site endeared me to her immediately after I first told her about the project. I am thankful for the questions she asked me, the suggestions she made, and the references she thought were crucial for my analysis and interpretations; they all improved the quality of the work. As an anthropologist who has studied the civic culture of the United States as well as issues of authenticity, identity, and charisma, Charles Lindholm offered important insights about uncovering the multiple ways that Fenway Park is consumed. I have admired Lyn Lofland's work throughout my graduate studies. I thank her not only for her academic contributions but also for her encouraging words as I began constructing a way of understanding the cultural importance of places.

Other faculty members of Boston University's Department of Sociology who provided me with guidance, discussion, and occasionally Red Sox tickets, include Jeff Coulter, David Swartz, Emily Barman, and Pat Rieker. My colleagues at Dartmouth College were always eager and excited to talk with me about my project, especially during the Red Sox championship run in October 2004. I'm grateful for my office and the key they gave me so I could stay there until the early hours of too many mornings. I thank Deborah King, Kathryn Lively, John Campbell, Denise Anthony, and Kim Albanese for their encouragement during the later stages of writing. Special thanks go to the Women in Leadership group at Dartmouth College's Rockefeller Center for Public Policy and the Social Sciences.

Leaving New England and moving to Greenville, South Carolina, to teach at Furman University provided a little needed distance from both the subject matter and from the anxieties of dissertationitis that infected earlier drafts. My colleagues in the Sociology Department and throughout the campus provided me with positive feedback and encouragement as I revised the manuscript. Special thanks go to deans Tom Kazee and Linda Bartlett, who provided some additional funding to help complete the book. The project became important locally because a mini–Fenway Park was built in the spring of 2006 to support the Red Sox Single A ballclub, the Greenville Drive.

Without the help of Dick Bresciani, the Red Sox vice president and club historian, I wouldn't have been able to get the bat on the ball, so to speak. "Bresch" provided me with access to the ballpark—the stands, the executive offices, the clubhouse—and to former and current Red Sox players and personnel. I am indebted to him for his willingness to support this project without asking for anything in return. Thanks go to Larry Lucchino, Janet Marie Smith, Larry Cancro, Lou Gorman, Johnny Pesky, Carl Yastrzemski, Jim Lonborg, Mike Andrews, Dick Beradino, Trot Nixon, Ellis Burks, Johnny Damon, Jason Varitek, and other members of the Red Sox organization, as well as to Jim Healey of the Yawkey Foundation, for being a part of this study.

I thank Richard Johnson, curator of the Sports Museum of New England in Boston, who knows more about Boston sports history than anyone. Erika Tarlin provided me with an entire set of Save Fenway Park! newsletters dating from 1999 to 2006. Ed Berliner put me on television to talk about the ballpark, Bruce Wood interviewed me and wrote two articles about my work, and Robin Young let me speak on NPR about the wonders of Fenway Park and Red Sox Nation. Through those media appearances, I met people who contributed to the breadth and scope of this project.

This book benefited from the precision editing and thoughtful advice and support from Ilene Kalish of NYU Press. Ilene and her staff, including her assistant, Salwa Jabado, and the anonymous readers, helped make me more comfortable as I cut out paragraphs and sometimes full pages that I had become attached to but that surely would confuse, bore, or even annoy the reader. So, for both the reader's sanity and my own, I thank them greatly.

To all my friends who attended baseball games at Fenway Park, as well as at other ballparks, I apologize for using you as test bunnies for my new ideas about this project. But, hey, you got to see some baseball. Witnessing the reaction of friends like Kris Nelson and Andrea Ryan when they entered Fenway Park for the first time provided important glimpses into the wonderment and mystique of the ol' ballpark. Harry Tower deserves thanks for his support. I would have had a much harder time understanding the passion of the Fenway Faithful if I hadn't spent so much time as a teenager and as a young adult watching and talking baseball with my grandfather, David Borer, and my fellow Mets maniacs, Dan Smalheiser, Tim Luceno, and Jon Yanovsky. I would have had a much harder time understanding people if I hadn't spent so much time during graduate school talking with Thomas Nesbit.

Alan and Elizabeth Borer are two of the smartest and most generous people I know. Elizabeth's friendship and support exceeds the boundaries of her role as a wicked stepmother. I know my father is proud of me. That alone makes my hard work and late-night writing worth it. I only wish my mother could read it, not because she was a baseball fan but because I know she would be proud too.

INTRODUCTION
The Sociology of Green Monsters and Broken Curses

I don't know what'll happen if we win [the World Series]. I mean, if we break the Curse, well, then what? What'll we talk about then? Maybe they'll get rid of the team, maybe they'll get rid of Fenway? I don't mean to sound like I don't want to win, but, what'll that do to Boston? I mean, Sox fans don't know what it's like to win. It'll change everything.
> —Pat S., Red Sox fan (comments made a few days
> before the Red Sox won the 2004 World Series)

I love this place! Look how happy everyone is right now. It's crazy out here! I just hope nobody tries to rip down the Monster or something because they're so happy we broke that damn Curse.
> —Jon O., Red Sox fan (comments made the night
> the Red Sox won the 2004 World Series)

Even though my apartment was only a five-minute walk to the T and then a fifteen-minute ride to Fenway Park, we decided to jump in my car and drive down Beacon Street. We had to be prepared for what we might encounter in the next twenty minutes and didn't want to get stuck in the crowd that we knew would flood Kenmore Square. When we turned off the television and left my apartment, it was the top of the eighth inning and the Red Sox were leading the St. Louis Cardinals three to nothing in the fourth and what proved to be the final game of the 2004 World Series. Although the game was a long way away, in St. Louis, my childhood friend Dan had driven up the night before from New York in anticipation of a hoped-for win and the potential chaos that a World Series would unleash throughout the city. Even though I lived there, we were children of suburban New York, Boston wasn't our city, and the Red Sox weren't our team, though, like many Mets fans, we tended to root for the Red Sox simply out of a shared dislike for the Yankees. The magnetism of the situation, however, was powerful enough to draw Dan north to join me and thousands of others who expected to share a memory together, even before we experienced it.

We parked near the St. Mary's T stop, about a five-minute walk to Fenway but far enough away from the ballpark just in case the post-win celebration escalated to include cars being turned over and set ablaze. Previous celebrations in Boston in the weeks prior had set an uncomfortable precedent for such acts. But the fear of a loose-trigger-fingered police force launching smoke bombs, tear gas, or rubber bullets into masses of intoxicated Red Sox fans and drunken college kids was not high enough to keep us away from being a part of history.[1] Whose history and why that history matters, however, were two questions swirling in my head as we ran through the parking lot across from Fenway, with a radio in hand, listening, as the Red Sox took the field in the bottom of the ninth for the last time in 2004.

Not many people who saw the Red Sox win the 1918 World Series were living in the fall of 2004, but all Red Sox fans with a pulse felt the burden of an eighty-six-year wait on their shoulders. One week earlier, as the Red Sox came back against the Yankees in the 2004 American League Championship Series, winning four straight games after being down three games to none, the Fenway faithful in Boston and beyond had enjoyed feelings of happiness and relief mixed with high degrees of caution and pessimism. "Let's not get ahead of ourselves," warned their collective voice. "We haven't reached our goal yet. We still need to win the World Series." Much of this trepidation was because of the supposed Curse on the Red Sox. Arguably, without understanding this contemporary urban legend we cannot understand the gravity of that night for the Red Sox, the fans, and the city. As such, I'll briefly introduce the origins of the Curse and then show a few examples of the often eccentric, and sometimes comedic, ways Red Sox fans have tried to either exorcise or anticipate an exorcism of the Curse from Fenway Park.

The Red Sox have been tortured by the stature of the Yankees, who have won twenty-five championships since the Red Sox's last World Series victory in 1918. The success of those Red Sox lay on the shoulders of their star pitcher and future homerun marvel, George Herman "Babe" Ruth, a.k.a. the "Bambino." Much of the Red Sox's World Series woes have been credited to the Bambino and the hex he left on Boston when he swapped his red socks for pinstripes.

Ruth was sold to the Yankees on January 5, 1920, marking a moment in Boston history that reached epic proportions after *Boston Globe* sportswriter Dan Shaughnessy popularized the idea of the "Curse of the Bambino" in 1989. The so-called Curse captivated many Red Sox fans, even those who only believe in it purely for the sake of believing or, for that matter, denying accountability for the litany of heartbreaking defeats since the Bambino's departure from Boston and his arrival in the Bronx. Although there has been debate about the actual sequence of events that led to Red Sox owner Harry Frazee's sale of Ruth to the Yankees, for $100,000 and a $300,000 loan to pay off the mortgage on Fenway Park, the tragic second-place history of the Red Sox after 1918 is indisputable.[2] Even though that history is factual, it is steeped in mythology and superstition. After Boston's heartbreak was given a name, and more importantly a cause, it took on a life of its own and in some cases began to resemble the likeness of a fact.

The Curse was the type of narrative that parents reluctantly passed on to their children along with their first Sox cap, warning them in anticipation of the disappointment and distress that comes along with being a Red Sox fan. The idea of the Curse was so commanding and widespread that House representative Silvio Conte (R-MA) read the following into the *Congressional Record* on February 2, 1989:

> those of us in New England have experienced something perhaps more profound than victory, something that has toyed with our emotions, teasing us into a frustrated state of hope and tension that has only become bearable through years of numbing and the company of generations of fellow Red Sox fans. Yes, it is the "near victory" that truly tries men's souls. Red Sox fans have felt the ecstasy of victory in their grasps so many times, have had their fists clenched, waiting for the final out in heady anticipation, only to be put through the agony of another lost victory. It is a ritual that has been repeated many more times than a kinder and gentler God would ever allow.[3]

Conte's comments clearly show how the power of mythology and the allure of the Red Sox pervade, permeate, and pummel the symbolic boundaries between politics, religion, sports, and popular culture.

Believing in the reality of the Curse, Red Sox fans have gone to great lengths to reverse it and restore Boston's once-prominent winning ways. Though many attempts were made with a touch of humor and a bit of sarcasm, these acts were real nonetheless. Repeatedly since the early 1990s, the "Reverse Curve" sign that hung above the outbound lanes of Storrow Drive on the Longfellow Bridge was ritually spray-painted by devoted fans to read "Reverse the Curse." In 1992, a local radio station sponsored an exorcism conducted by Father Guido Sarducci, a character played by comedian Don Novello, at the corner of Ipswich and Van Ness streets in front of Fenway Park's Gate B. This was "the first exorcism of a baseball stadium ever in the history of ever," the good father told the crowd of over two hundred scarlet-and-blue-clad parishioners. Pictures of the Bambino were burned, a "virgin" wearing a plaid skirt was symbolically sacrificed, and red and white balloons were released into the air while fans in parked cars honked their horns in celebration.

In 2001, a thirty-seven-year-old Red Sox fan from Auburn, Massachusetts, reached the summit of Mount Everest carrying a Red Sox cap and a Yankees cap. Taking the advice of a Tibetan Buddhist lama, he devised a way to bury the Curse for good, or so he thought. He left the Red Sox cap attached to a flagpole buried deep into the snow, leaving it, literally, on top of the world (at 29,028 feet). And when he returned to his base camp, nearly 10,000 feet below the summit, he dowsed the Yankees cap in kerosene and lit it aflame.

Diane Dalpe and Daphne Weld Nichols performed "energy rituals" at the ballpark in both 2001 and 2003. The two Arlington, Massachusetts, residents used the principles of feng shui and reiki to channel positive energy into Fenway Park. Using bits of broken glass, sage, sweet grass, red candles, pictures of the Babe, rattles, bells, and a big pot fit for a witch's brew, they performed various rituals throughout the ballpark in order to help the ballpark's natural "chi" flow more freely.

With the permission of the state of Massachusetts, in 2002, a diving expedition was organized in Sudbury, Massachusetts, to retrieve a grand piano allegedly dumped into a pond by Babe Ruth when he left New England to play baseball for the Yankees. The group hoped to refurbish the piano and play it again, just as the Babe did in 1918, the last time the Red Sox won a World Series. "We're confident we can save it and play it again," said Kevin Kennedy, a member of the expedition. "The last person to play this piano was Babe Ruth. Who knows—it could end up at Fenway Park."

The Fenway faithful would have to wait until October 2004 to see, and feel, the supposed Curse lifted and their suffering redeemed. "This is the year" became a mantra echoed throughout Red Sox Nation at the start of each new baseball season, but 2004 proved to be "the year." Some claimed that they saw it coming. A little prophecy can go a long way for people whose distress and suffering is equally matched by their hope and faith. In September, a month before the Red Sox's championship run, two beer vendors at Fenway Park received what they interpreted as an irrefutable sign that the Curse was soon to be relinquished from the heart and soul of Boston and the rest of Red Sox Nation. Just before the Red Sox took the field to play the Texas Rangers, the vendors found a penny stuck to the corner of their Heineken and Miller beer stand. The penny was from 1918. And that day, Gabe Kapler and Johnny Damon were playing outfield for the Red Sox. Occasionally, they would stand next to each other. Their respective numbers: 19 and 18. 1918!

Although members of the Red Sox organization, from all levels, repeatedly told me, "We officially do not believe in the Curse," the mystique that it brought to the ballpark is undeniable. Curses or not, no one was quite prepared for the magic that emanated from Boston during the 2004 playoffs.

After winning four straight games against the Yankees, the Red Sox reached the World Series since 1986, when they had lost to the New York Mets after Mookie Wilson's careening groundball rolled through the legs of Sox first-baseman Bill Buckner in Game 6. The Red Sox took the loss, but Buckner took the blame for another generation's misery and torment. Buckner wasn't far from many fans' thoughts that night in October 2004. Many hoped that the lunar eclipse that glared above them would keep the ghosts of Buckner and, of course, the Bambino away from their beloved and often beleaguered Red Sox.[4]

Even though the fourth and final game of the series was played in St. Louis, hordes of hopeful fans flooded the streets around Fenway Park. Many stood with hand-held radios or with cell phones so they could talk to their friends and families as the game reached its desperately anticipated conclusion. With two outs in the bottom of the ninth, the Cardinals' Edgar Renteria (wearing number 3 on his jersey, just like

During the majority of the 2004 season, a billboard stood outside the ballpark with the Red Sox player David "Big Papi" Ortiz looming over Brookline Ave. demanding Red Sox fans to "Keep the Faith." (Photo by the author)

the Babe) hit a weak groundball back to Red Sox relief pitcher Keith Foulke. Foulke tossed the ball underhand to first base. Renteria was called out. The Red Sox win! The Red Sox win! And in that very moment the ballpark took on a new meaning, or at least a meaning that had not been connected to Fenway Park since 1918: Home of the World Series Champions.

The city screamed with pangs of joy.

Boston would never be the same again.

THE IMPORTANCE OF SHARING STORIES AND PLACES

When I began doing research for this project in 2001, I wanted to know what Fenway Park means for Boston and the people who revere the ballpark, are near it, or hope one day to sit in one of its wooden seats. At that time, the future of Fenway was a heated subject of debate in Boston that only those who tried could avoid. Fenway's future is more secure now than it was then, but the debate still continues, though it's less about knocking Fenway down and more about building Fenway up, and out. Either way, the meaning of Fenway Park remains an oft-discussed subject in and around Boston. Moreover, delving into the depths of Fenway Park's importance for the city and those who revere the ballpark provided me with a unique opportunity to explore the meaningful relationships between people and places.

Yet, although I began the project by questioning the loss of Fenway, I was able to witness the loss of something other than the ballpark. I witnessed the loss of one of Boston's most powerful cultural narratives: the Curse of the Bambino. But as we will see, it is the presence of Fenway Park, as a place to commune and tell such tall tales as the Curse, that made and will continue to make the Curse important, and not the other way around. According to anthropologist S. Elizabeth Bird, "local narratives are . . . about how people construct their sense of place and cultural identity. . . . [They] are not just about the site itself but about the particular concerns of the people who tell the legends."[5] In this case, the Curse wasn't about Fenway, but what happened at Fenway certainly affected the perceived validity and vitality of the Curse. Fenway Park outlived the beginning and ending of the Curse, providing a place where the narrative could be passed from one generation to the next, told and retold, believed in and broken. As such, members of the "community of believers" known as Red Sox Nation gathered near the ol' ballpark as the Curse was broken and put away as a relic of the past along with thousands of other local stories, dreams, and nightmares that constitute Boston folklore. Fenway Park survived the Curse and now stands as a reminder not of failure but of triumph.

The day after the Red Sox won the World Series was a truly strange and unique day in Boston. I went back to Fenway Park about twelve hours after the streets were filled with Red Sox revelers and riot police. Though Kenmore Square and the streets that encase the ballpark were far less populated than they had been the night before, there were now many people eating victory lunches and buying souvenirs. A few hundred people waited in line to enter the Souvenir Store on Yawkey Way to be one of the first people in eighty-six years to wear the words "Boston Red Sox" and "World Series Champions" on the same shirt. The line stretched down the street, around the corner, and continued several hundred feet down Brookline Avenue. The timing (the day after the Red Sox won the World Series) and the place (outside Fenway Park) added to the mystique of the sought-after treasures.

The Red Sox and slugger Manny Ramirez thanks the Fenway Faithful for believing in and supporting them throughout the team's eighty-six year championship drought. (Photo by the author)

The sun shone brightly above Fenway Park that day, causing some to speak of divine intervention. But the most striking evidence that things had changed in Boston from one day to the next was in the form of a billboard directly outside the ballpark on the corner of Brookline Avenue and Lansdowne Street. A billboard with a picture of Red Sox designated hitter David Ortiz with the slogan "Keep the Faith" across the top peered out at onlookers throughout most of the 2004 season and into the postseason. It was replaced sometime between the end of the celebration, which ended prematurely at about 1:30 a.m., and noon the next day. The new billboard showed a picture of Red Sox left-fielder Manny Ramirez with his arms stretched out in front of him and his fingers pointing outward. The sign simply read, "Thank You."

This exchange between the organization, the team, the ballpark, the city, and the fans is about something that transcends sports and transcends the individuals in the executive offices, on the field, in the stands, on the streets, and at home in front of the television or playing Wiffle ball in their backyards. In some ways, it was an exchange of ownership. By thanking their fans, the same fans who had kept their faith in the team, the city, and the ballpark, the Red Sox recognized that they were in possession of something that they did not, nor could not, fully own by themselves. What was being exchanged was not a material object or artifact. It was something much more symbolic and ethereal.

They were sharing a sense of belonging, a sense of place, and a sense of the sacred. And they shared it with the same people who had been sharing their time, money, and beliefs with the Red Sox for over a century. Fenway Park not only helped make that sharing possible. It helped make it important.

The ways that people make sense of the world they live in, once lived in, or hope to build are tied to cultural places like ballparks, museums, taverns, and soda shops. Many observers of contemporary American culture doubt that people appreciate such locations today. Such places are assumed to be either mere backdrops like movie sets or signs of Americans' forged and fabricated culture. We are told today that the American landscape is littered with historical façades and "theme parks" that are devoid of spirit or authenticity. These claims give rise to criticisms that American culture is superficial, depthless, fake, and full of kitsch.[6] But many of these claims come from those who stand at too far a distance from the places where people live, work, and play and who are too far away from the culture that people make for themselves in those places.

Newspaper clippings announcing the 2004 World Series win adorn the Copley T stop in Boston. (Photo courtesy of Julian Paul Keenan)

Regardless of the reality of the Curse, there is no doubt that Fenway Park is real, both physically and symbolically. You can put your hands on it, and it won't fall down. And, apparently, you can believe in its importance, and it won't go away. I spent a lot of time at Fenway trying to figure out what, why, and how a ballpark became and remains the most cherished shrine of a city and a community of believers. What I found was not only that Fenway Park was a place that people believed in but also that important places help make believing possible, and necessary.

THE ON-DECK CIRCLE

The ways that people use, act in, and act toward an important place like Fenway Park reveal some of the most skillful ways that people care about, and for, their culture. Through the use of multiple methods, I sought to uncover the logic of urban culture as it is manifested through persons' uses of, attachments to, and sacred reverence for Fenway Park.

Even though Fenway Park is the main subject of inquiry, it is merely the empirical case that I am using to discuss other issues about the ways people live in cities (and the ways cities still matter for those who live outside them). Moreover, I am interested in how people use places to make sense of the urban world they live in. The theoretical position that I adopted in order to recognize the multiple and diverse uses of the ol' ballpark is what I refer to as the *urban culturalist perspective.*[7] I "discovered" this perspective during the gathering of data through fieldwork and while trying to make sense of both expected and unexpected findings.

The places where we work, play, and sleep at night are culturally important. Common and historic places, including local diners, coffee shops, birthplaces of famous people, commemorative landmarks, emblematic streets and neighborhoods, sports facilities and other recreation spots, provide locals, newcomers, and visitors with a "sense of place."[8] The fact that people care about the loss of particular places shows at least one way that people make the city, or any area for that matter, less "strange," less anonymous, and less chaotic. How these attachments are fostered and what places are deemed as irreplaceable and immutable, and for what reasons and purposes, are crucial for maintaining and reconstructing cultures inside and outside cities. And they are crucial as subjects of inquiry for students of urbanism, civic life, and culture in general.

Whereas most sociologists begin with a social problem or phenomenon and then seek out places where that problem or phenomenon happens or happened, the urban culturalist perspective prompts the researcher to begin with a place and ask an open and inductive question: What happens or happened here? Starting from a place and *then* moving outward can yield important findings. Even though most sociologists take for granted the fact that culture happens somewhere, the examination of those somewheres can reveal important insights about the use of places as meaningful community "building blocks" and personal-identity markers. Groups and individuals use *shared* places for celebration, commemoration, dialogue, and protest.[9] Such places function as meaning holders that constitute "webs of significance" to be "suspended" by and to reflect on.[10] These places are more than simply grist for the cultural mill; they are, in actuality, where culture is empirically located.

There are six areas of research that urban culturalists have contributed to and continue to cultivate: (1) images and representations of the city; (2) urban community and civic culture; (3) place-based myths, narratives, and collective memories; (4) sentiment and meaning *of* and *for* places; (5) urban identities and lifestyles; and (6) interaction places and practices. These six domains, though overlapping somewhat, provide a comparative model for studying culture-place relationships in general, while allowing for distinctions between types of places and the people who use and inhabit them. The city and the smaller public and semipublic places that constitute it are both symbolic and material locales that, literally and figuratively, ground people in history and tradition and help them make sense of their world.

In what follows, I present a narrative about Fenway Park that begins with the rise of urban ballparks as important places steeped with meaning and mythology and ends with the realization that reverence, which itself is not a matter of pure consensus, does not guarantee the survival of such places, though it certainly helps.

The first chapter introduces Fenway Park as "America's Most Beloved Ballpark" and poses questions about the relationships that people have developed with and at the ballpark. Chapter 2 connects the development of professional baseball with the growth and rise of American cities and shows how beliefs behind both developments left an indelible mark on the urban environment in the form of the ballpark. The same motivations for building urban ballparks are still present at Fenway Park today and are linked to what has been called the "baseball creed." Chapter 3 shows how the ballpark remains important even when it is not in use as the home playing ground of the Boston Red Sox. A civic partnership exists between the city, the organization, and Fenway's patrons and onlookers that is mediated through various events and people at the ballpark. As such, Fenway Park is discussed as a place where civic culture is practiced and negotiated. Chapter 4 demonstrates another way that important places like Fenway Park are endowed with meaning and value, namely through the consumption of replicas, souvenirs, and other types of memorabilia. These "objects of devotion" and "articles of faith" are part of a feedback loop whereby they help enhance the meaning and importance of the original. Chapter 5 picks apart the different approaches to the debate about the future of Fenway and uses the debate to make an argument about the ways that people choose to construct, maintain, and/or reconstruct their culture through material products that express their way of life. Chapter 6, the concluding chapter, shows how the meanings of Fenway Park are not inherently fixed, but by using the urban culturalist perspective we can see how and why many people choose to make them appear permanent.

While trying to answer why Fenway Park is important, people I interviewed spoke in both personal and general terms with specificity and ambiguity. In the end, we can be sure that Fenway Park's importance has something to do with history and longevity. It has something to do with beliefs about leisure time. It has something to do with the ways that people use the ballpark for both private and public purposes. It has something to do with feelings of ownership of the place, even if only through buying or constructing replicas and souvenirs. It has something to do with the ways that people construct their own relationships to a place through personal experiences and collective memories. Taken together, these elements, along with others, constitute the complex connections that people foster with places. Throughout the pages that follow, let's not take for granted the attachments that people have to the places that help define them both individually and collectively. Rather, let's explore *what* makes a place important, *how* it becomes important, and *why* important places are necessary for the construction, maintenance, and reconstruction of urban cultures and communities.

So as they say at the beginning of each baseball game at Fenway Park and in every other ballpark, stadium, sandlot, and backyard: "Play ball!"

BOSTON BELIEVES
Fenway Park, a "Lyrical Little Bandbox"

At any time of the day when you're around that ballpark, it personifies the city. Fenway's worn at the edges like its occupants and fans. It's like the womb that Bostonians and New Englanders are birthed from; it's as if there's a piece of Fenway in them.
> —Ed Berliner, host and managing editor
> of CN8 Sports New England

May the Red Sox always play at Fenway Park, and may they win the World Series in my lifetime.
> —message written on a prayer book in an ancient temple in Tokyo

Fenway Park is short on comfort but long on character. It lacks the amenities of many of the newer sports stadiums. There is no Hard Rock Café (as at Toronto's Skydome), no swimming pool (as at Arizona's Chase Field), and definitely no sushi (which has become a fan favorite from Seattle to Baltimore). All Fenway Park has are cramped seats, poles that obstruct spectators' view of the game, a daunting big green wall in left field, a hand-operated scoreboard, and a slew of devoted patrons, pilgrims, and parishioners. It is an old-fashioned ballpark in an old-fashioned city. As the *Boston Globe*'s Dan Shaughnessy wrote, "There is nothing trendy or hip about Fenway. It is NPR in an MTV world."[1] And yet there is something about Fenway Park, with its feet

13

firmly planted in the past, that makes complete sense, even in today's newer-than-thou world.

Walking around the outside of Fenway Park, even during the off-season or when the Red Sox are out of town, you get the feeling that you are treading on sacred ground and that, simply by being there, you are a part of something special. Unlike most buildings in most cities, Fenway Park brings you into it, even if you're only observing it from the outside. You get the feeling that something has happened there and that "something" is significant. There is a certain but hard-to-define buzz emanating from the ballpark that demands onlookers to take notice of it and recognize it as a place that is important to the people of Boston who, since 1912, have invested not only time and money but meaning and value into it.

Fenway is nothing less than a national icon, and for many people it is Boston's most treasured local attraction and delicacy. Not only do people pack the ballpark on game days, but hordes of baseball fans also flock to the bars and restaurants that surround Fenway and flow into Kenmore Square, which is only a stone's throw away. Certainly they could watch the televised broadcast elsewhere, but they are drawn to or near the park even when the team is out of town. The closer you get to Fenway and, once inside, the closer you get to the lush green field, the closer you are to "history." Just by being there, you become part of a shared history of triumph and tragedy, heroes and villains, beer and hot dogs.

People from outside of Boston, from places well beyond commutable distances, regularly make pilgrimages to Fenway to pay homage to one of American culture's most cherished shrines. They take the tours, touch the Wall and the new seats on top of it, and try to remember the things that happened there that they only know about second-hand. They try to imagine players of yesterday, from stories that their grandfathers told or that they only vaguely recall themselves. Memories and stories are shared about childhood heroes hitting, running, making diving catches, or being carried off the field by excited fans after a victory the way Jim Lonborg was after he pitched the Red Sox into the playoffs on the last day of the regular season in 1967.

Lonborg himself still gets a bit red in the face with excitement when he talks about that day. He was so proud to have helped Boston take a giant leap toward the championship and share the celebration with local fans and the city, even though people stole articles of clothes, like his belt, while they hoisted him above their shoulders in a joyous frenzy.

"I never understood why they would want my belt," he told me. "I guess they were as overjoyed as I was. Probably even more so."

Today, so much of Fenway Park's appeal is about the past, the triumph of nostalgia perhaps. Despite the tragic second-place tradition of the Red Sox, which was upended in 2004 in dramatic fashion, Fenway Park is still standing because of the veneration believers continue to bestow on it. Although that reverence has not guaranteed Fenway's survival, it still plays a large role in the ballpark's longevity. As one of New England's greatest landmarks, Fenway still captures the hearts and imaginations of a deferential and devoted public. There are T-shirts, bumpers stickers, banners, and snow globes that honor the ballpark. Fenway shows up in popular films, novels, television commercials, and in replicated form in people's backyards and community recreation fields. Some people even have dogs and tattoos that bear the name "Fenway."

Perhaps John Updike captured the essence of the place best in a short essay about Boston legend Ted Williams's last game, one that far more than the six thousand or so who were in attendance that night claim to have seen in person. Updike's description was so apt that it is prominently displayed in green letters in the lobby of the Red Sox executive offices at Fenway. A portion of the passage reads,

> Fenway Park is a lyrical bandbox of a ballpark. Everything is painted green and seems in curiously sharp focus like the inside of an old fashioned Easter Egg. It was built in 1912 and rebuilt in 1934 and offers, as do most Boston artifacts, a compromise between man's Euclidean determinations and nature's beguiling irregularities.[2]

The compromise that Updike speaks of is the one between culture and nature, between the built environment and the virgin landscape, between America's rural past and its urban present. One of the marvels of urban ballparks is their ability to reconcile these differences, or at least to provide a place for us to do so.

Putting poetry and personal memoirs aside, this book takes a sober look at a place drunk with nostalgia, sentimentality, and superstition. My objective is to recognize the roles that Fenway Park plays in the city of Boston, and throughout New England and American culture in general, in order to understand the ways that physical places become anchors of meaning that help build symbolic communities and collective identities. That is, I am interested in the ways that people use places like

As Updike notes, everything, from the field, to the outfield walls, to the press box, and the metal limbs that block views and keep the ballpark standing, is painted green. (Photo by the author)

Fenway Park as cornerstones for understanding both cities and themselves. As such, I have attempted to document, interpret, and explain the vast array of ways that people use Fenway Park as a place of worship, reverence, community, antipathy, catharsis, and joy. How can this place, still standing after many attempts have been made to tear it down, hold such sacred and revered meanings to so many people? Where do those sacred values come from, and why are they important?

Part of the reason that Fenway Park is still in operation is because so many people, spanning three and four generations, have come to cherish its space through important shared experiences and through private ones as well. When we take a step back, we can see that even private experiences contain a lot of shared moments. That is, the commonalities between and across individuals' subjective experiences with and at Fenway Park give the meaning of Fenway Park an objective reality, a presence outside individuals' minds and heart. In other words, it becomes what Émile Durkheim, one of the founders of sociology, called a social fact.[3]

The lessons that we can learn from persons' relationships to and with Fenway Park can give us clues into the ways people use important shared places to understand and represent their city and themselves. Exploring the public life of Fenway Park can tell us a lot about what contemporary Americans believe in, why they believe, and how they believe. And we can see how important places like Fenway Park help make that believing possible.

Common and shared places are not only the settings for cultural legends, narratives, rituals, and ceremonies. Sometimes they become the main characters in the stories we tell about ourselves. The types of places that people adopt and adapt as place-based identity markers can range from the mundane, like a local department store, coffee shop, cafeteria, bar, or sidewalk, to the spectacular, legendary, or sacred, like Colonial Williamsburg, the Vietnam Veteran's Memorial, or Graceland.[4] People are drawn to those places where a culture's narratives not only are told but also play an important role in defining that town's or city's or nation's character and identity. They help remind community members not only who they are but *why* who they are is important.

Throughout this book, I addresses the cultural issues and contexts that have made, and continue to make, Fenway Park an important place and a continued subject of public discussion and debate in Boston and across the American cultural landscape. There are about as many opinions about Fenway Park as there are people who have sat in its wooden seats or dreamed of doing so one day. Those opinions remain of paramount importance because plans for tearing Fenway Park down and building a new ballpark have played a large role in its story since the mid-1990s. And with Yankee Stadium coming down in the Bronx, meeting the same fate as most of its now defunct early-twentieth-century cousins, some people believe that it is only a matter of time until a bulldozer runs the bases in Boston.

From the end of the 2003 season through the entirety of the now legendary 2004 season that ended with the Red Sox's first World Series championship since 1918, I spent a lot of time at Fenway Park. I roamed the surrounding streets before, during, and after games. I hung out on Yawkey Way and Landsdowne Street when the Red Sox were out of town just to see if Fenway could still draw people in without the team. It did.

I walked around the inside of the park, from the executive offices through the tunnel behind home and first and up to the standing-room-only section, where I conducted many on-the-fly interviews with cheering and jeering fans. I sat in the front row of the coveted Green Monster seats. Thirty feet above the field and only 310 feet away from home plate, they are among the best seats in baseball. Like so many others, I touched the Wall, even though signs told us not to. "It's the Green Monster" seemed like a strong enough argument for most people. I went up to the newly built right-field roof seats and was greeted by fans giddy about the Sox, the city's skyline behind them and the looming red Budweiser sign above their heads. One fan confessed that he never thought a Budweiser sign could be beautiful. Apparently this one was.

That fan was far from the only person who used words like "beautiful," "sacred," "mystical," "unique," "home," "intimate," and "authentic" to describe Fenway Park and its various nooks and crannies. For the "community of believers" known as Red Sox Nation, Fenway Park is revered as hallowed ground, where people come from both far and near to pay homage to the ghosts of the past and the heroes, and goats, of today. Former Red Sox pitcher Bill "Spaceman" Lee, known for spouting Eastern philosophy and sprinkling marijuana on his buckwheat pancakes, underscored that sentiment by declaring that "Fenway Park is a shrine where people come for religious rites." What that statement means, for the city of Boston and the people whose eyes are turned to Fenway, is important for recognizing that the "religious rites" that Lee refers to are about the faith and devotion of Fenway Park's deferential patrons. These rites, which serve to highlight ideas and beliefs about community membership, values, and ideals, are reenacted on a regular basis in special places, like Fenway Park, across American cities, where people are afforded multiple opportunities to negotiate their identities and celebrate themselves. These places provide bases for people to stand on, or slide into, and reach toward the sacred.

THE MOST BELOVED BALLPARK IN AMERICA

"You want to know what Fenway Park is? It's the beating heart of fucking Boston. You better believe it!"

"The 'beating heart' or the 'bleeding heart'?" I ask.

"Yeah, 'bleeding heart' works too. I mean, being a Red Sox fan has definitely taken years off my life. . . . Thankfully, Fenway Park's still there. You know, they were going to knock it down a few years ago. I just want to see 'em win it in Fenway. Could you imagine?"

—from my conversation with Tom S., Red Sox fan, Medford, Massachusetts

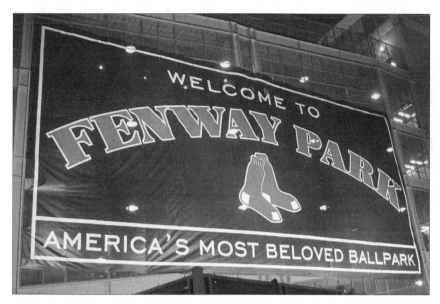

This enormous banner was placed along the side of the ballpark facing the corner of Van Ness Street and Yawkey Way during the last month of the 2004 season. (Photo by the author)

In late November 2004, the Red Sox still occupied the front page of the local newspapers despite the reality that the season had been over for more than a month and that the New England Patriots were in first place in the National Football League's Eastern Division with a 9–2 record. The Patriots actually ended up winning the Super Bowl that season, their second in three years. The joy from a Pats' Super Bowl victory pales in comparison to the pangs of ecstasy that had rung through New England, from Boston to Burlington to Bangor, when the Red Sox were crowned World Series Champions.

Minutes after the Patriots had won the Super Bowl in January 2004, many fans crowded the streets near Fenway Park. According to one postgame reveler, "All anyone was doing was pointing at Fenway and saying: 'The next one's there. The next one's there.' . . . It's just made us more hungry."[5] Even at the parade and celebration for the Patriots a few days later that culminated with a rally in downtown Boston with a reported 1.5 million in attendance, Red Sox fans could be heard howling their contentious war cry: "Yankees suck! Yankees suck!"

Mike Andrews, who played second base for the Sox from 1966 to 1970, reiterated a similar sentiment, not about the Yankees but about the position or status of the Red Sox in Boston and throughout New England: "With all do respect to the Patriots, Celtics, and Bruins . . . I'm totally convinced that this is Red Sox country. At its deepest roots, baseball is still the number-one sport of all of New England, and it is the Red Sox, and it is the Red Sox in Fenway Park." In early 2004, when the Patriots won their third Super Bowl in four years, a great achievement by any standard, it was merely a light appetizer to the hearty meal the Red Sox served Boston by winning their first Worlds Series since 1918 later that year.

Fenway Park is a place that connects individuals to one another, past and present. It is the site where Boston's civic rituals are practiced on a greater scale and at a greater frequency than any other institution in the city and throughout the New England region. There are few, if any, places where about thirty-five thousand people show up eighty times a year. But is this something that is unique to Fenway Park, to its idiosyncrasies and storied past, to its weathered red brick façade and looming Green Monster, that garners such appreciation? Or can the "Fenway experience" be transferred, so to speak, to another site if the wrecking ball has its way? More importantly, why does it matter at all?

Of course we could look at the grown men on the field, with their gloves and bats (and overflowing wallets), or the different kinds of people that fill the seats, with their Fenway Franks and peanuts, and say, "It's just a game." That might be the case in some other cities. But at Fenway Park and in Boston, where non-ticket holders stay glued to their television sets or have their radio dials steadied at 850 AM to listen to WEEI's play-by-play broadcast, it is a good deal more than that. As sportswriter Mike Barnicle once wrote, "Baseball isn't a life-and-death matter, but the Red Sox are."[6] When a million and half tickets are sold the first weekend they go on sale, it is a clear indication that something else is going on here.[7]

Sometimes a ballpark is more than just a place to watch baseball when there's nothing better to do. Sometimes it can be an important place, a symbol that signifies the culture of an entire city. Sometimes that symbol marks the identity of a city and the people who live, work, and play in it. And when that symbol is threatened, so too is the image and culture of the city.

At Fenway, Boston's culture is played with every time the ballpark is renovated or "improved," as the current ownership has dubbed each recent addition to the ballpark.[8] That culture is played with even more so when talk of removing Fenway and building a new ballpark makes its way into public discourse in the media, at local taverns, or across the dinner table. And it is played with even further when people organize together to thwart its demolition and "save" Fenway Park. We can learn a great deal about a culture by considering the importance people give to their buildings. The relationship between Fenway Park and contemporary American culture is no exception. And the debate over Fenway's renovation or removal highlights the meanings people invest in important and iconic places.

Fenway Park functions as a "symbolic representation" of Boston's urban culture, a "coded, shorthand expression [that] is at once understood by the audience."[9] Soon after buying the Red Sox and their playing grounds, current owner John Henry told an eagerly awaiting public that "Fenway Park is one of the great landmarks of New England. When I think of Paris, I think of the Eiffel Tower. When I think of Boston, I think of Fenway."[10]

Fenway Park symbolizes the city's and region's identity, even more so than the Old North Church or Walden Pond or the Old Man of the Mountain, whose stone face saw its last sunrise on May 3, 2003.[11] Like the Old Man of the Mountain, the Old Ballpark of the City will eventually meet its crumbling fate at the hands of Mother Nature and Father Time. How soon, though, is hard to say. What that loss will mean for Boston, New England, and for anyone else who has dreamed of stepping into one of American popular culture's most treasured shrines is even harder for some people to talk about. The trepidation about Fenway Park's future is an important part of what my investigation is about.

In many respects, Fenway Park is a completely irrational stadium for today's urban culture. It is a place where a family of four can easily spend a week's pay to rub elbows, and knees, with strangers and eat boiled hot dogs wrapped in Wonder Bread. For the price of admission, you can spend approximately three hours in a wooden seat fit for an adolescent, jockeying for position with other spectators and imposing columns alike to get a peek at the baseball team you came there to root for, or against. The seats are cramped, often face the wrong way, are overpriced, and worst of all, there are not enough of them. Because seating capacity is so limited, you have to either plan ahead well in advance or press your luck and rely on an anonymous scalper's candor in order to get a valid, unobstructed seat in the ballpark. Even though Red Sox tickets are the most expensive in baseball, Fenway Park sells out more than any other ballpark in the majors—and it is not because the Red Sox keep winning championships, nor is it about the individual players who are regularly swapped and shopped to other teams.

Why then have Red Sox fans and patrons fought against the building of a new ballpark and fought to "save" Fenway Park with such ardent devotion? What is it about Fenway Park that generates such fierce pride and loyalty? Should the oldest active stadium in Major League Baseball be renovated or removed? Is it Fenway Park, rather than some curse, that was responsible for an eighty-six-year World Series championship drought in Boston? Will renovation squelch the supposed "aura" of the aged and aging ballpark? Will the past be lost if the Red Sox have to play their home games in a new stadium, possibly outside the borders of Boston in a town like Somerville or as far away as Foxboro? Will Boston be the same place without Fenway Park? These were some of the questions that were of paramount importance to the people I talked to, in and outside of Boston.

Although some of these questions can at least partially be answered by considering the economic value either lost or gained by building a new ballpark, economic models cannot access the cultural value of seemingly sacred objects. Economics certainly plays an important role in the decision-making process for the Red Sox owners and administration, the City of Boston, local businesses in the Fenway area, and the tax-paying public. Most of the recent studies about new ballparks and stadiums, as well as other leisure sites, have focused primarily on the economics of construction and urban redevelopment.[12] They have done a good job of showing how cities use cultural institutions and amenities as means of attracting tourists and regenerating local economies.

Still, a ballpark is only economically valuable because it is culturally valuable, or at least if people believe it is somehow important to their lives or the lives of others. In other words, its fiscal worth is dependent on its "cultural capital."[13] A monetary figure can be assigned to it only if there is an audience, a consumer population that deems it worthy, endows it with meaning, and is willing and/or able to pay for it. The economic market for leisure products and activities exists because people, the same people that pay to sit in Fenway's stroller-like seats, make it so. And at Fenway, they do so in droves.

The future of Fenway and the construction of a new ballpark are, currently, matters of speculation. As the saying goes, "you never know what you have until it's gone." I heard this repeated from more than a

few devotees of the ol' ballpark, from members of the grassroots preservationist group Save Fenway Park! and others. But the future does not
just happen by itself. So much of what the future will look like depends
on the way we see our present circumstances.

We are not lamenting a paradise lost, yet. But words that hold a certain reverence for the past like "nostalgia," "history," "collective memory," and "tradition" are tied to and shaped by Fenway Park in the present.[14] Such language gives us clues about the future of Fenway Park and
the city, or at least how people envision life in the city with or without
Boston's "lyrical little bandbox." The undeniable fact that so many people care so much about Fenway Park reveals a lot about the various
ways urban Americans experience, maintain, reconstruct, and practice
their culture. The issues become complicated once we recognize that
not everyone who cares about Fenway Park necessarily wants to "save"
it. Save it as a symbol and save the memories attached to it, yes, but as
a material, physical edifice, perhaps not.

If everyone agreed, there wouldn't be much of a debate. It has been
a long time since the world was black and white. It probably never was.
The urban world we live in is a complex hybrid of beliefs and attitudes,
convictions and concerns, values and tastes. Culture is never a matter
of pure consensus, and, in the city, consensus is both untenable and un-
wanted. Urban culture is an odd amalgam of past beliefs, present perceptions, and future speculations. The debate over the future of "America's Most Beloved Ballpark" shows how the culture of a city is dependent on ideas that are handed down *and* ideas that emerge within it.
In this case, people are struggling with the paradox of needing to preserve and learn from the past while not becoming stuck in it.

AUTHENTICITY AND THE FUTURE OF FENWAY PARK

I don't know. I'm torn. I love this place. I mean, my father used to take
me here every year for my birthday. I loved Wade Boggs and the hot
dogs and the way they'd throw us those bags of peanuts. I still love
that stuff. . . . But, I don't know, Fenway's getting old, you know? I
mean, maybe it's time for something new. Maybe not. I don't know. I
mean, what would a new Fenway be like? Would it even be like the
"real" Fenway. I mean, I really do love this place.

—Jane H., Red Sox fan, Lowell, Massachusetts

This place is great and keeps getting better. The new additions are good, like the Monster seats. They should do something about some of those seats though. Section 5 in right field have to be the worst possible seats to watch anything. I'd rather sit behind one of those damn poles.
—Pete L., Red Sox fan, Boston, Massachusetts

Over the past decade, there has been a considerable amount of heated debate in and around the city of Boston concerning the future of Fenway Park. The fate of Fenway may not be in the hands of everyone, but as a public symbol, it is open to debate for anyone, making it a highly contentious and common subject of popular discussion. That is, everyone is allowed to make claims about what should or should not happen to the ballpark.

Debates over the status of the ballpark are not new in Boston. The Red Sox have been interested in a new ballpark since the 1960s. Tom Yawkey, who owned the club from 1933 until his death in 1976, wanted to build a new stadium. Yawkey was a hands-on owner, always trying to improve the ball club, even if that meant having the Red Sox play on new grounds. Yawkey developed friendships with many of his players. Sam Mele, who played for the Red Sox from 1946 to 1953, mentioned in passing during our conversation about the ballpark that Yawkey included many of his players, including Mele, in his will. Yawkey often asked their opinions about the ballpark. Maybe it was the short porch in right field or the lack of foul territory, but apparently Yawkey's players liked their old home.

Yawkey thought that a new stadium would help draw more fans and revenue that would subsequently make the team better. He flirted with the idea of building a multiple-sport arena, which was the dominant trend from the early 1960s until the late 1980s. Most of Fenway's original "Golden Age" cousins were demolished during that period and were replaced by large, standardized, multisport cookie-cutter stadiums outside of the city. These stadiums followed their migrating public from the city to the suburbs. Those efforts never came to fruition in Boston.

While a few people have suggested building a new home for the Red Sox outside of Boston, such as in New Hampshire or in Foxboro, Massachusetts, where the New England Patriots play their home football games, the majority of plans have sought to find a worthy, accessible, and affordable space in the city. The proposed "Hubdome" idea in the late 1980s and early 1990s would have brought the Pats back to Boston, doubling as a football and baseball stadium in Boston's South End.[15] The "New Fenway Park" plan that was officially announced by the Red Sox to the public on May 15, 1999, would have kept the Red Sox in the Fens, only moving home plate about 206 yards southwest of its current and original location. These proposals, however, never advanced beyond the stages of talk and neat-looking miniature models.

Riding on the coattails of the newly constructed retro-style ballparks in Baltimore and Cleveland, the "New Fenway Park" plan went the furthest of the proposed plans. Actually, it went just about as far as it could go without employing wrecking balls, cement mixers, and governmental power to take by eminent domain the land needed to expand the ballpark's footprint from 7.9 acres to 15.5 acres.

People were, and still are, decidedly mixed about the prospect of losing Fenway Park, the "old" Fenway Park, even if the new ballpark was supposed to look like the old one, though with about ten thousand more seats. The "New Fenway Park" was designed as "a classic open-air ballpark modeled after Fenway Park, recreating the intimacy and unique dimensions, while providing better views, more comfortable seats, easier access, and more concession and restroom facilities."[16] This approach satisfied some people and troubled others.

Some people were downright confused about the proposed changes. In an article in *Sports Illustrated*, the most well known and widely read national sports magazine, journalist Rick Reilly decried, "Let me get this straight: We're bulldozing real vintage ballparks like Tiger Stadium [in Detroit] and Fenway Park to put up fake vintage ballparks?"[17] It is somewhat ironic that the new retro ballparks used Fenway Park as their muse, trying to emulate and capture some of its magical appeal. Why, then, would we want to replace the original with a copy? Perhaps simply because the old ballpark is, well, old.

As historian John Demos writes in his homage to Fenway, "Boston remains a place where older is frequently seen as better."[18] What happens when cultural objects that are older are destroyed and replicated? Do they still hold the same status? Does authenticity in contemporary American culture simply mean old or older or even extinct? Can "authentic reproductions" (certainly an awkward, oxymoronic term) evoke the same types of meanings and attachment that the originals once did or, probably more accurately, were thought to be able to induce?

The authenticity of a place is wrapped up in and dictated by the culture that endears it. The perceptions of a place's authenticity, which, as sociologist David Grazian correctly states in his study of contemporary Chicago blues clubs, "are never evaluated in absolute terms but measured comparatively along a *sliding scale of authenticity*,"[19] affect the experience of and in that place. In the debate about Fenway Park's future, the various parties are often explicitly concerned with its "authentic" past, and how the ol' ballpark can fit into Boston's urban culture today.

The idea and ideal of *authenticity* has been left relatively unexplored by sociologists. The term, however, has been part of the lexicon of scholars and critics of popular culture and has also been a key concern for both producers and consumers of cultural products. Studies of contemporary culture have tended to be drenched in pessimism stemming from the belief that "pure" forms of culture have been debased and defiled.[20] Debates about the commodification of culture often presume that authenticity must lie somewhere outside of, away from, and untouched by the marketplace.[21] Such analyses are troubled by an essentialist vocabulary that pits the authentic (the real, the pure, the original) above and against the inauthentic (the fake, the tainted, the copy). This leads to assumptions about authenticity as an inherent property of things or people, which thereby ignores and diminishes the social conditions that influence persons' ideas about and quest for the authentic experience. As cultural critic Lionel Trilling once noted, authenticity becomes an issue only after a doubt arises.[22]

I side with anthropologist Edward Bruner's "social constructivist" position on authenticity. This position aims at moving away from both postmodern and Marxian cultural analysis by focusing on the way that culture emerges through the way that people practice it. That is, instead of trying to locate the authentic in a particular style of culture as if that style contains its own inherent meaning, Bruner posits that "each new performance or expression of cultural heritage is a copy in that it always looks back to a prior performance, but also that each is an original in that it adapts to new circumstances and conditions. . . . the distinction between the original and the reproduction could just be abandoned."[23] Applied to Fenway Park, we can then say that the ol' ballpark today is no more authentic than, say, Camden Yards, since patrons of each ballpark are looking back to the same period in the past. Even though Fenway Park is the original, regardless of the modifications and renovations made to it over the years, it becomes a copy each time it is used, each time a game is played there, each time someone experiences a new performance within and outside Fenway's hallowed ground.

I do not want to make the claim, as some theorists have, that "the search for authenticity is always a failing prospect,"[24] nor do I want to treat authenticity as a fantasy that is controlled, manipulated, and fabricated by producers, marketers, and distributors of cultural commodities.[25] By attending to the *experience* of authenticity, tourism theorists like Dean MacCannell and Richard Handler offer a needed corrective to analyses that focus too heavily on the institutional production of culture. But I see no need to assume that such experiences only exist outside of or away from everyday life.[26] Instead, I defer to the people who, from their varying perspectives, have sought to produce, transmit, and consume Fenway Park's authenticity. By focusing on the ways people practice culture and use authenticity as a motivation for such actions, the criteria of what constitutes authenticity lie in the crack between objectivity and subjectivity. Again, I find it instructive to follow Bruner's lead:

> No longer is authenticity a property inherent in an object, forever fixed in time; instead it is a social process, a struggle in which competing interests argue for their own interpretations of history. Culture is seen as contested, emergent, and constructed, and agency and desire become part of the discourse. When actors use the term authenticity, ethnographers may then ask what segment of society has raised a doubt, what is no longer taken for granted, what are the societal struggles, and what are the cultural issues at work. These are ethnographic questions, empirical questions, requiring investigation and research. Grand theorizing thus gives way to ethnography.[27]

Investigating the ways that authenticity is used as an ideal and as a desired quality at Fenway Park reveals more than would simply making judgment claims about the various plans for the ballpark. While some cultural analysts are comfortable making claims about "McDonaldized" and "de-McDonaldized" baseball theme parks and chastising "the implosion of leisure and consumption,"[28] I am more concerned with persons' perceptions of ballparks. Moreover, the ways that people use Fenway Park show how the realms of leisure, consumption, authenticity, and the sacred are not always easily definable, or condemnable. These connections are certainly complex and, as such, require "investigation and research."

APPROACHING THE BALLPARK FROM THE GROUND UP

Most of the recent studies about ballparks and stadiums take for granted the symbolic attachments people have with their city's teams and the places they play. Studies usually do this in order to focus on the economic and political conflicts surrounding processes of neighborhood redevelopment and public investment schemes. Rarely do these studies approach stadium debates from the ground up. As such, they easily lose sight of the people in the seats, waiting on line for tickets, at home watching the game on television and wishing they were *at* the game, or cranking the dial on their Fenway Park snow globe to hear another rendition of "Take Me Out to the Ballgame." Such practices constitute a small sample of the variety of ways that people use Fenway Park and actively make it important. The practices, and the motivations and beliefs that foster them, are not easily calculable or quantifiable, nor are they always about money and governmental power.

Because the reach of Fenway Park extends beyond street corners and neighborhood bars, findings could presumably be more generalizable simply because the population involved is vastly larger than a handful of regulars at a local hangout. Such a large, albeit ill-defined, population—that includes the three million people a year who watch the Red Sox at Fenway; the eighty-five thousand people a year who take the tours; the more than five hundred people who work for the Red Sox organization (from the players to the ushers to the club historian); the innumerable producers of new articles, websites, and online blogs; and the countless others who pass by the ballpark on their way to somewhere else—makes the task of ethnography especially difficult.

Whereas most researchers are interested in a specific and well-defined population, I began with a place and then asked an open and inductive question: What happens here? Rather than making assumptions about the population and the theoretical problems we might encounter when studying its social behaviors and belief systems, my approach provided enough room for the unexpected to be recognized and included. As anthropologist Ruth Behar writes,

> the beauty and mystery of the ethnographer's quest is to find the unexpected stories, the stories that challenge our theories. Isn't that the reason why we still go to the field—even as we question where the

field is located—in the 21st century? We go to find stories we didn't
know we were looking for in the first place.[29]

Theoretical and methodological models are intended to shape our
analysis, not our findings.

I employed separate but related methods that provided more than
enough information to grant me at least some semblance of an authoritative voice to speak about Fenway Park and the roles it plays in and
outside the city. (See the appendix for an extended discussion of my
methodology and the rationale behind it.) The power of sociological
methods helped me be *in* the place, learn *about* the place, but not be *of*
the place. That is, I was able to get close enough to the subject through
the research process and not because I was a member of the tribe. I was
not and am not a member of Red Sox Nation. My personal and professional lives did, however, help shape my analysis. As a child and as a
teenager, I went to baseball games with my grandfather, father, and
friends. So, I get what baseball means as a familial and communal activity, exemplifying and enhancing some of the strongest bonds of
male-to-male relationships.[30] Even though I lived in Boston for six years
(as a graduate student), I am not a Bostonian, nor am I a Red Sox fan. I
grew up in the suburbs just north of New York City. I am a New York
Mets fan. So I get what it means to hate the Yankees. Yet as a trained sociologist, going to Fenway Park was never just about baseball. But as I
learned throughout my research, it's rarely just about baseball for anyone.

My research began in the fall of 2003. I attended a few games that
season, including Game 5 of the American League Championship Series (the Red Sox lost to the Yankees, 4–2, two days after the infamous
bench-clearing brawl that included Red Sox ace Pedro Martinez throwing seventy-two-year-old Yankees coach Don Zimmer to the ground by
the head). Like the players and the organization, the 2004 season started
early for me. I flew down to Ft. Myers, Florida, where the Red Sox hold
spring training. I attended two games, which were both sold out, at City
of Palms Park. But that trip was less about watching the games or the
fans watching the games and was more about doing interviews with
fans outside Boston and with Red Sox players, coaches, and personnel.
Many former players still work for the Red Sox in some capacity as
coaches at the different levels of minor- and major-league ball. Having

been granted access to the Red Sox practice facilities, I was able to hear stories about Fenway Park from a number of old-timers, like Charlie Wagner (who broke into the big leagues with the Red Sox in 1935 and roomed with Ted Williams during road trips) and Red Sox legend Carl Yastrzemski (the last player to win the Triple Crown).

Throughout the 2004 season, Red Sox vice president and club historian Dick Bresciani signed off on almost twenty guest passes that gave me access to the ballpark during home games. I was supposed to wear the guest pass around my neck as I roamed around the ballpark before, during, and after games, stomping on peanut shells, grabbing a hot dog and a beer every now and then, and trying to grasp all the details of Fenway Park, from the most grand to the most minute. Occasionally, I would stop to watch an inning or two, especially when Manny Ramirez stepped to the plate.

During the 2004 regular season, I was exposed to a few heartbreaking loses and a few heroic wins, like the Red Sox–Yankees battle on July 24. It began with a fifty-four-minute rain delay, gained steam from a bench-clearing brawl in the third inning, then evolved into an intrepid duel settled in the most dramatic fashion: a two-run homer by Bill Mueller off the Yankees seemingly invincible All-Star closer, Mariano Rivera. Someone kept handing me fresh drafts of Harpoon IPA. I danced in the aisles with the rest of the Fenway faithful as the PA ritually blasted "Dirty Water" by the Standells: "Well I love that dirty water, oh, Boston you're my home!"

Watching baseball games, however, is not the only way to participate in or observe the practices associated with Fenway Park. Tours of Fenway Park and charity events are other ways to get inside the ballpark. Some cultural practices take place outside and around Fenway, so admittance to the ballpark was not always necessary or sought after. For example, Opening Day brings people to Fenway Park from all over the country. While much of the crowd searches for scalpers' tickets outside the ballpark on Brookline Avenue, Lansdowne Street, and Van Ness Street (Yawkey Way, a purposely contrived circuslike street fair that lines the southern side of Fenway, is now open to ticket-holders only), there are an equal, if not greater, number who are satisfied by just being there.

In order to gain some comparative perspective about the architectural elements and community dynamics that supposedly make Fenway Park special, unique, and important, I visited a variety of other ballparks. I sat in the bleachers at Chicago's Wrigley Field, the other active "Golden Age" ballpark, and attended a few games at one "second wave" 1960s cookie-cutter stadium—Shea Stadium (it was admittedly strange to be there as a researcher instead of a fan).

I also attended games at six of the most recently constructed retro ballparks: Oriole Park at Camden Yards in Baltimore (opened in 1992), Turner Field in Atlanta (opened in 1997), Angels Stadium in Anaheim (renovated between 1997 and 1999), Chase Field in Phoenix (opened in 1998), SBC Park in San Francisco (opened in 2000), Miller Park in Milwaukee (opened in 2001), PNC Park in Pittsburgh (opened in 2001), Citizen's Bank Park in Philadelphia (opened in 2004), and Petco Park in San Diego (opened in 2004).[31] Because the architects of these ballparks purposely tried to emulate the "feel" of the ballparks of an earlier time and generation, like Fenway, it was important to see how they attempted to do so. That is, I was interested in which elements they tried to keep (like the asymmetrical outfield dimensions and steep seating bowl) and which they chose to disregard (like the cramped wooden seats and aisles). So, I sniffed around the insides and outsides of these ballparks for clues from the past, sampled the local treats and delicacies, and casually chatted with fans about their hometown team's playing grounds.

Exploring the things that people believe are important is at the heart of what sociologists should be doing. Going into the field and discussing people's beliefs with those who hold them is a key component of the way I envision "public sociology." During the first decade of the twenty-first century, the idea of public sociology has become a popular subject of discussion throughout the discipline, so much so that public sociology was the overarching theme of the 2004 American Sociological Association annual meeting.[32] Most of the discussions revolve around sociologists' potential impact on local, national, international, and global public policy. There are a few sociologists, however, who have acquired and applied their insights at more grounded levels. The way of practicing public sociology that I espouse is through a purposeful engagement with popular culture. And by popular culture, I mean everything from BMWs to VFWs, from Barney to Barney's to Matthew Barney, from collard greens to collared shirts, from diamond rings to baseball diamonds.

This study of Fenway Park stands as an example of an alternative public sociology to those that set out to change public policies and agendas. My public sociology aims to provide a thorough exploration of the material and symbolic cultural products, however esoteric or popular, that people believe in, fight for, and care about. It is not about putting up academic walls around popular phenomena and dressing them up with elitist or cynical jargon. Rather, it is about thinking and writing in a clear and concise manner about the complexities of American culture in a way that neither offends the rigor of the discipline nor alienates the public at large. It's a tricky line to tiptoe, but it's the one I've tried to stay on throughout this analysis of Fenway Park and the people whose reverence has endowed the ol' ballpark with meaning and value to the point of consecration.

Just because some people define something as sacred doesn't mean that it's necessarily sacred for everyone. But it does make that something worthy of study and analysis. I have tried my best to present Fenway Park in a way that maintains the "aura" of it for those who believe and demonstrates its significance for those who don't.

THE BIRTH OF AN
URBAN BALLPARK
Leisure, Nostalgia, and the Baseball Creed

> It's old baseball, how it used to be, and there's so much history at Fenway. The legend has grown over the years. . . . Historical monuments are important; they bring back old memories, the real field of dreams.
> —Lou Gorman, former Red Sox general manager
> (1984–1993)

> Fenway, the fans, the city, they all need each other. . . . they always needed each other. It's been that way since 1912.
> —Tom T., Red Sox fan, Brookline, Massachusetts

Like many of those fortunate enough to get their hands on a ticket to the see the Red Sox host the Yankees for the fifth game of the 2003 American League Championship Series, I was pacing back and forth on the concourse just above the single-level infield grandstand on the third-base side. Like some, I was able to sneak my ticket stub in front of Billy Crystal for his autograph. A renowned Yankee fan who had made the trip north to find himself in one of Fenway Park's not-so-cozy box seats, Crystal's celebrity status seemed to trump his baseball allegiance. But most of the Red Sox fans at Fenway that chilly October evening had other things on their mind than the chance to chat it up with the "ma*h*velous" comedian.

A pronounced tension filled the air, accentuated by the strangely quiet drone that stretched from Pesky's Pole in right field to the .406 Club behind home plate, down the third-base line, around the Green Monster, and back again. Everyone seemed to be somewhere within their own heads and hearts, doing their best to will a win for the home team. Rarely are we privy to such open displays of collective prayer on a Tuesday night. Their vigil made the cool autumn New England air feel as thick as a hot August night.

Boston fans are knowledgeable devotees. Baseball has been a part of Boston's cultural makeup since the mid-1800s. The "Massachusetts Game" was one of the first codified base and ball games, and as was revealed in 2004, Pittsfield, Massachusetts, may have been the birthplace of American baseball.[1] Also, the first World Series was played, and won, in Boston in 1903. Baseball has long been a part of the region's and city's cultural DNA. I heard that sentiment repeated from one interview to the next. "There is no such thing as a casual Red Sox fan," one interviewee told me. "It just doesn't happen; they get too caught up in the history of it all." The fans at Fenway that October night understood the significance of the game.

The series was tied two games a piece. With a win, the Red Sox would take a one-game lead going back to New York for the final two games of the series to determine which team would represent the American League in the 2003 World Series. Whereas the "Evil Empire," the moniker that Red Sox CEO Larry Lucchino and the Boston sports media have branded the Yankees, seems to make it this far every year, this was as close to the prize that the Red Sox had come in over a decade.[2] This is to say nothing of the ever-present fact that Boston had not won the World Series since 1918. They had been there five times since then, only to lose the seventh game in some of the most heartbreaking and storied ways possible.

"They're in the business of almost," said one fan, which was echoed by another who sarcastically asked, "How many different flavors of excruciatingly almost are there in the Red Sox ice cream store?" Some might say that over the years the Red Sox have run the gamut on bitter flavors of disappointment. And 2003 would offer up another spoonful to Red Sox Nation, right off of Aaron Boone's bat.[3]

Waiting for the Ataris, a one-hit-wonder garage rock-pop band, to finish their rendition of Don Henley's "Boys of Summer" being belted out from atop the right-field roof, I found myself in the middle of a conversation, an unprompted interview. A man standing next to me was talking, apparently to me, about tonight's game's starting pitchers. Although this type of discourse between strangers is very common (to the point of expectation and sometimes even annoyance) at the ol' ballpark, there was very little chatter that night. It was eerily quiet both inside the park and outside on Yawkey Way. It would have been less eerie if no one was around. But the place was packed.

The man, who must have been in his late sixties or early seventies, made stiff eye-contact with me. Looking back at him, I could tell that he was not having fun. And it seemed that baseball had not been fun for him for quite some time. There was something else going on here. With a look of utter desperation, if not despair, he interrupted his own rant about Red Sox pitcher Derek Lowe's poor postseason win percentage and Yankees pitcher David Wells's well-publicized drinking habits. "[The Red Sox] have to win tonight," he exclaimed. "They have to win tonight," he emphasized as he reached out and grabbed my forearm. "I don't know how much more of this I can take."

While this type of pain or devotion derived from spectator sports or any other leisure activity may seem undeserved or misplaced to the outsider, it is hardly trivial or, for that matter, new. To understand this man's emotional attachment to the successes and failures of his hometown team, it is necessary to uncover the processes and events that fostered a cultural milieu that inspires, if not demands, such ardent devotion. From a historical point of view, it was this same context that made the construction of Fenway Park both possible and desired and continues to make the ol' ballpark a subject of dedication and debate.

The modern tribal angst of the Red Sox fan is not unprecedented in Boston, or in baseball. Of course, baseball is not the only sport that elicits devoted fans, as sports fandom has become ubiquitous in much of Americans' public culture. But baseball and its playing grounds have a unique relationship with its fans. Of the four major professional sports —baseball, football, basketball, and hockey—baseball's season is the longest, creating more opportunities for fans to attend games or even watch them on television. It is the only sport that is played, and watched, throughout the summer, even though it begins in the spring and ends in the fall. Moreover, there is a strong historical connection between baseball and modern American culture. The rise of professional baseball and the building of the first permanent ballparks coincided with the processes of urbanization and the first appearance of a widely acknowledged, though not necessarily widely accepted, American consumer culture.[4]

Fenway Park was built in 1912 in the midst of baseball's "Golden Age," when the first permanent steel-and-concrete ballparks were constructed in the then-budding metropolises that, today, seem almost inevitably stationed across the American urban landscape.[5] Since its inception as the "national pastime," baseball has been steeped in a nostalgic mythology about olden games and olden times. It is a collective mythology that connects today's fans to past generations, to past players, and to past places. The remarkable thing about Fenway Park is that it not only reminds people of the past, but it is actually *from* it. It functions as an *artifactual* witness to and of a time we can only touch with our imaginations and through the stories we're told by others. The values and beliefs represented by Fenway Park symbolically constitute its "aura," which gains strength over time as it no longer merely represents tradition but is a part of tradition itself.

The symbolic quality of Fenway Park beholds "a public and cultural relation among object, tradition, and audience"[6] that allows present-day Fenway visitors to be a part of its history each time they enter the ballpark, stand for the seventh-inning stretch and sing "Take Me Out to the Ballgame," pump their fists and sing along with Neil Diamond's "Sweet Caroline" between the top and bottom of the eighth inning (a relatively new tradition), and cheer for their team together.

In many ways, Fenway Park functions like a museum, itself being its most prized possession, holding, and offering. Throughout my interviews, the word "museum" was often used to describe or characterize Fenway Park. For example, Richard Johnson, curator of the Sports Museum of New England in Boston and coauthor of *Red Sox Century*, described the ballpark to me as follows:

> Fenway Park is really the village green writ large. Because of the tether, because of the connection to history, because part of that real estate is the same earth that was trod by Ruth and Kerrigan, Speaker and Hooper, Williams and Yastrzemski, it is one of the few places in the region that has this wonderful inter-generational appeal. . . . it's hard to get kids really turned on to symphony hall, say, though you might like them to. . . . *Whether folks know it or not, they're really experiencing the game in a museum,* . . . a utilitarian, historic place. . . . We have history at every corner, at every turn here, and Fenway is just another

part of that fabric, another piece of the mosaic that connects this area historically.

It is not difficult to understand why some people refer to Fenway Park as a museum. If the park is ever demolished, many of its parts, from the wooden seats to the famed left-field wall to the various signs that adorn the park's skin and underbelly, will surely become instant and coveted additions to any number of local and national museums and archives.

But calling Fenway Park a museum is not an entirely accurate designation. The roots of the term are consistent with the roots of "mausoleum."[7] Anyone who steps into the ballpark today will surely recognize that it is much more than a space to house dead objects. Perhaps qualifying the term "museum" with an adjective like "living," "vibrant," or "animated" would be more appropriate. This may seem to be just a matter of semantics, but the words that people use to describe a place provide clues about the meaning they ascribe to that place and enhance its "local color."[8]

One local Red Sox fan, a Rhode Island native in his late twenties who now lives a few miles from the ballpark, actually dealt with this issue from one sentence to another. First, he claimed that Fenway Park is "like a museum, an artifact." Following that statement, he recognized Fenway Park as a place that "keeps Boston on the map by bringing people to the city to have a good time. . . . it's a place that is passed down from our grandparents' parents; it has a lot of history."

Not only does it have history; it *is* history. And while it still continues to be the home of the Boston Red Sox and their fans and patrons, history is being made there every day. When we speak of history, we are often talking about the events and places that become markers of our cultural narratives and collective memories.[9] We are talking about the stuff that makes a people, well, a people, and not merely a collection of autonomous individuals running around and into one another.

Here, we are primarily interested in the ways that history is used and revered today as a means for creating meaning. When we talk about the ways that history is used and practiced we begin to enter the realm of "collective memory." Sociologist Barry Schwartz contends that "collective memory is based on two sources of belief about the past— *history* and *commemoration*. Collective memory is a representation of the past embodied in *both* historical evidence and commemorative symbolism."[10] It is sociologically valuable to analyze the ways that collective memory connects people in the present to the facts of yesterday and how those facts are ascertained and received. Fenway Park is an excellent example of the way an important place can become a part of a culture's symbolic system and help foster collective memories that span across generations, social classes, and lifestyles.

It will soon become clear that some of the memories that Fenway Park evokes are external to the ballpark itself and are, in part, derived from the general emerging spirit and worldview of turn-of-the-century urban America. Later, we will explore the historical relationship between baseball, American culture, and "the largest things that human beings build that actually work,"[11] the cities where we live, work, and play. This relationship was enhanced by modern acts of popular *mythopoesis*, or mythmaking, whereby baseball became an influential part of an emergent urban culture that required a reconstructed mythos/ethos that made sense in the new social organizational and behavioral practices of America's sweltering cities. Baseball has played, and continues to play, a significant role as part of a national nostalgia drenched in the paradoxical "yearning for and dismissal of the rural past."[12]

THE (SOCIAL) CONSTRUCTION OF FENWAY PARK

Fenway Park has two histories, at least. First, there is the tale of its birth, its adolescence, its adulthood, and so on. That story begins with then-owner John I. Taylor's decision to build a modern steel-and-concrete ballpark in a less populated area than the team's former residence in South Boston (actually Roxbury), symbolizing both "a recognition of the maturity and stability of the baseball business"[13] and the advancement of construction and transportation technologies. This laundry list of events details the team's move from the Huntington Avenue Grounds to their home in the drained but still swampy "Fens." Next, the story includes the continued struggle to renovate the ballpark after fires burned down the left-field bleachers in 1926 and then, on January 5, 1934 (fourteen years to the day after Babe Ruth had been sold to the Yankees), helping the Red Sox and arguably baseball's greatest hitter, Ted Williams, by building a bullpen in right field that brought the fence twenty-three feet closer to the plate.

Bringing the tale up-to-date, we'd note the recent construction by John Henry and Co. and their multiple attempts at making Fenway economically viable by adding seats without sacrificing the historical integrity and structural stability of the ol' ballpark. Despite the necessary changes and facelifts made to the ballpark, Fenway Park looks very much the same as it did in 1912.

The second history is really more like collective memory. That is, it is the story, or stories, that people know and generally accept as history. Most of the people who care about Fenway Park do not know all the facts and details about its past, despite the almost universal acknowledgment that Fenway Park is important because of its history. When I asked people why Fenway Park was important, many of their first responses had something to do with history: "because of its history," "because of all of the history that happened there," "it has a history like no other ballpark or place in Boston, for that matter," or "it a historical treasure." The next question I would ask—"Why is history important?"—fostered some confused looks and yielded some very inarticulate answers. Admittedly, it's a tough question to answer.

A good portion of a person's knowledge of the ballpark is personal or primary history, built over time through his or her individual experiences with and at the ballpark. These stories are not any less real than the raw data of social facts. They may even be more real because they are directly felt and told. As anthropologist Barbara Johnstone notes, "stories do not simply describe worlds; stories also create worlds."[14] The factual accuracy of a story is often less important than the purpose of the story, the way it's used, and why certain stories are repeated while others are forgotten.

The facts that persons know about Fenway Park tend either to corroborate their own experiences or to be the fodder of Red Sox folklore. Nearly 90 percent of the people I interviewed, including some local sportswriters and persons affiliated with the Red Sox organization, repeated the commonly uttered and accepted story of Fenway Park's name. As the story goes, and the way it is told and retold, when Taylor was asked what the new ballpark would be called, he replied, "It's in the Fenway, isn't it? Then let's call it Fenway Park." Although this seems logical, and, I suppose, could demonstrate the instant and intimate connection between the ballpark and the neighborhood, rather than naming it after the team's owner (like Shibe in Philadelphia,

Ebbets in Brooklyn, or Crosley in Cincinnati), Taylor's reasons were far more self-serving than is often acknowledged.

Taylor's family owned the *Boston Globe* and then the Red Sox, though they weren't called the Red Sox yet. The team was called either the Pilgrims or Americans until 1907, three years after Taylor's father, Civil War veteran General Charles Henry Taylor, bought his reportedly rowdy son the team. The family also owned the Fenway Realty Company, which secured land in the formerly ill-smelling marshlands west of Boston's downtown central business district.

The urban-design maverick Frederick Law Olmsted, who designed New York City's Central Park, drained the Fens in the mid-1880s as part of his collection of parks that weave through and around the city. These parks are still known as the "Emerald Necklace."[15] By the turn of the century some of the land originally allotted as part of the necklace park scheme had turned into a needed residential area, some owned by the Taylors' real-estate company. In effect, the Taylors sold themselves a chunk of cheap land, conveniently located near the city's expanding trolley lines.

As historian Glenn Stout writes, "The enterprise was first and foremost a real estate venture; [Taylor] used the ballpark to help draw attention to the surrounding area and enhance its value."[16] Naming the ballpark "Fenway Park" increased the visibility and speculated value of the Fenway Realty Company and its holdings. Not unlike Chicago's Wrigley Field and chewing gum or Denver's relatively young Coors Field and beer, Fenway Park was used to help sell real estate that the Taylors owned in the Fens. Taylor guessed correctly. At the time of its inception, two streetcar lines were available to transport people to and from Fenway Park. Two years later, a subway line was extended past the park to accommodate Boston's growing population and the hordes of spectators that attended games at the new steel-and-concrete ballpark.[17] Today, the D train of Boston's Green Line has its own Fenway Park stop.

This piece of Fenway Park history is significant for two reasons. First, it highlights the difference between actual history and a word-of-mouth oral and vernacular history, and how the two do not always match up or mirror each other. Second, the naming of a potential new ballpark in Boston is one of the great concerns voiced by many people on both sides of the fence. Opponents of the new ballpark and baseball purists who laud the authenticity of Fenway Park and decry the commingling of cultural and commercial interests should be aware of the full story of Fenway's namesake. If the Red Sox built a new ballpark or if they decided to rename Fenway Park something like Bank of America Park, it would be in keeping with the tradition the Taylors started in 1912. And, perhaps, selling the naming rights of the old ballpark would provide the necessary funds to save it.

The Philadelphia Phillies and Citizens Bank entered into a naming-rights agreement for their new stadium that opened for the 2004 season. Citizens Bank will pay $57.5 million over twenty-five years to name the ballpark after the company. The bank will also pay the Phillies an additional $37 million to advertise on the Phillies radio and television broadcasts.[18] Certainly, that type of money could be used to help renovate Fenway or decrease ticket prices or both, rather than using public tax dollars. Then again, it is also money that could be used to build a new ballpark. In fact, when the Red Sox were aggressively pursuing the "New Fenway Park" plan in 2000, they were hoping to raise nearly $128 million dollars from naming rights.

Because this study of Fenway Park is not meant to shoot down cultural myths and legends but rather to recognize them and elucidate the reasons for their persistence, my intent is not to point a finger or distribute blame for misinformation. It should be noted, however, that the "Taylor—it's in the Fenway" story is a myth perpetuated by the Red Sox organization. On the official website of the Red Sox, the claim is made that "Taylor dubbed the new ballpark Fenway Park because of its location in the Fenway section of Boston." No reference is made to the Taylor family business. Also, this same claim is repeated during official tours of the ballpark. In 2003, the approximately eighty-five thousand people who took the tour left Fenway Park with only half the story.[19]

Oddly enough, Glenn Stout's outing of the Taylors' business interests in the naming of the ballpark was printed in the 1987 Red Sox yearbook, where he plainly states that "the park's name . . . served to promote real estate instead of baseball." Although that statement may be a little heavy-handed because the ballpark clearly promoted, and continues to promote, both private and public interests, the point remains that the Red Sox have chosen to ignore this valuable piece of information. Or at least they have kept it hidden in the corner like that cousin nobody talks about. The reasons why the Red Sox have done so are complicated. But it surely has something to do with enhancing or retaining the mystique and authenticity of Fenway Park for both commercial and cultural purposes. This supports sociologist Anselm Strauss's claim that people "bring their pasts into line with their presents."[20]

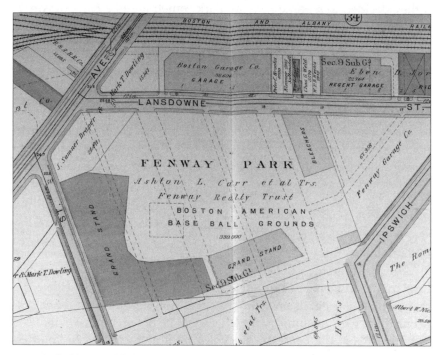

Detail of plate 33 of the 1912 *Atlas of the City of Boston*. Note the way the ballpark was squeezed tightly into an already existing city block. Because the atlas was printed for 1912, the team's name had not yet changed from the Americans to the Red Sox and the ballpark had not yet been properly named. (Photo courtesy of the Boston Public Library)

Putting the exact origins of the name aside, Fenway Park's location is of paramount importance for its original acceptance, devoted reverence, and continued relevance. In the fall of 1911, architect James McLaughlin's plans for Fenway Park were virtually complete, but his original conception for the ballpark was much different from the structure that was built during that winter and subsequent spring. The original design had to fit the oblique urban block owned by the Taylors. A more symmetrical ballpark would have been even smaller than the one they built and would not have taken up the entire parcel of land that the Taylor family business intended to utilize. Fenway was shoehorned into this small piece of real estate, bounded by Brookline Avenue and Jersey, Lansdowne, Ipswich, and Van Ness streets.

McLaughlin was ordered to design a park that completely enclosed the site, resulting in a field of play being much larger than that required by the way the game was played at the time. He was further ordered to retain the orientation of the Huntington Avenue Grounds in relation to the sun, with the third-base line pointing almost due north. This placed the left-field fence hard against Landsdowne Street, barely 300 feet from home plate.[21]

Landsdowne Street could not be moved or eliminated because the Boston & Albany Railroad was on the other side. Today, the Massachusetts Turnpike runs parallel to the rail tracks.

The short left-field fence was not a concern for hitters, who could barely reach it in the "dead-ball era." For the most part, the twenty-five-foot wooden wall was built to keep fans from climbing in without tickets or watching the game from the roof of the buildings across the street the way fans in Chicago still do today outside Wrigley Field. Duffy's Cliff, a sloping ten-foot-high grassy hill in front of the wall, named after Red Sox left-fielder George "Duffy" Lewis, was more about making it harder for outfielders than it was about impeding batters' long flies and scorching "worm burners." The hill also allowed the ticket-holding standing-room crowd to see over the heads of one another. In those days, there was no need to put seats on top of the wall; people just stood in front of it.

Fenway Park's original left-field wall was much smaller than the one that stands today. Because of the importance of the wall as one of the starkest defining features of the ballpark, it's worth jumping ahead chronologically in the story of Fenway to note that along with a considerable number of other renovations to the ballpark at the same time, the current left-field wall was born in 1934.[22] Made of thirty thousand tons of Toncan iron, the wall was dubbed the "Green Monster" a decade later when it was slathered in green paint (the formula for the color is still an organization secret). After the National Football League's Boston Redskins ended their season in December 1933, the then new owner of the Red Sox, Tom Yawkey (the Yawkeys and/or the Yawkey family trust owned the Red Sox and Fenway Park from 1933 to 2001), collaborated with the Osborn Engineering Company (the builders of the original ballpark) and the Boston-based Coleman Brothers Corp. to undergo the second-largest building project in Boston during the Depression. As Yawkey reconstructed the ballpark, leaving little more than the original steel supports in the grandstand (the same poles that still obstruct fans' views of the playing field) and the quirky left-field wall, the cost reached $1.5 million.

Yawkey knew he needed to fix the aging ballpark because fans were threatening to boycott games, regardless of the players Yawkey put on the field. "Renovate be damned," Yawkey told a reporter. "Let's build a new ballpark and have it right."[23] Even though people were worried that money spent on a ballpark would mean less money would be available to spend on players, there were no impassioned pleas for Fenway Park's preservation before Yawkey's reconstruction project got under way during the blustery winter of 1934. No one waxed poetic about the aura, magic, or authenticity of the dilapidated and decaying ballpark. There were no campaigns to "save" the ballpark, no nostalgic memoirs, and no public laments.

When Fenway Park was opened for the 1912 season, Bostonians did, however, make nostalgia-driven public lamentations. These laments were not about Fenway but about its predecessor. The Red Sox first took the field at Fenway Park on April 8, 1912, for a preseason exhibition game against Harvard University that the Red Sox won 2–0 in front of just over three thousand snow-drenched fans. Little was said about the new ballpark in the press. Most newspaper reporters were busy scrambling for the names of survivors and victims of the 2,340 passengers expecting to make their way across the Atlantic on the SS *Titanic*.

The tragic sinking of the *Titanic* was still on people's minds when the new ballpark opened three days behind schedule, due to three days of incessant rain. But, then as it is now, once the baseball season starts in Boston, the Red Sox take precedence over almost anything else. As Paul Shannon wrote in his *Boston Post* analysis of the game:

> Into the mammoth stands, out upon the sun-kissed bleachers and swarming over the field, forming a human fringe to the expansive playing space where the Red Sox were to make their initial bow of the 1912 season, the fans of Boston forced their way, until when the umpire gave the word for play to begin more than 24,000 loyal Red Sox supporters were waiting to pass judgment upon the park and the team.[24]

Those twenty-four thousand fans saw Boston mayor John "Honey Fitz" Fitzgerald throw out the ceremonial first pitch. The Red Sox beat the New York Highlanders, later known as the Yankees, 7–6 in eleven innings.

As Boston eased into the 1912 season, the *Sporting News* reported that home attendance was down 25 percent.[25] Like Shannon, who used words like "mammoth" and "expansive" to describe the ballpark, Tim Murnane, a renowned Boston sportswriter for the *Sporting News*, disparaged the enormous size of the park, which almost doubled that of the old Huntington Avenue Grounds, and lamented the replacement of the old single common entrance with two widely separated entrances. "I find much of the old sociability gone. At the old grounds you were continually running into old friends as grandstand and bleacher patrons passed through one long runway to be distributed like a lot mail at various stations." Murnane also complained that "the new park is not as handy to reach and get away from as the old park."[26]

These comments reveal much about how baseball fans interpreted and feared the growing scale of professional baseball and its playing grounds and how people's perceptions and renderings of size and space are context dependent. Arguing that Fenway Park is too big, that it is what the *Boston Post* the day after it opened called a "mammoth plant," seems practically absurd from our contemporary perspective.[27] In fact, by today's standards Fenway's petite confines and the intimacy of such close quarters are some of the most repeated reasons for keeping or "saving" the ballpark.

URBAN ORIGINS AND PASTORAL DREAMS

Today, ballparks are expensive to build, expensive to maintain, and expensive to get into. Regardless, they have been mainstays across urban landscapes for the past century or so. Virtually all of today's major sports evolved, or were even invented, in cities.[28] In the early decades of the nineteenth century, urban settings provided the necessary wealth and population to create and sustain professional teams. Cities have been important for professional sports since the organization of the first baseball leagues in the 1870s. Baseball's pastoral origins are part of the pastime's mythology, enshrined and perpetuated in the location of the Baseball Hall of Fame in rural upstate New York as well as in popular films like *Field of Dreams*, with its images of an Iowa cornfield sacrificed for the sake of the game.[29] The ideas that continue to laud the agrarian qualities of baseball, like running around on lush green grass, have successfully trumped the real origins of the game. Such agrarian and pas-

Aerial view of Boston from 1945 showing Fenway Park encased by Kenmore Square to its left and the Fens just above the ballpark. Other prominent buildings include the Christian Science Church and the Museum of Fine Arts. (Photo courtesy of the Boston Public Library)

toral notions are planted firmly in America's public memory and are part of the mythos about baseball that coincides with the sport's presumed virtues constructed from both a lived present and a nostalgic past.

The first permanent steel-and-concrete, fire-resistant ballparks, known as the "Golden Age" ballparks, became some of the most important semipublic edifices in the growing American cities at the beginning of the twentieth century.[30] Today, Fenway Park and Chicago's Wrigley Field are the only surviving members. Fenway Park has been able to maintain its status as an important place for almost a century. For the most part, it has become even more important as the ballpark and city of Boston, one of America's first, have aged together.

There is little disagreement among social historians about the role of cities as engines for the evolution and rise of contemporary sports. This "urban paradigm," as historian Stephen Hardy calls it, "has dominated sport historiography since at least 1917, when Fredrick Paxson argued . . . that burgeoning businesses like baseball, tennis, boxing, and golf had recently emerged as a new safety valve for a congested America that no longer had a frontier."[31] While Americans continued to hold on to the frontier as a powerful symbol of nation building and rugged individualism,[32] a mythology developed around baseball. Baseball was presented as an activity that could ease the growing contradictions of life in early American cities. Journalists, politicians, progressive social activists, and creative authors wrote about baseball in glowing terms. Together, these narratives helped create and substantiate an emerging ethos for an urban public presumably fettered by the loss of the vast "wilderness" that had succumbed to urban expansion. The new urbanites were willing to embrace new sports like baseball as part of their new urban ethos.

What this American ethos was or, more accurately, what it was supposed to be is exactly what was at stake when the Special Base Ball Commission, as it was officially called, convened in 1907 to declare the "true" origins of baseball. Headed by the former president of professional baseball's National League, Abraham G. Mills (though there is some controversy about his actual role as the panel's leader),[33] this specially designated and entrusted group of baseball executives, sportswriters, and other influential persons was "charged with deciding the true origins of America's national pastime, that is, whether baseball derived from the English schoolyard game of rounders or whether it was a purely native product."[34]

In many ways, the Mills Commission, as it has since been remembered, was more concerned with constructing a mythology of baseball under the guise of scientific discovery than with making a scientific discovery based on actual facts. Mills and his cronies were determined to portray the national pastime as an American creation. The commission very explicitly recognized that baseball contained the proper types of symbols, myths, and rituals that a relatively young nation would need in order to bind members of its increasingly diverse population together. But their conclusions were as bad as their intentions were good.

The committee was heavily influenced by Albert G. Spalding, an American-born baseball player and sporting-goods entrepreneur, who strongly supported the creation myth that baseball had a "purely American origin." Spalding was a staunch opponent of Henry Chadwick, an English-born sportswriter, and sought to discredit his evolutionary "rounders theory." Yet Spalding admitted, "It certainly appeals to an American's pride to have the great national game of Base Ball created and named by a Major General in the United States Army."[35] Luckily, for Spalding, Abner Graves presented what was then a believable story that would substantiate the committee's desires to "discover" the "American" origins of the game.[36]

The committee's endorsement of Abner Graves's testimony made his claims legitimate. Graves credited Abner Doubleday as principle inventor of the modern rules of baseball, claiming that the former Civil War hero had laid out the first baseball diamond in rural Cooperstown, New York, in 1839. Despite being debunked a year later by journalist Will Irwin, as well as by others over the years since the first decade of the twentieth century,[37] Graves's Cooperstown creation story is still the one that most people know. And despite an effort by historians to thwart the myth and search for the true origins of the game, it

> nonetheless remains powerful in the American imagination due to the efforts of major league baseball and the Hall of Fame in Cooperstown. For the record, however, one must acknowledge that research has proven that Abner Doubleday enrolled as a cadet at West Point in the fall of 1838 and possibly never even visited Cooperstown. . . . in his published writings [Doubleday] never mentioned anything about his role in the creation of modern baseball. Furthermore, Mills had known Doubleday ever since their service in the Civil War, but his friend had apparently never told him about his notable brainstorm in Cooperstown.[38]

Many of the people I interviewed, from fans to players, repeated Graves's farce, albeit without knowing or without calling Graves by name. Yet they knew where the Baseball Hall of Fame was located, in Cooperstown, New York, and, as if reciting old Sunday School lessons, told me why the Hall of Fame was there: because that's where baseball was invented. But baseball was not invented by one person at one time in one place. It evolved over time and across borders.[39]

The continued mythology and debate surrounding the rural origins of baseball shows one way that today's urban culture, which is not strictly confined to the physical geography of cities, is made up of a dynamic hybrid of unquestioned beliefs, half-truths, and fables. This is not to say that such sentiments and narratives are false. It does tell us, however, that urban culture, as seen through the social institution of baseball and the physical edifice of the urban ballpark, actively blurs the boundaries between traditional dichotomies. Urban culture can be understood in dialectical terms, as the melding of opposing ideas or states into a new and emergent formation. Such symbolically powerful dichotomies as rural/urban, sacred/profane, business/community, and work/leisure lose their assumed permanence when we pay attention to the ideas, beliefs, and practices of urban Americans.

Like the fans of yesterday, today's fans further deconstruct these dichotomies, not consciously but through their actions of faith and devotion toward their teams and playing grounds. Even though they paid on average $44.56 a ticket in 2004, not including parking, hats, T-shirts, beer, and hot dogs, fans treat Fenway Park as a place for communal interaction, civic engagement, and urban respite.

Professional baseball emerged as a "commercialized amusement business" along with the massive population growth in cities between 1880 and 1920. It was used as an escapist retreat from the confines of the city even though the business was dependent on the urban marketplace.[40] Professional baseball was a business, and the building of permanent ballparks during the early decades of the twentieth century was a sign of its acceptance as potentially stable and lucrative. Yet it still functioned for spectators as a diversion from the increasing rationality of the urban environs. According to historian G. Edward White,

> the central attractions of baseball as a spectator sport . . . lay in the fact that it *was* a diversion from the business world, a game echoing the associations of childhood play and leisured, sporting pursuits. Paradoxically, the more baseball was thought of as a pastime, a retreat from urban life as much as a confirmation of its vitality, a vicarious experience as much as an observational experience for the "cranks" and "bugs" (later "fans") who attend games, the more it appeared to become a spectacle that was socially desirable, as well as emotionally uplifting, to attend. From its earliest modern decades, baseball was thought of as a business, a form of entertainment for profit, but implicitly presented as a much more engaging spectacle than a circus or an opera or a play.[41]

From the start, then, professional baseball embodied paradoxical attributes as a way to get out of the city without leaving it and still participate in its culture. Baseball, too, contained within it a home for individualist and collectivist values, statistical calculations and nonrational emotions, and business and community interests. Baseball's urban ballparks not only provided places for people to cheer and jeer but also acted as mediums for urban Americans to negotiate their accepted and prevalent work ethic with their new-fangled and budding leisure ethic.

JUSTIFYING LEISURE

Before baseball became widely acknowledged as the national pastime, a designation that originated in the late 1850s and was popularized in the 1880s,[42] it took a number of forms, each with its own rules and regulations. In some cases, baseball looked very different from the sport we recognize today, especially the folk versions of the game that included "plugging" or hitting runners with the ball.[43] Baseball grew up in and out of an era in American history that fostered an entrepreneurial ethic that made its way into the realms of work, play, and religious worship. Late-nineteenth- and early-twentieth-century America was a time of great technological innovations, progressive politics, religious awakenings, and thriving new consumption practices.

In the introduction to the second volume of his detailed history of baseball, historian David Quentin Voigt writes that baseball did not simply spring to life by chance. "Rather, it evolved from various childish games and play and grew to fit the leisureways of an increasingly urban America where an ethic of fun was gaining at the expense of such values as religious sobriety and commitment to toil."[44] As baseball grew from its initial stages of experimentation and rule tinkering into an organized sport, eventually budding into a lucrative commercial industry and popular public amusement, it was promoted as an activity, to supplement, rather than replace, traditional civic institutions, that encouraged both individual and collective values. Sociologist Claude Fischer found that the increase in types of leisure and recreation from 1890 to 1940 did not displace traditional collective activities but actually aided the increase of group and public activities.[45]

As baseball became a civic pastime, the notion of the "civic" expanded and continues to expand to take in or edify new pursuits. Moreover, just as the individual and the community are not mutually exclusive categories that somehow operate outside and independent of each other, baseball and urban America neither mimicked nor mirrored each other. They came into being together, neither securing an ultimate causal position over the other. As such, baseball and other emerging organized sports were not simply vehicles for the expression of values, as if persons' actions are mere containers for their beliefs, but were vital activities that helped solidify and promulgate the core values of an overarching American ethos.

Connecting ball playing to a wider set of values has been a consistent practice for Americans who felt the need to justify or rationalize the time they spent not working. Its populist appeal was an effective advertising mechanism for those, first, who believed in the latent social functions of baseball and, later, for those who profited financially from its appeal. Baseball was presented as a group activity that makes better people, better citizens, and better Americans and that thereby benefits the nation as a whole. At least that is what social reformers and baseball enthusiasts hoped then and what many still believe today. Examples of this type of sentiment run rampant in newspapers and personal memoirs of the mid- to late nineteenth century and into present times.[46]

In today's media, when the negative aspects of baseball are reported—usually having something to do with the presumed overcommercialization of the sport, misbehaving fans and crowd violence, players' salaries, or, most recently, players' use and abuse of steroids and performance-enhancing drugs—they are often compared to a misbegotten time when the game was supposedly purer and more authentic.[47] In effect, such negative stories often use the "baseball teaches values" paradigm as a point of comparison, as a yardstick, to juxtapose what *is* to what *should be*, which is often misrepresented as what *was*. In other words, the crimes of today are often compared to the virtues of yesterday, regardless of whether knowledge of the past is based on evidence or belief.

Still, there are many who see the "baseball teaches values" argument as one of the key connections between the past and the present. Using this argument as a resource for justifying their own leisure activities, fans today often see the good in spectator sports when recalling their own affiliations and experiences. During a game at Fenway against the Anaheim Angels, I met a Red Sox fan eating a Fenway Frank in the standing-room-only section behind home plate who told me about her experience as a recently converted Red Sox fan. More than once, she mentioned the solidarity she felt with strangers who, in turn, became less strange through their common loyalty to the Red Sox.

> It happens here at Fenway, but also on the T, or on the street, or when I'm throwing a frisbee on the Commons. I'll see someone wearing a Red Sox hat or a T-shirt, or they'll see me wearing my hat or shirt, and we'll strike up a conversation. "Did you see the game last night? How's Nomar's ankle? Do you think they'll trade for another starting pitcher?" Sure, the conversations don't go too much further than that, but, hey, it's something, right? I don't know, I think that's probably pretty common in most cities. People can always talk about baseball. . . . as someone who's not from here, the Red Sox, Fenway, the fans, it just all made me feel like this was my home now, and maybe for a long time.

From the most heralded literati to the proverbial "Man at the Bar" who is always several stools away and several drinks gone, baseball is one of those cultural phenomena, and perhaps more so than any other activity or institution, that Americans love to wax poetic about. Such romantic discussions of baseball often envision the sport as the great social leveler, providing all those who choose to participate and believe in it with a shared history and a national mythology. Baseball becomes the medium for morality tales, offering characters and events on a regular basis for strangers to talk about and debate.

This type of discourse may appear to be merely idle talk, barroom banter, or narrow-minded vitriol, an impression that many of the popular call-in talk-radio shows help paint. But there is a longstanding history of sports talk. We can easily recognize sports talk as one of the types of *sociability* that classical social theorist Georg Simmel described. Arguing against views that saw people as rationally motivated, utilitarian actors, Simmel recognized that we do not always engage in conversations for strategic purposes, but, rather, we often interact with others simply for the sake of interacting itself.[48]

As more than one interviewee made clear, next to the weather, baseball is one of the few things that people can talk to complete strangers about in public. A good proportion of that talk is not about players' statistics and win percentages. When conversations about baseball begin to evoke feelings of city or hometown pride, or summon personal recollections of attended games or even those watched on television, or lead to laments on the lack of upstanding heroes in the game today, the social importance of baseball is substantiated and validated.

The great American poet Walt Whitman grew up in the throes of baseball's growing popularity in Brooklyn. Whitman's praise of baseball is widely cited, acting as a mantra of sorts for past and contemporary sportswriters and urban reformers. "I see great things in baseball, it's our game—the American game," Whitman gleamed. "It will take our people out of doors, fill them with oxygen, give them a larger physical stoicism . . . and be a blessing to us."[49] This quote, however lofty the terms and sentiment may be, actually reveals a fact of baseball history that is widely overlooked, if not forgotten or even ignored, namely, that baseball is a city sport. Whitman implicitly acknowledges the urban context of baseball and the early reform movements that encouraged people to spend time outside when they leave their office and factory jobs, breathe fresh air, and partake in a game that could potentially aid the development and maintenance of healthy minds and healthy bodies.

Whitman was also showing his own cultural heritage by echoing the same rationalizations about leisure activities that concerned past American generations. In historian Steven A. Riess's discussion of the budding "baseball creed" that emerged in the years immediately following the Civil War and became more widespread in the twentieth century, he acknowledges the typical functional requirements that "respectable" Americans had always placed on their recreational activities:

> Since the days of the Puritans, it had always been essential for a person to demonstrate that his free time was spent usefully and not merely for fun and amusement. Puritan and other upstanding colonists stressed that free-time activities were fine as long as they were moral and performed in moderation and provided a worthwhile function. Rifle-shooting contests were positively sanctioned because they helped train colonists to be better marksmen and thus better prepared for hunting and defense. But a sport like billiards had to be stopped because it was a waste of time which did not improve the participants and was sinful because of the gambling involved.[50]

Baseball, though certainly not the only sport that attracted participants and spectators, appealed to a cross-section of the general population, cutting through traditional social dividing lines. Baseball fit nicely into the emerging urban world, where the ideals of "prosperity and order" were both lauded and threatened.[51] This made sense in Boston, where the Puritan emphases on discipline and order still held significant weight but had lost their authoritative hold on the culture.[52]

Organized recreation and play were part of a growing movement among urban residents at the turn of the century to recognize the benefits of physical activity. Alongside the industrial and commercial work ethic that is often used to describe city life was an equally important *leisure ethic*. This spirit of play was of great interest to reformers who saw that selected sporting activities could help promote team work, discipline, order, and self-sacrifice.

As American cities grew in both size and population, sports became a cathartic enterprise, an institution allegedly able to combat the ills of industrialization and the loss of traditional rural activities. Baseball, as Whitman pronounced, could provide a means for physical activity that would both benefit the individual and be a "blessing" for society as a whole. The great American poet was a bearer of an Enlightenment tradition that touted the Greek ideal of the unity of sound body and sound mind. This tradition was at the heart of a new philosophy of sport and athleticism that was superseding, or at least countering, the traditional religious and social objections to sport and other active leisure activities. Those who espoused this new standpoint saw fitness, recreation, and sport as positive means for helping people successfully manage the changing cultural norms and social structure.[53]

Whitman was also a native city dweller, growing up on the edges of Brooklyn, home of some of the first organized teams. Whereas Brooklyn was once known as the "City of Churches," the *Porter's Spirit of the Times* declared in 1857 that it was "fast earning the title of the 'City of Base Ball Clubs.'" The article continued by assuring the compatible goals of baseball and church piety. The ball clubs provided both "innocent amusement and healthful exercise" and were "valuable adjuncts to the church, inasmuch as healthy bodily condition is undoubtedly essential to the enjoyment of a peaceful and religious state of mind."[54] The contours and content of the urbanite's "state of mind"—peaceful, religious, or otherwise—was part of the public discourse in places like Brooklyn, New York, Philadelphia, Cincinnati, Cleveland, Chicago, and Boston. These places became America's first "major league" cities, homes to some of the first professional baseball teams. The way of life espoused and garnered in these cities is still a part of today's urban culture, and social scientists and social commentators are still wrestling over the "state of mind" of the city and its people.

The need to get "out of doors" that Whitman spoke of was not counter to the emerging urban way of life; it was already a part of it. Many observers of American cities have, traditionally, characterized urban life in negatives terms, spending significant amounts of time, paper, and ink describing the poverty and squalor, the feeble tenements and feeble bodies of urban dwellers, and the social decay and disorganization that became apparent in certain parts of cities with the onset and rise of industrial work and bureaucratic organization.

But this only tells one part of the story. The other part is about the things that people did to counteract the social ills of a newly unsettled and often unsettling environment. This is the part about a culture that was not willing to be swept away by the powerful forces of urbanization. Instead, there were groups and individuals who sought to harness it, change it, and mold an urban way of life that would be conducive to the changing world around them.

Seeking to retain certain aspects of a traditional lifestyle in the midst of rapid social change, urbanites joined voluntary organizations as a way to fend off the presumed, and often psychologically and physiologically damaging, "anomic" aspects of industrialized cities.[55] "In the antebellum city, sport became an important focal point for the formation of urban subcommunities that provided both ready-made associations of people who shared the same interests and values and facilities and organizations for their common interests."[56] It has been well documented that the formally and informally organized sports clubs or "sporting fraternities" (also known as "fancies" for the upper echelon of more distinguished fellows) provided the roots for the rise and growth of professional baseball.[57]

Many of the groups were throw-back organizations that managed to survive and thrive in the new urban settings, but they were not necessarily holdovers from the past. The sporting fraternities purposely sought to relieve certain aspects of city life and were less binding and constrictive and more willing to accept transients and newcomers than the type of close-knit, often hereditary and exclusive, groups of small rural villages. "In this democratic and anonymous environment, men of different backgrounds rubbed shoulders and entertained each other, forming a transient community in which sharing jokes and paying for drinks made for temporary acquaintanceships but not necessarily lifelong friendships."[58] The earliest baseball clubs were true social clubs and civic associations, where the playing of baseball was only one of a host of other activities the groups took part in. Because groups gathered after regular work hours and on weekends, members of these clubs usually came from the same occupation or had the same work schedule.[59]

The early sporting clubs often met in social halls and taverns. The tavern has a storied history as a meeting place for various groups, often centered around particular trades or neighborhood interests.[60] It was also a place for conducting indoor sports that did not require too much space, though it was not unusual for bloody bird fights to take place in dark alleys just behind or adjacent to the "watering hole." Aware of the draw that certain sports had, for both participants and spectators, tavern owners were willing to host events like boxing and its less genteel and less rule governed cousin "gouging," pedestrian races, endurance contests, and animal fights (rats, dogs, chickens, etc.). Even though these activities were illegal or would soon become illegal because of public outcry, they proved to be commercially valuable and, to a certain extent, community sanctioned. Because of their popularity among men who sought out camaraderie and sociability in an environment that helped them escape "femininity, domesticity, and the demanding routines of the new economy,"[61] owners and barkeepers often went to great lengths to keep these activities under the authorities' radar.

BELIEVING IN BASEBALL AND ITS CIVIC VIRTUES

Although members of the upper sectors of urban society did make their way into the seedier parts of the city to experience the less "respectable" forms of sport and play, the demographic makeup of the crowds at cockfighting and other similar events was far from evenly distributed. Some men of wealth and "standing" used sporting groups and athletics as ways to define social status. Wealthy folk were the only people who had the access and financial ability to participate in sports like thoroughbred racing and yachting. Baseball, however, from its beginnings as an organized sport in the 1850s, appealed to the middle class. This was evident in regard to its players and fans, and in the values baseball came to stand for and promote.

Baseball emerged as a likely, and perhaps the most appropriate, candidate to be a socializing institution that could teach "positive" values, rather than the hedonistic and escapist attributes linked to the indoor tavern spectacles discussed in the preceding section. Baseball was hailed as an assimilation tool for working-class immigrants and native-born urbanites alike.[62] Some historians have argued that workers found in baseball a confirmation of their work ethic and behaviors, rather than a retreat from them.[63] Indeed, baseball was promoted as an institution whose greatest value was to teach the practical importance of individual skill and success for the greater good of the team. Of course "team" could mean anything from an actual ball club to a commercial company to an entire nation. This idea was made explicit by Henry Curtis of the Playground Association in his discussion of the relationship between the individual players and his "team":

> A long hit or a daring run may not be what is needed. The judgment of his play is a social judgment. It is estimated not on the basis of its individual excellence, but by its effect on the success of the team. The boy must come out and practice when he wants to go fishing. He must bat out in order that the man on third may run in. Many a time he must sacrifice himself to the team. This type of loyalty is the same thing we call good citizenship as applied to the city, that we call patriotism as applied to the country. The team game is undoubtedly the best training for these civic virtues.[64]

This quote is from a manuscript written by Curtis and published in 1915. He was a full-time believer in the sporting creed that sprouted in the second half of the nineteenth century and was in full bloom at the time of his book's publication. This creed was remarkably able to retain its vibrancy even as baseball shifted from an amateur hobby to a lucrative business. Moreover, the belief in this creed is still evident today, despite the fact that such egalitarian ideals have not been fully realized at the ballpark, in the workplace, or in many of our homes.

Curtis was one of many who touted baseball as a source of civic pride for spectators. Amateur clubs in the 1850s began encouraging local residents to attend games and root for their team against opposing out-of-towners. As the amateur clubs and fraternities gave way to professional teams and leagues, there was a growing concern about baseball's commercialization and its effects on community involvement. But as teams and matches within and between cities became more and more competitive and skill driven, professional baseball was nearly inevitable, and was highly profitable for certain franchises and their home cities. Still, the move from amateur play to professional baseball was met with some uneasy resistance.

Sportswriters, other journalists, franchise owners, local businessmen, and public officials like Curtis used the new and improved means of transportation and communication to wage a massive public-relations campaign for the tenets of baseball. Though they had different personal objectives and motivations, together, though not in any conspiratorial sense, they provided the public with firm justifications that

> attending baseball games was not a waste of time but an enjoyable and useful leisure activity. *Baseball was an edifying institution that taught traditional nineteenth century frontier qualities, such as courage, honesty, individualism, patience, and temperance, as well as contemporary values, like teamwork.*[65]

The concerted effort to show that baseball was a wholesome recreation and not merely an idle amusement or frivolous waste of time was successful. Moreover, baseball's proponents were able to capitalize on the fact that professional baseball was nothing less that a skilled trade. As such, because baseball was still baseball, even if it was now a business, it was worth spending one's hard-earned money to watch, and root for or against, baseball players, who themselves labored at their craft. Envisioning ball players as hard-working laborers, perhaps, made them easier to admire, celebrate, chastise, and emulate.

By 1913, professional baseball was well established and practically nationalized. Big-league baseball had not only flourished in the northeastern cities; it had also gained increasing popularity in the burgeoning cities in the Midwest. According to political scientist Michael Danielson, "Baseball's cities [also] dominated the industrial heartland; they were the urban dynamo of the rapidly expanding American economy."[66]

During the first decades of the twentieth century, writing about baseball shifted from the effects of the sport on players to concerns about spectators and fans. Journalist H. Addington Bruce's article "Baseball and the National Life," published in 1913, clearly states baseball's (alleged) latent social functions, providing a good summation statement for the current discussion and a template for analysis of the game's mythological role in American culture today.[67] Bruce identified four ways that baseball was far more than a simple idle amusement and, especially in urban areas, was a necessary means of stress relief, character building, community building, and physical well-being for enthusiastic spectators. "Baseball," wrote Bruce, "from the spectators' standpoint, is to be regarded as a means of catharsis, or perhaps better, as a safety-valve. And it performs this service the more readily because of the appeal it makes to the basic instincts, with resultant removal of the inhibitions that ordinarily cause tenseness and restraint."[68]

Baseball provided a setting where fans could get out in the fresh air, jump up and cheer for their team, and participate "in such socially sanctioned rituals as booing opponents and cursing umpires."[69] Releasing pent-up emotions in a safe, public environment, Bruce contended, was better than directing the tensions of everyday life toward one's family, employers, co-workers, or innocent strangers.

As evidence that this creed has been appropriated by contemporary baseball fans, many interviewees made unacknowledged testaments to the "baseball creed." "I like coming here with my kids, but I've had some of my greatest times just going and getting loud with my boys and rooting for the Sox," said one fan, as he sipped his Bud Light between innings outside on Yawkey Way. A Red Sox fan who drives north from Connecticut four or five times a year said that Fenway Park is a great place "to come have fun, let it out, cheer for your team, you know, get drunk and be rowdy." When asked about his favorite moments at Fenway, another fan said he didn't think about actual events, that it was more like a feeling. "It's the whole experience of being there with my buddies and just letting loose," he explained.

Not everyone approves of the rowdy Red Sox fans who often stretch the limits of safe venting. A few persons I interviewed talked quite openly and disparagingly about teenage and young-adult fans, especially those who attend night games on weekends. During such times, Fenway Park can feel more like one of the bars or nightclubs that surround the ballpark. On a Friday night, it often seems like there are more sober people a block away from Fenway in Baseball Tavern than there are at the ballpark.

This sort of letting loose, however, is a part of Fenway's tradition. Sam Mele, who played outfield for the Sox from 1946 to 1952, remembers smelling both "booze and marijuana coming from the bleachers." Indeed, this tradition, for better or for worse, plays a role, to varying degrees, in the Fenway experience. Although fights do occur in the stands, they are the exception rather than the rule, and the Fenway faithful have never reached the height of violence associated with the "hooliganism" surrounding European soccer.[70] In 2004, fearing what the excitement of a World Series victory could bring along with it, Boston police went out of their way to oversee the situation. The celebrations that took place outside Fenway Park after the Red Sox won the Series were accompanied by mounted police armed with pepper spray, plastic-bullet guns, and smoke bombs because of previous public carousing that led to damage of both public and private property and included one fatality.

The second tenet of Bruce's depiction of the American "baseball creed" could be conceived of as a direct opposite of the first. Bruce believed that young men and women who watched baseball would learn important social values and gain personal traits such as hard work, respect for authority, judgment, patience, and teamwork. Jon C. of Peabody, Massachusetts, has two sons, ages nine and eleven. He talked about bringing his boys to Fenway so they can see what it takes to become a great athlete, qualities he attributes to patience when at bat or on the mound, as well as good sportsmanship.

> Even when the players get out of hand and do something foolish, I can use it to show my boys what not to do. . . . We were at that game when [former Red Sox outfielder] Carl Everett was called out looking, and he got in the ump's face and bumped him. I told them that was the wrong thing do and asked them if Nomar would ever do anything like that, and they said "No." They loved Nomar. It's a shame he's gone. He was a good role model. . . . coming to Fenway to see guys like that, that's giving my kids a good education about working hard and doing your job.

The idea that the ballpark can be used as a medium for civic education has been fostered by owners, players, journalists, and fans alike.

A third theme Bruce discussed was the democratizing value of baseball. The sport was regarded as a wonderful leveler of people. "The spectator at a ballgame is no longer a statesman, lawyer, broker, doctor, merchant, or artisan, but just a plain everyday man."[71] According to historian Gunther Barth, immigrants and other newcomers to the budding cities of the late-nineteenth and early-twentieth centuries found in baseball, as players and fans, a common language (box scores and batting averages), a common history (team records), and a common creed (individualism within defined rules and regulations).[72] Perhaps most important, baseball provided a common place: the ballpark. And the ballpark provided a locus for the advent of sustainable and believable ethos and mythos.

In recent years, historians and sociologists have questioned the ability of baseball, or any sport for that matter, to promote community or character building and have tried to upend the notion that the ballpark was a hotbed of democratic egalitarian values.[73] It is true that baseball's magnates carefully manipulated ticket prices, specialized seating, and game time to control and segregate crowds. The division of ballparks, today and yesterday, into separately priced sections is clearly a matter of economic segregation that was once motivated by ethnic and racial tension and separatism.[74] Irish and German Americans occupied the cheap seats. The bleachers in St. Louis were known as the "Kerry Patch" and in New York's Polo Grounds as "Burkeville" for the hordes of Irishmen that sat there. When they were allowed to attend, African Americans of every income group were restricted to "segregated sections . . . usually in the less favorable locations."[75]

Many recent studies have sought to debunk the egalitarian myth of baseball in the name of or for the sake of a more accurate picture of historical and contemporary American culture, but they have done so at the risk of losing an important element of American culture—the *persistence* of such myths. My interviews and my participant observations at the ballpark revealed a strong belief in Fenway Park, at least today's Fenway Park, as a place where individuals of different descent and income can rub elbows with one another, despite the disillusionment with professional players' salaries and alleged steroid abuse, use of public funding for stadium building, and climbing ticket prices.

In the eyes of those who attend the games, and for some who hope to someday, they see friends rather than foes at the ballpark, that is, if they're rooting for the Red Sox (or against the Yankees). Regardless of whether or not such mixing happens or at what frequency, the *belief* that it happens is irrefutably true. Granted, such beliefs might stem from the fact that the stands are filled with an overwhelming proportion of white faces. But to assume that white faces constitute a homogeneous population is as misguided as the assumption that a place must be shared equally to be considered shared at all.

Although the Red Sox and the city have made significant advances in their openness and inclusion of ethnic and racial minorities, both on the field and in the stands, questions about race still remain.[76] And we know that it is not simply about class. Blue-collar, working-class whites often save their money to make a trip or two a year to Fenway Park. But African American attendance at Fenway Park remains disproportionately lower than other populations, especially when compared to the rising attendance of Latinos in Boston and other urban ballparks.

THE URBAN BALLPARK:
AN ENDURING SYMBOL OF THE CITY

The City Beautiful movement of the early twentieth century, itself an outgrowth of the emerging sporting ethos, was prompted by the idea that the civic life of cities could be enhanced and nourished through the construction of monumental buildings, parks, and public spaces. Such places became the material basis for literally and symbolically building the identity of reborn neighborhoods and entire cities.[77]

Ballparks can help cities present themselves as "big time" or "major league," regardless of whether they are or not.[78] These places continue to play important roles as integral symbols within what sociologist Gerald Suttles calls a city's "urban iconography," aiding the selective preservation of a city's character and local culture.[79] The "cumulative texture of local urban culture" is constituted by a hybrid of beliefs about what ideas and objects to preserve from the past, how they fit with the city today, and how they will make room for the emergent ideas that accompany the inclusion of more diverse populations, technological advancements, and the changing boundaries of work and leisure time.

In his historical analysis of American cities, sociologist Daniel Monti found that the paradoxical nature of urban culture demands that "persons who follow an urban way of life [fashion] a world that mixes principle with the need to make practical accommodations."[80] As an enduring symbol of the city, ballparks act as mediums for the negotiation of cultural paradoxes both within its walls and through the building of those walls, stands, and sometimes domes as well.

When the Astrodome, lauded as "the eighth wonder of the world," was built in 1965, it helped reshape Houston's image "from sleepy bayou town to space-age Sunbelt dynamo."[81] It was the first indoor, air-conditioned stadium, and it introduced AstroTurf, artificial grass that at the time was thought to be a major technological breakthrough but, soon enough, was proved to be good for little more than hard bounces and nasty rug burns. But AstroTurf was easy to maintain, did not need sunlight, and shined on television. The Dome quickly became a symbol of America's sterile, automobile-dependent, air-conditioned nightmare.

Houston, again, tried to rectify its image by building a new downtown ballpark in 2000 in the neotraditional style of Baltimore's Camden Yards, Cleveland's Jacobs Field, and San Francisco's SBC Park. The new ballpark began life as Enron Field, but when the giant utility company was caught in the midst of a huge financial scandal in 2002, the Astros moved quickly to terminate the naming-rights deal and renamed the stadium Astros Field for the 2002 season. The team promptly came to an agreement with the Coca-Cola Company to rename the stadium Minute Maid Park. Hosting the 2004 MLB All-Star game, the new ballpark, which features a ten-degree grass-covered incline in the deepest part of center field as a tribute to Cincinnati's old Crosley Field (which was built in 1912, the same year as Fenway, and demolished in 1972), showed the rest of the baseball-watching public that Houston could be a major player in the world of entertainment and tourism.

Eli Jacobs, owner of the Baltimore Orioles when Camden Yards was built in 1992, maintained that it was "very important that the park have a personality, an identity, so people could say, 'This is Baltimore's baseball park,' and if you're in it you have no doubt where you are."[82] The identities of the ballpark and the city were supposed to play off each other.

Trying to test the "If you build it, they will come" Hollywood (or Iowa) principle, St. Petersburg searched for a team after it built the Florida Suncoast Dome in 1991. The fancy new domed stadium was reportedly intended to lure already established teams (including the San Francisco Giants and the Chicago White Sox), as well as change the city's image as "heaven's waiting room" for the retired and aged.

> In Florida, the quest for the legendary Fountain of Youth has often merged with the state's quest for development and renewal. For many, the quest for a major league team and the construction of the domed stadium on speculation are just modern-day version of the same wide-eyed vision.[83]

Though the National Hockey League's Tampa Bay Lightning played there from 1994 to 1997, the Suncoast Dome, which was renamed the Thunderdome (perhaps trying to live out more Hollywood dreams) did not host baseball until 1998. Along with an expansion team, the Devil Rays, came another new name for the stadium, Tropicana Field, and an $85 million renovation to make the "field" more baseball-specific and architecturally interesting. In an attempt to connect Tropicana Field, the Devil Rays, and St. Petersburg to the history of baseball, the city built an eight-story-high rotunda entrance that was designed from the very blueprints used for the rotunda at Ebbets Field.

St. Petersburg's attempt to emulate Brooklyn is surely a worthy effort. The tradition of baseball in Brooklyn is so strong that even the construction of a relatively small minor-league ballpark was able to boost the city's civic pride and enhance and display the community's identity. In the summer of 2001, professional baseball was played in Brooklyn for the first time since 1957. Though the wounds from losing not only Ebbets Field but the entire Dodgers franchise are still not completely healed, the Brooklyn Cyclones, a minor-league affiliate of the major league's New York Mets, helped mend the forty-four-year-old gash.[84]

The Cyclone's Keyspan Park was built on the edge of Brooklyn, bordering the historic Coney Island area and its "Cyclone" wooden roller coaster. Since it opened, the team regularly plays in front of sellout crowds that easily fill the 6,500-seat ballpark. "I love it," said Dionne Durant, a local Brooklyn resident. "I think it's great. It really enhances the community and gives real life to Brooklyn."[85]

Ballparks are urban identity markers and have been since the late nineteenth century. They are one of the great tools that people use to present their city to outsiders, newcomers, tourists, and themselves. Although a city's identity may never be entirely stable, persons' desires to maintain a degree of continuity in the built environment show the significance of important places for sustaining past beliefs and ideals.

The leisure ethic that emerged in American cities during the first decades of the twentieth century remains strong today as cities continue to build new ballparks and other public amusements. The "baseball creed," which played a significant role in establishing the American leisure ethic as a supplement to rather than replacement for the traditional (Protestant) work ethic, was what theologian Michael Novak once referred to as the "consecration of the American spirit."[86] And that spirit emerged from the urban ballparks of the early twentieth century

—the "Golden Age" of baseball. As such, the ideals of the "baseball creed" are still connected to Fenway Park, more so than to newer ballparks, because it helped institutionalize the perceived values of spectator sports. Because Fenway grew out of and grew up in the time when baseball was cherished as a social and civic institution, it is a physical embodiment of that era. Instead of the Doubleday Cooperstown myth that acts as reminder of our lost rural past and continues to thrive because of the Hall of Fame locations in upstate New York, Fenway Park is a more accurate depiction of the early urban sporting ethos.

In today's urban culture, Fenway Park is a nostalgic reminder of our urban past. And Fenway Park thrives because it still functions today in very much the same way that it has since 1912. The tale of those years is not written in stone. The way the story is told is affected by our present urban condition— a condition defined by an ever-changing blend of past beliefs and new situations. Whereas Cooperstown stands still as an "imagined" place, Fenway Park is a living testament to the paradoxical culture of American cities.

THE BALLPARK AT REST
The Civic Partnership between Boston, the Red Sox, and the Fenway Faithful

I've always had a feeling that baseball teams are civic institutions and therefore should celebrate civic holidays. So we wanted to do something for Halloween and Thanksgiving, during the winter holidays, Martin Luther King Day, Father's Day, Mother's Day. Part of it is a marketing disposition. The other part seemed that it was self-evident to share it with the people who feel connected to it.
> —Larry Lucchino, Red Sox president/CEO

Sometimes I like to come here during the winter or in the spring just before the season starts and walk around the ballpark, maybe stand for a few minutes or so behind the Green Monster [on Landsdowne Street]. It's like my second home. . . . Fenway tells me I'm home. Fenway tells me I'm in Boston.
> —Pete S., Red Sox fan, Cambridge, Massachusetts

Between April and September, the Red Sox play eighty-one games at Fenway Park. Even though baseball games usually last around three hours, Red Sox games are more like full-day events, perhaps more so for the organization than for the fans. Consider the amount of time needed for pre- and postgame warm-ups, cool-downs, preparation, and cleaning. For night games, the players are in their uniforms at 4:00 p.m.

for a 7:05 p.m. start. The field and stands must be in pristine condition before any player takes the field for batting practice or any fan finds his or her seat. After the game ends, while the grounds crew waters and rakes the grass and infield, Fenway's clean-up crew combs the narrow aisles to dispose of sausage wrappers, used packets of mustard, abandoned plastic beer cups, and the ever-present piles of tattered peanut shells.

The fan, too, can stretch the Fenway experience beyond the ceremonial first pitch and the last out. I have seen, and participated in, many of the rituals that take place before and after Red Sox home games. Groups of cheering and jeering Red Sox fans, adorned in scarlet red and navy blue, in anticipation of a Sox win, make their way toward Fenway Park, many via Kenmore Square, sometimes stopping for snacks and beverages from one of the many bars, restaurants, or vendors that circle the park. Flooding the nearby streets and stopping traffic in the name of baseball, before and after the game, the fans themselves enhance Fenway Park's visibility. No one needs to look at a calendar or schedule to know when the Red Sox are in town. Home games do not make good secrets.

But what happens the rest of the time at Fenway Park, and how does what happens at those times affect the ballpark's importance? In short, a lot happens at Fenway Park, on the inside and outside. A consistent fixture in and feature of Boston, Fenway Park does not have an off-season. Charity events, political rallies, concerts, holiday celebrations, and tours take people inside Fenway's storied confines with increased frequency since the new ownership group took over in 2002.

The red brick façade and towering lights, the scoreboard and the Green Monster, and the Citgo sign that looms over the ballpark resting high above Kenmore Square, all visible from the Massachusetts Turnpike, are constant and continuous reminders of the fact that you are in Boston. The unique layout of the ballpark and the surrounding area is part of its character and charm. As historian Philip Lowry observes, "No one can ever mistake Fenway Park for Yankee Stadium, as they might Busch Stadium for Riverfront [two symmetrical, "cookie-cutter" stadiums]."[1]

Lou Gorman, the general manager of the Red Sox from 1984 to 1993, reiterated this point during my interview with him. "You can walk into a lot of ballparks but never get the same feeling you get when you walk into Fenway. It's that unique," said Gorman as we sat in the press box before a Red Sox–Orioles spring training game in Ft. Myers, Florida. A transplanted Red Sox fan who now lives outside Houston, Texas, reaffirmed this sentiment from her own "dislocated" position:

> Every time I come back to Boston, I go to Fenway Park. If the Sox are playing, that's great, and if I can get a ticket, even better. . . . I always make sure to visit Fenway, even if it's just to go take a walk around the park, stop in and buy a souvenir or something. I don't know, I just like seeing it and being near it when I come back here. It's Boston; it ain't like anything else. It's home. My parents don't even live in the same house anymore. Luckily the Red Sox still do. Boston just wouldn't be the same without Fenway Park.

This native Bostonian uses Fenway Park as a means to continue her sense of identity even though she now lives in Texas. Sociologists have found that places can help maintain "identity continuity" between different phases of one's life.[2] When this fan said that "Boston just wouldn't be the same without Fenway Park," she was also telling me that *she* wouldn't be the same either.

Even when the ballpark is completely empty, it still maintains a great deal of significance for individuals and for the city at large. For the city, the ballpark acts as a landmark amid Boston's historic landscape. Fenway Park has symbolic significance as a shorthand emblem that denotes the identity of twentieth-century Boston and provides an introduction to an important part of its culture.[3] It also holds everyday significance as a place that defines an area of the city for individuals as both a "memorialized locale" and a "familiarized locale."[4] That is, Fenway Park is a place that people both pay homage to and are accustomed to as an everyday feature of their daily commute or as a fixture in their local neighborhood. These relationships can be both personally and socially beneficial, though their intensity can vary between individuals and social groups.

From their seminal study of domestic spaces and material things, environmental psychologists Mihaly Csikszentmihalyi and Eugene Rochberg-Halton found that "although we live in physical environments, we create cultural environments within them. We continually personalize and humanize the environment as a way of both adapting to it and creating order and significance."[5] The creation of this "order and significance," however, is not a solitary act but a social practice fashioned in both public and private places and for both public and private purposes.

One important type of shared place where shared meanings are constructed and where interactions are of a social and civic nature is the "third place." Sociologist Ray Oldenburg defines a "third place" as a public leisure setting used for informal social interactions, engagements, and encounters. Third places are social spaces "beyond the realms of work and home."[6] They are most commonly places like corner shops, coffee houses, hair salons, barbershops, local pubs, taverns, bars, and other varieties of watering holes and other hangouts. Although the notion that third places are "beyond the realms of work and home" misses the fact that people work in these places (e.g., waiters, waitresses, bartenders, bouncers, cashiers), the main point still stands: third places are important for the construction, maintenance, and reconstruction of a city's civic culture. Even though third places are often privately owned, they are still shared. They do not have to be shared equally or all the time for the place to serve a broader, more common good.[7]

Fenway Park is a *big* third place. Most of the analyses about such places focus on small, neighborhood-specific places or, comparatively, on public locales that are so large that membership is so inclusive that the symbolic boundaries of the population are almost totally amorphous.[8] Even though the cost of tickets keeps many people from attending as many games as they wish or, for some, any games at all, becoming a member of the Fenway faithful is still liberally open. Even though there are some regulars at the ballpark, for the most part the population is individually dynamic and inconsistent.

Some of Fenway's regulars qualify as "familiar strangers," people who we see routinely on our daily or regular commute from one place to another.[9] Sometimes we cross paths with the same persons so much that we notice them more when they're not there than when they are. One qualification of the familiar stranger is the lack of verbal interaction with him or her. This qualification separates the familiar stranger from what urban planner Jane Jacobs identifies as the "public character," as does the intentions and motivations of the individual in question.[10] For Jacobs, public characters are small business owners, local shop keepers, pamphleteers, and sidewalk souvenir, food, and book vendors.[11] Though she emphasizes the *publicness* of the character as an outward expression from the character's point of view, she does not address the actual relationship between the character and *the public,* the community that consumes his or her service and presence.

Many of the people whose presence is important in and around Fenway Park are more than familiar strangers and are something akin to but still different from public characters; they are what I call *shared human landmarks.* This term, which I admit is somewhat awkward, still gets at something that both of the other terms for the most part ignore or, at best, only faintly convey. These shared human landmarks both help define a place and are defined by it, and they are attached to such places through other persons' shared recognition of them. In short, *a shared human landmark is any person who acts as a medium for social cohesion between others in public within a defined and distinct local area.* These public characters are readily recognized and often become the focal point of conversations between strangers, even if those conversations are fleeting and nothing more.[12] But such conversations *are* something more; they create a connection, however minimal, between people who do not know each other personally. And when shared human landmarks are geographically rooted, they become markers of that territory and the culture of that place.

The shared human landmarks at Fenway Park include ticket holders, people who use the large public gathering for other purposes—like the "Jesus Saves" guy and the typically teenaged plastic-pail drummers —and those who work inside and outside the ballpark such as longtime ushers, ticket takers, and concessions vendors.

A week after Opening Day of the 2004 season, an article in the *Boston Globe* had the following title: "Absence of 'George the Peanut Guy,' a Fixture for Three Decades, Leaves Void in Fenway Lineup."[13] For the first time in thirty-one years, seventy-year-old George Tsardounis was not outside the ballpark on Opening Day. Since 1973, the Fenway Faithful were greeted by George's endless hollers from behind his pushcart on Yawkey Way: "Pea-nuts! Pis-tach-i-os! Cash-ews! Hot Pretzels! And Craaaaaacker Jaaaaaacks!" His customers knew him as "George the Greek," "George the Peanut Guy," or "The Peanut Man." "There are few people who know Fenway Park who don't mimic George in some way," said an owner of one of the local bars. "'Peanuts, Pistachios, Cashews.' They know his spiel."[14]

The "Sausage Guy" and his encased-pork-slinging rival, the "Sausage King," have become Lansdowne Street institutions for pre- and postgame munchies. Indeed, the "Sausage Guy" has become so much a staple of the Fenway experience outside the ballpark that Mitt Romney stopped to slop out a few sausages and onions five months before the 2002 Massachusetts gubernatorial election. This was a well-timed and well-placed strategic move on Romney's part. In the weeks prior to his sausagefest, Romney had been slammed in the local press for being an out-of-state resident, paying taxes for two years to Utah while he headed the organizing committee of the 2002 Winter Olympics. Serving sausages with one of the most well-known vendors in Boston outside one of the most cherished places in Boston afforded Romney an easy opportunity to ingratiate himself to the local constituency. "[It] portrays him as regular person," said Richard Lane, a resident of Somerville, Massachusetts, as he stopped for a snack before entering the ballpark. "Instead of kissing babies, he's serving sausages."[15] In this case, Romney used both the "Sausage Guy" and Fenway Park as a "rite of inversion" to blur his high cultural status and present himself to the public as a "regular person."[16]

In the same way that a coffee shop is used for more than just drinking coffee and a pub is used for more than just drinking alcohol, Fenway Park is used for more than just playing baseball.[17] Although baseball is the primary activity that happens there, there are plenty of other important activities that involve the ballpark. These may be secondary activities in that they are not the initial purpose or intention of the ballpark, but they are hardly secondary when we again consider that for 278 day out of the year the Red Sox do not take the field. And even though it was baseball that originally generated the aura and mystique of Fenway Park, the other things that happen there and the other ways that the ballpark is used help rekindle its character. In this sense, Fenway's status does not depreciate without the Red Sox. In some ways, the ballpark's status may even increase when it is at rest.

THE PLACE OF SPORT AND THE BUSINESS OF COMMUNITY

Since its rise in popularity as a public amusement in the early decades of the twentieth century, professional baseball has provided a commercial medium for the practice of community in cities. Historian Warren Goldstein argues that historical studies of baseball have taken two distinct paths. One deals with the enterprise or business of baseball, what Goldstein refers to as the "linear" history of the game. The other deals with baseball's emotional and sentimental attributes, which pertain to the game's "cyclical" history and fans' attempt to re-create or relive a lost past.[18]

While this bifurcation is evident in the literature and may be useful as an analytic distinction, the division does not exist in reality. This is especially true regarding the building or placement of ballparks within cities, which was always about tying private business to civic identity and community sentiment. Sociologist Daniel Monti contends that "commercial communalism" and "consumer communalism" are two of the important ways that contemporary Americans practice community.

> Shopping and investing of the sort we associate with a modern "consumer culture" and market economy actually helps make communities better. Both are updated versions of voluntary subscription campaigns in which individuals give up part of their wealth so that they might improve their own situation or the lives of other persons they know only slightly or maybe not at all. . . . After all, they may know a manufacturer, merchant, shopper, or investor only by reputation, and sometimes not even that well. It is for this reason that the customs and codes built up around investing, buying goods, and using services are among the most widely shared, most intricately prescribed, and carefully managed that we have.[19]

Of course, claims of civic pride and community-building can be used to mask the business interests of elite firms and groups, but that does not address the motivations behind the business that fans and spectators bring to the ballpark. Are consumption and fan loyalty that far apart? Not at all. Sure, fans complain about ticket prices, but they also complain about losing games, losing teams, and sitting in hard wooden seats without enough leg room. They spend a good amount of money on souvenirs and memorabilia as markers of their devotion. It is remarkable to see how many people are wearing at least one piece of Red Sox apparel at the games, not to mention every day on the streets of Boston. Such individual adornment gives off messages of team loyalty, community membership, and purchasing power. Consumer and community interests are therefore intricately intertwined in urban areas as expressed through these "articles of faith."[20]

The sports industry is different from other business ventures because of the sentiment and symbolism, rituals and myths, and civic

During the 2004 playoffs, the Prudential Building cheered for the Red Sox and ensured a World Series victory. As a way of showing civic pride, the message "Go Sox" was displayed by keeping specific office lights on during the games played at Fenway. (Photo by the author)

pride and self-image connected to hometown teams and their home playing grounds. More mundane businesses do not have the same type of connection to the community as sports teams.

"It is hard to imagine Baltimoreans rooting for the Esskay meat company, a local firm, over a rival cold-cuts firm like Oscar Mayer of Madison, Wisconsin," writes economist Charles Euchner. "The two firms do not carry the city's name and do not confront each other as symbols of their communities the way sports teams do."[21] This is not to say that cities do not support local industries, because they do, regardless of how cosmopolitan or global they appear to be. Consider urban community interests and local culinary customs. Boston and New York certainly battle over the superiority of their respective clam chowders. But, without a great leap of the imagination, the two styles will never meet and fight it out themselves.

Sports teams, however, foster inter-city competition and provide forums for such battles to be played out. As historian Benjamin Rader argues, "Determining urban supremacy in terms of population growth, community leadership, or quality of life might be difficult, but baseball games offered an unambiguous test of urban supremacy in the form of a symbolic contest."[22]

The players themselves often feel like they are the foot soldiers in these symbolic contests between cities. I interviewed Red Sox right-fielder Trot Nixon during spring training before the 2004 season, picking his brain about the ballpark and the fans he's been playing in front of since 1996. When I asked him what it would mean to win a championship with the Red Sox, he properly rephrased my question by talking about what it would mean to win it for the city:

> I'd like to win a championship for Boston. But, I'm not going to lie, I'd like to win one for myself too, and everybody else would say that as well. Honestly, with me and most of the guys who have played here for a few years, they want to win it for the city too. We see how much this organization means to Boston; they know how much baseball means to them. I see people who are eighty-five years old who say, "I haven't seen a championship. Is this the year?" When you play in this organization, you're not just playing for the organization or your teammates or yourself; you're playing for a greater group of people. And we're not just talking about the Greater Boston area; we're talking about all of Massachusetts, Vermont, New Hampshire, Rhode Island, the entire Northeast. I think what makes it even better is that, you know, Boston's greatest rival is only four hours south, and they're trying to do the same thing for the entire Northeast too. . . . It's not just two teams playing; it's two cities . . . battling it out.

Kevin Millar, the Red Sox on-and-off first-baseman, outfielder, and designated hitter, walked by at this point in our conversation, overheard what Nixon had just said, and let out an affirming "Yee hah!" Millar was responsible for the "Cowboy Up!" rally cry that swept across Boston during the Red Sox playoff run in 2003. Power hitting aside, Millar's popularity was so great that urban Bostonians bought cowboy hats and wore them to the ballpark.[23]

Nixon continued: "It's a whole lot more than just a game. You might actually like for it to be just a baseball game, but, more or less, when we play the [New York] Yankees, it's one nation against another nation." Nixon is making a reference here to the now popular nomenclature of the team's "community of believers": Red Sox Nation. It is easy for the players to get caught up and involved in the storied history of the Red Sox and passion of their fans.

The Red Sox were able to obtain a significant acquisition during the 2003 off-season because of that rivalry and those historic tales. About a month after they suffered another heartbreaking playoff-series defeat to the locally dreaded Yankees, the Red Sox signed ace pitcher and future Hall of Famer Curt Schilling, who helped the Arizona Diamondbacks win a World Series in 2001. According to Schilling, he decided to come to Boston, the team he was originally drafted by, to help them win a World Series for the city and "end the franchise's 85-year championship famine."[24] And, as the *Boston Globe*'s Jackie MacMullan wrote shortly after Schilling's mission was completed, "The city of Boston immediately embraced Schilling. The fans liked his outspoken nature, his meticulous preparation, and his appreciation for the history and the culture of the city."[25]

Because of the intimate connection between the city and the Red Sox, the team and the ballpark serve their public through charity work as well. The public exposure that Schilling received after he signed with the Red Sox aided his fundraising efforts for his charity, Curt's Pitch for ALS, an organization that Schilling founded to raise awareness of and money for research and patient care for people with Amyotrophic Lateral Sclerosis (ALS, or Lou Gehrig's Disease).[26]

Schilling's cause shined brightly in the national spotlight during the Red Sox playoff and World Series Championship run. In heroic fashion, Schilling came back from an injury to a tendon in his right ankle to beat the St. Louis Cardinals in Game 2 of the World Series at Fenway Park. The blood-stained sock that he wore during that game now sits in the Baseball Hall of Fame as a symbol of Boston's persistence and perseverance. As the television cameras zoomed in on Schilling's literal "red sock," not missing a chance to exploit the overt symbolism of the moment, they also picked up on a message inscribed on his shoe: "K ALS," short for "strikeout ALS." That shoe will sit alongside the "red sock" in Cooperstown with all the other treasured, nostalgia-soaked relics that make up the Hall of Fame.

Although much of what constitutes the civic partnership between the Red Sox and the city is mediated through the ballpark, not all the Red Sox good works take place there. In addition to Schilling's charity, past and current players make regular trips to hospitals and schools in and outside Boston. In 1998, the Red Sox sponsored a program in neighbor-hoods that lacked the funds and facilities to manage their own youth baseball leagues. The RBI League, or Reviving Baseball in Inner Cities, is a national program founded in 1989 by former major-leaguer John Young in South Central Los Angeles. As of 2004, RBI programs are up and run-ning in 185 cities worldwide, serving over 120,000 boys and girls.

Other charitable activities include donations of tickets to home games and sponsorship of literacy programs. Over the past few years, the Red Sox have worked with the Massachusetts Teachers Association and Verizon to promote literacy, sponsoring a summer reading contest for public school children. The Sox have also worked with the Boston Public Library, sponsoring a similar contest called "Read Your Way to Fenway" for children between the ages of five and seventeen. Students who read three books and write essays about them over the summer are given the opportunity to attend a home game free of charge.

On one afternoon before a home game during the 2004 season, I was in the Red Sox clubhouse interviewing players about the ballpark. Jason Varitek, the Red Sox captain and All-Star catcher, was sitting in front of his locker lacing up his spikes. I walked over to him and asked if he had a few minutes to chat about Fenway. He looked up at me and said he didn't have time then but maybe another day: "I have to go up and see my kids right now." OK, I thought, he must be a family man, and I went on with my business. It wasn't until I went up to the field myself that I realized what Varitek meant.

While his teammates were taking their pregame batting practice, Varitek was standing between the on-deck circle and the dugout. He was surrounded by a group of children wearing red T-shirts with "Varitek" above a big "33" on the back and "Red Sox" in navy blue across the front. These were his "kids"; they were "Tek's 33s." This was one of five games to which the catcher invites ten patients from the Chil-dren's Hospital of Boston to Fenway Park to watch batting practice from the dugout, get autographs, and then stay for the game. Varitek and his wife, Karen, pay for the tickets. As I watched him talk and laugh with the children—all of whom, as I later found out, had either under-gone or were about to undergo major surgeries—he seemed genuinely happy to be there. Later, Varitek said, "Just by bringing them here to see a game, I hope I can help them feel normal again."

Bringing children to Fenway Park or using a trip there as a prize for reading contests are some of the ways that the Red Sox have explicitly demonstrated their civic responsibilities and the importance of the ballpark for Boston's civic culture. Places become important through the ways that people use them. The physical edifice of Fenway Park holds symbolic meanings, not by itself but through the actions of both the organization and the people who use the ballpark for various reasons.

Fenway Park plays an active role, by design and by consequence, in the civic partnership between the city and the team. By opening up the ballpark for charity events, like the Jimmy Fund "Fantasy Day," or for Father's Day, Mother's Day, Halloween, or a Bruce Springsteen or Jimmy Buffet concert, the organization is practicing civic culture and community. Likewise, by attending such events and by appropriating the ballpark for their own purposes, Fenway Park patrons are also practicing civic culture and community.

PRIVATE MOMENTS IN CIVIC SPACE

The civic partnership between the ballpark and the city is constructed and maintained both with and without the Red Sox. Like any partnership, it must be actively worked on. On the ground, every day, that work is done by individuals and not simply through corporate entities like the "team" or the "city." People often use the ballpark for their own personalized forms of civic engagement. It is common for people to include Fenway Park, like an old friend, in the most significant and celebrated moments of their lives.

Take a story I was told by Mike Andrews. It is a story that highlights both an official public giving of the ballpark and an unconventional, private taking of it. Andrews played second base for the Red Sox from 1966 to 1970 and retired from baseball in 1973. Since 1979 he has been the chairman for the Jimmy Fund, the official charity of the Red Sox and the prime fundraising arm of the Dana Farber Cancer Institute. When I met Andrews at his Brookline office, which is about a twenty-minute walk from the ballpark, Red Sox Nation was still coping with another playoff loss to the Yankees. In order to remedy their ills, the Red Sox had entered trade negotiations that would have sent their star shortstop, Nomar Garciaparra (locally referred to, affectionately, as "Nomah!"), elsewhere in order to sign the most coveted and expensive player in the league, Alex Rodriguez (locally referred to, spitefully, as "Pay-Rod" for his continuously record-breaking contracts).

Andrews and I talked baseball for a while, and then Andrews answered some more pointed questions that I posed about the ballpark. He talked about Fenway Park as a landmark, calling it "a historical treasure, ingrained in Boston and all over the world." He talked about his mixed emotions about Fenway and how a new ballpark on the waterfront could be nice, like San Francisco's new ballpark (revealing his California roots, perhaps). He talked about the seating problems at Fenway for anyone six feet tall and over. He talked about playing at Fenway and recalled fondly the celebration after the 1967 pennant victory. "It was inside the park, it was outside the park, it was all over the city. I've never seen a celebration like that. . . . it was an amazing thing to behold and be a part of." He talked about the pressures of playing in Boston and how sad he was when he was traded.

We spent the rest of our time discussing the Jimmy Fund and the events that the organization has held at Fenway Park. Along with luncheons and conferences in the executive offices or the luxurious .406 Club, the Jimmy Fund has been organizing an annual "Fantasy Day" at Fenway Park since 1991 to benefit children with cancer. Andrews said that the organization raised over $400,000 in 2003. In 2004, Fantasy Day brought in $580,000 from both corporate charities and individuals eager to swing away at the Green Monster.

The John Hancock Fantasy Day at Fenway Park brings people together to support the Jimmy Fund, but it also gives people the chance to play on the field they have only watched from afar. There are a few packages that participants can choose from, including a "Fan Package" that allows people to watch friends, family, and other philanthropic baller-wannabes from a prime seat. Children under three are allowed in for free, children between three and ten need $50 to get in, and adults pay $100 to sit in the ballpark and watch grown men and women trot around Fenway's hallowed grounds.

According to Andrews, the "Batting Package" is the most coveted. It does not take a stretch of the imagination to know why. Participants take a few warm-up swings in the cages and then step up to home plate and take fifteen swings at the most beloved, and hated, left-field wall in baseball—the Green Monster. Stepping to the plate wearing an official Red Sox jersey and cap, the participant's name and picture are projected on the center-field scoreboard while the announcement of the at-bat rings through the ballpark: "Now batting, ——." The crowd roars, or at least you pretend it does. And if you manage to add a new dent among the thousands that dimple the big green wall, you can walk away with an "I Hit the Wall at Fenway Park" T-shirt. Individuals pay about $1,800, and teams of five pay about $9,000. If one would rather shag fly balls or turn double plays, the "Fielding Package" is a less expensive option (individuals, $800; teams of five, $4,000). The Batting, Fielding, and combo Batting/Fielding packages were sold out in each year from 2003 to 2005.

"It's common for people to pick up infield dirt and put it in their pocket or slide into second and never wash those pants again," said Andrews. "Getting something that is so historical, there's really nowhere else that you can do that." Andrews then interrupts himself, and his eyes brighten up in anticipation of the story he's about to tell me. "Oh yeah, you're definitely going to like this one." After the Fantasy Day participants take their fifteen swings, regardless of the results of their hacking, they run the bases. While a particular participant was rounding first base, Andrews and company saw a clear plastic bag, containing what looked like a white powdery substance, drop out of his back pocket and onto the field.

> It was a plastic baggy with some sort of white substance. We didn't know what it was, maybe drugs or something. Naturally, we were concerned. As I walked towards him, the guy said, "Hey, don't worry, this is, this is my buddy. He passed away, and I promised him that I would make sure that he was a part of Fenway Park forever." So, as he ran around the bases he sprinkled the ashes around the infield. His friend said this was his last wish, so he figured out a way how to get him there.

This example is far from the only one of its kind. According to a vendor outside the ballpark on Yawkey Way, "It happens all the time. People come in for tours and they drop ashes on the field." A Red Sox fan who looked as if he was in either high school or college overheard what the vendor and I were talking about and interjected that he "would definitely want [his] ashes dumped at Fenway. What would be cooler than that? It's like having season tickets at Fenway forever."

Another telling example is the story of late "superfan" Mary Ennis, of Arlington, and her remains.[27] Before she died in 1997, she was one of the Red Sox fan elite because she was one of the few who could remember the last time the Red Sox won the World Series. She was 31 in

1918 and died at the grand age of 103. A longtime season-ticket holder, she was twice named "Fan of the Year" by the Red Sox in the 1980s. Five years after her death and subsequent cremation, her grandnephews decided to make Aunt Mary's beloved Fenway Park her eternal resting place. Six relatives, each with baggies filled with ashes in their pockets, took the train into the city from nearby Wellesley, showed their tickets at the gate, and made their way through the ballpark. Coincidentally, the pregame ceremonies began with an impromptu tribute to Ted Williams, Aunt Mary's favorite Red Sox player, who died earlier that day, July 5, 2002.[28]

During the Williams tribute, the six relatives spread out all over the ballpark, marching up and down the first- and third-base lines, leaving a trail of ash behind them. A few went to sprinkle some ashes near the seats where Aunt Mary and her brother sat throughout the years. They made their way through the front rows, passed the dugouts, and each one leaned over the short padded fence between the field and the seats. Because everyone around them was distracted by the tribute, some learning for the first time that Williams had died, they were able to lean over the fence and casually dump bits of Aunt Mary onto the field.

Although these somewhat macabre tales of sowed remains may seem odd at first, the notion of spreading ashes on sacred and revered places is hardly unusual or unconventional, highlighting one of the ways that symbolic places are used and consecrated. Although burial is more common than cremation and affects the landscape on a more physically dramatic scale through the construction of large tombs and mausoleums or headstones and statues on land purposely set aside from everyday activities, cremation implies nuanced relationships between material, symbolic, and spiritual worlds.[29] Nonetheless, decisions concerning postcrematory remains are often about finding the right place for them.

Cremation has existed on American soil for centuries, but its practice only reached the mainstream in 1980 with the sudden murder and subsequent cremation of The Beatles' John Lennon. According to historian of religion Stephen Prothero, "Lennon's cremation highlights an important turn in American religion and culture. But that turn is not secularization. It is the rise of religious pluralism and the concomitant customization of religious rituals."[30] Self-fashioned "death rites" have become popular, with celebrities often as the forerunners. "*Star Trek* creator Gene Roddenberry and LSD guru Timothy Leary had their ashes rocketed into outer space, while John F. Kennedy Jr.'s were dispatched in the opposite direction: to the bottom of the ocean, after a shipboard ceremony attended by a small gathering of Kennedys."[31]

The same argument that Prothero makes about Lennon and the "customization of religious rituals" can be applied to the sprinkling of ashes at Fenway Park. Such practices not only demonstrate the wealth of possibilities of objects and practices that can be customized to suit individual, familial, and communal needs; they also show how people "sacralize" the ballpark and engage the ballpark as a civic partner in a way that goes beyond officially sanctioned charity events.

Despite the moaning and groaning from Red Sox fans when their team falls behind by a run or two, the civic rites and rituals at Fenway Park are not only about ways of dealing with the dead. The Fenway faithful have also followed Americans' newly customized ways of birthing and marriage as well. Most Fenway patrons are well aware of the birthday and anniversary announcements (and the occasional marriage proposal) that are flashed between innings at each home game on the "big screen" above the bleacher seats in center field.

The many storied spots inside the ballpark offer a variety of options for the Fenway faithful to profess their love to their partners, and for the Red Sox. The Green Monster seats, looming above left field and granting spectacular views of Fenway's lush green field and the surrounding neighborhood and city, is the last stop on the Fenway Park Tour. After the tour guide brings the group up and atop the great wall, he or she routinely asks if anyone has any questions. On one sunny summer afternoon in 2004, Jon, a diehard Red Sox fan, raised his hand and shouted that he had an important question to ask. Jon tugged on Sarah's swivel chair, spinning her around so she could see him kneeling on one knee with a small red jewelry box in hand. Sarah recalls the moment:

> I covered my face in absolute shock and listened as he made a heartfelt speech to me, our friends, and the fifty strangers on the tour with us. Tears started flowing, and I couldn't speak, but I hugged him and celebrated while one of our friends took pictures to capture each beautiful moment. From the crowd a man shouted, "Did she say yes?" and the crowd erupted into cheers and clapping when I replied, "Of course!"[32]

Red Sox fans have found creative ways to use the ballpark to show their love for their soon-to-be husbands and wives.

The Red Sox's current equipment manager, Joe Cochran, has worked for the Red Sox organization since 1984. He has worked inside the Green Monster operating the manual scoreboard, sometimes working in only his boxer shorts because "it gets like 120 degrees in there in August." His name will forever be etched among the thousands that adorn the inside of the wall. For Cochran, "Fenway Park is a magical place," a place he wanted to be a part of his wedding ceremony.

Even though Cochran was married across the Mass Turnpike at Boston University's Marsh Chapel, he wanted to share the ballpark with his groomsmen. They used the Red Sox clubhouse as their changing room before the wedding and then entered the playing field in their formal attire. Cochran joked that there is something strange about tuxedos and baseball together. They took a host of photographs out on the field. The group posed together in the dugout, each with one leg bent, resting on the top step of the dugout.[33] Cochran framed a copy of the photograph for each of his groomsmen. He admits that his buddies all have the photo prominently displayed in their homes less as a memento of his wedding and more as a souvenir of Fenway Park.

When I asked Cochran why he didn't have the wedding ceremony at the ballpark, he said, "That's all right for some people, but not for me and my family. As much of a Sox fan as my mother is, and my father was, neither of them would have wanted me to do it there. But, you know that some people have been married at Fenway, right?" I said that I did.

A few weddings have taken place at Fenway Park, but the first was a fictional wedding. Two characters on the television show *The Practice*, which takes place in Boston, were married at home plate. The fictional priest who married the fictional couple announces, "This is not a cathedral known for happy endings, . . . but Fenway Park is known for its lifelong commitment to joy and pain." After the episode aired in May 2000, the Red Sox received a number of requests from real people, but at the time Red Sox spokesperson Kevin Shea did not expect that Fenway would ever host any weddings.[34] Since then, however, a small handful of people have been married at Fenway, and the Red Sox plan to host even more in the near future.[35]

Sharla Collier and Dennis Hennessy, who are self-proclaimed "big Red Sox fans," were one of the first couples to wed at Fenway. They were married at the ballpark on November 1, 2003. "We just called the Red Sox and asked if we could be married in Fenway Park," said Sharla. "They said OK. It was something they were trying out."[36]

Kelly Carlson and Jimmy Theobald were the first couple married at Fenway after the Red Sox "broke the curse" and ended their eighty-six-year World Series Championship drought. In fact, they chose to get married at the ballpark as a result of the Red Sox win. Earlier in the year, they promised each other that they would get married at Fenway Park if the Red Sox won the World Series. The Sox did their part. Kelly and Jimmy both wore white for their wedding—white home Red Sox uniforms.[37]

Hosting marriage ceremonies at Fenway Park adds weight that drives historian Philip Lowry's designation of ballparks as "green cathedrals" beyond a simple metaphor. "The more I have studied ballparks," writes Lowry, "the more they have begun to resemble mosques, or synagogues, or churches, or similar such places of worship."[38] Lowry is primarily concerned with the ability of ballparks to summon feelings of past memories "where the soul of the game of baseball resides,"[39] but we can see how ballparks can also become mediums for important rites and rituals in the present.

The passion of Red Sox fandom coupled with the allure of Fenway Park, Boston's "green cathedral," has also attained a bit of local cultural capital as "date bait." For example, a personal ad published in the *Boston Phoenix*, under "Gals Seeking Guys" reads, "Smart, wacky, fun SWF, 25, 5'3", brunette, hopeless romantic, into rock-n-roll, football, history. Want to see the Red Sox?" From the *Improper Bostonian*: "I also overheard you talking about the Red Sox. . . . You were wearing a Garciaparra T-shirt. Hopefully you will see this and respond to it so I can accompany you to a Sox game!"[40] A few fans I interviewed had been on dates that included catching a ballgame at Fenway Park. And a few fans I interviewed told me that they had heard stories about people having sex in the bathrooms, though none of these stories was substantiated.

Although sex might be hard to find at Fenway Park,[41] which probably has more to do with smells of stale beer and urine than with Boston's Puritan heritage, I was, however, told one story in which the ol' ballpark was believed to help induce labor. Patton D., a native of Colorado, moved to Boston during the summer of 2001, was quickly swept up in the excitement of the Red Sox, and during the next season became a converted Red Sox fan.

> Just living here in Boston, and hearing people talk about it on the T and in bars, people dropping Red Sox references everywhere you go,

Kimberly Kissam, David Lucchino

Michele McDonald/The Boston Globe

Kimberly Elizabeth Kissam, a daughter of Nancy L. Kissam and the late James B. Kissam of Wellesley Hills, Mass., was married yesterday to David Lawrence Lucchino, a son of Roberta F. Lucchino and Judge Frank J. Lucchino of Pittsburgh. The Rev. Shannan R. Vance-Ocampo, a Presbyterian minister, officiated at the Country Club in Brookline, Mass.

The bride, 39, is the president and a founder of Isabel Harvey, an online company in Boston that specializes in the importing and retailing of designer jewelry. She graduated from Wittenberg University.

Kimberly Kissam and David Lucchino (nephew of Larry Lucchino, president and chief executive of the Boston Red Sox) were engaged at Fenway Park, on second base. After Ms. Kissam said yes, her mother and sister leaped out of the Red Sox dugout to congratulate them and a passing tour group cheered them on. Ms. Kissam said of the ball on which Mr. Lucchino wrote with instructions to meet him at the ballpark, "It's a piece of memorabilia I'll treasure my entire life." (Photo and article from the *New York Times*, Weddings/Celebrations section, 27 May 2007)

it's so much a part of Boston. It's just in the air. It's so easy to get excited about it. . . . Before we moved here, even though I wasn't a big baseball fan, Fenway Park was already a part of my imagination about Boston; it already had a mythical appeal. It was one of the first places we went when we got here.

Even before Patton and his wife, Michaela, moved to Boston, they knew about Fenway Park, but not as intimately as they would after living in the city for just a few years.

"So many of our memories here are wrapped up with the ballpark," Patton said fondly. One memory in particular is connected to an old tale about the ballpark. When Michaela was about a week overdue with her pregnancy, they tried to do everything they could to help the baby arrive and to pass the time.

> We took long walks, ate Indian food, saw just about every movie, anything to pass the time. So I called Joe [a friend of Patton's who works for the Red Sox] to see if he could get us tickets to a game, anything for a distraction for Michaela. . . . We went to the game, Sox won, and later in the middle of the night, labor started. We didn't know about the myth until we are at the hospital and we were telling a nurse about where we were that day, and she asked, "So who told you to go to Fenway?" No one, we just went. And she said, "Oh, that's what people do when they're overdue—it's an old wives' tale—they go to Fenway."

About a week later, a friend of Patton and Michaela's told them about another friend whose labor was also overdue and went to the same Red Sox game specifically for the purpose of inducing labor. She had her baby the same night.

> Since then, when we've told the story to Bostonians, we've heard the story confirmed a lot. We live in Southie now, and, you know, that's about as Boston as you can get, and a lot of our neighbors knew about the myth and joke with us about our "Fenway baby."

Stories like these that are about the private taking of the ballpark are part of a rich vernacular oral tradition. Historian John Bodnar writes that "vernacular expressions convey what social reality feels like rather than what it should be like."[42] Bodnar contrasts what he calls "vernacular culture" with "official culture," which is primarily a "restatement of reality in ideal rather than complex or ambiguous terms."[43] Here, we can understand Fenway Park as a place where the feelings and ideals of Boston's civic culture are negotiated between vernacular and official expressions and practices.

WALKING ON HALLOWED GROUND

Since the new ownership took over the Red Sox in 2002, they have not only added seats to the ballpark; they have also offered the ballpark as a venue for various community, promotional, and charitable events, all of which add to Fenway Park's status as an important civic space. Using the ballpark for events other than baseball brings in both more money for the team and more "cultural capital" for the ballpark.

Making Fenway Park *feel* like everyone's place reconstructs and reinforces its meaning *as* everyone's place. Ian Browne, a sportswriter for redsox.com and mlb.com, said that opening up the place for more occasions than just baseball makes "Fenway Park the backyard of Boston and New England and not a high and mighty place that nobody can touch unless they pay $40 for a ticket and $20 for parking." When I asked Browne if turning Fenway Park into the city's "backyard" would squelch some of its mystique, he said, "No, if anything it will increase it. Instead of this pristine thing that no one can touch, people feel even closer to it." And that is what the new ownership thinks as well. They have not only recognized the allure of the ballpark as, perhaps, their primary marketing tool, but they also understand that their ownership is really a stewardship. "Fenway Park was here before us, and if the people of Boston want to keep it as their home, it will be here after we're gone," said Larry Lucchino. "We're just steering the ship right now."

Opening up the ballpark for nonbaseball events provides more opportunities to bring in money for the team and for the city, though some of this money is also donated to charities like the Jimmy Fund through the Red Sox Foundation. The money generated by nonbaseball events goes directly to the team's bottom line, as opposed to ticket sales, which are part of Major League Baseball's revenue-sharing agreement. Because the Red Sox do not release an itemized list of their revenue earnings, it is hard to estimate how much money they bring in from these events. Some observers have guessed that the number might be around $20 million, a substantial though small piece of the overall revenues, which, according to *Forbes* magazine, were about $190 million in 2003, making the Red Sox the second most profitable organization in baseball (the Yankees are first).[44]

Although there is a financial incentive for the Red Sox to open up the ballpark when the Red Sox are not playing, they are also making a civic investment by sharing Fenway's hallowed ground. Allowing people to come into the ballpark for a variety of events, from political rallies to high school all-star games to Christian revivals to rock concerts, gives people a feeling of ownership. It gives them the feeling that Fenway Park is their place, or as Bill S., a devoted Red Sox fan since the late 1960s, put it, "It makes us feel like it can really be a place for the Common Man and not just some yuppie diversion." By offering the ballpark

TABLE 3.1.
PLAYING HOST: OFFICIAL NONBASEBALL EVENTS AT FENWAY PARK

Arts and Entertainment	Newport Jazz Festival
	Bruce Springsteen concert
	Rolling Stones concert
	Jimmy Buffet Concert
Philanthropic	"Field of Dreams" softball tournament, Action for Boston Community Development
	Adoption "party," MA Adoption Resource Exchange
Political	1944 Rally for President Franklin Delano Roosevelt
	1964 Rally for presidential candidate Barry Goldwater
	1968 Rally for presidential candidate Eugene McCarthy
Conventional Religious	Jehovah's Witness revival
	Catholic Church Jubilee
Civil Religious	Father's Day
	Mother's Day; Halloween
	Thanksgiving
	Tours*
	Opening Day*

* The tours of Fenway Park and Opening Day are placed in the "civil religious" category because they both serve as opportunities for people to celebrate and revere the ballpark and the city together.

for other activities, the Red Sox give the city a chance to showcase one of its most prized possessions.

Fenway Park houses a few special-event rooms and suites that can accommodate corporate meetings, seminars, birthday parties, reunions, and other formal gatherings, but I am interested in those events that give people access to the hallowed ground of Fenway's manicured outfield and precious diamond. The other-than-baseball activities at Fenway Park have come in a variety of forms over the years, and each of them highlights a specific way that the ballpark is a medium for expressing, negotiating, and practicing civic life in a contemporary American city. These activities can be grouped into five substantive categories: Arts and Entertainment, Philanthropic, Political, Conventional Religious, and Civil Religious (see table 3.1). All of these types are part of an active "commercial communalism" that the Red Sox practice by providing and following socially sanctioned rules of behavior, making themselves publicly accountable, and sharing their place with other groups and individuals.[45]

Some events are designed specifically for fundraising and charity work, resembling the "subscription campaigns" of early American urban business leaders,[46] but the giving of money is not the sole criterion for having a nonbaseball event at Fenway. Sometimes the Red Sox organization even gains revenue through these events. Most important, providing the use of their ballpark ennobles the Red Sox organization and pushes Fenway Park into the public domain for reasons the organization finds socially and culturally beneficial and worthwhile. As such, the ballpark begins to resemble the "village green writ large" where local residents are able to contribute to something bigger than themselves.

Arts and Entertainment

For two nights in early September 2003, Bruce Springsteen took the field at Fenway Park. Entering the stage set up in center field, Springsteen announced to the thirty-six thousand fans inside the ballpark, as well as to the thousands on the other side of the Green Monster and those watching from nearby apartments, fire escapes, and rooftops, that he planned to give Boston "a good old rock 'n' roll house party, a rock 'n' roll baptism, a rock 'n' roll bar mitzvah, a rock 'n' roll exorcism."[47]

For a number of years in the late 1950s and early 1960s, the Boston Jazz Festival took place at Fenway. The last full-fledged concert before Springsteen's arrival, however, was thirty years earlier in 1973, when the Newport Jazz Festival was relocated to Fenway Park due to severe flooding on the coast of Rhode Island. About thirty thousand people in total showed up for the two-day concert that featured Ray Charles, Stevie Wonder, and War. Sir Paul McCartney requested to play at the ballpark in the early 1990s but was turned down by the owners, who were concerned about the potential damage to the field. So when Springsteen was granted permission by the Red Sox and the city to play at Fenway, he knew what a special honor he had been given and tried to make it into a special night for the people of Boston. Caught in the excitement as well, city official put up temporary street signs near the ballpark that read "Welcome to Boss-ton," in homage to Springsteen's nickname, "the Boss."

Springsteen showed just the right amount of deference to the people and the place. He tailored the show for the Boston crowd, opening his three-hour set with a "Take Me Out to the Ballgame" sing-along, followed by a cover of Boston's Barry and the Remains' 1960s hit "Diddy

Workers assemble giant speakers on the field at Fenway Park for the 1959 Boston Jazz Festival. (Photo courtesy of the Boston Public Library)

Wah Diddy." He ended the set with an excited rendition of the Standells' "Dirty Water," which blares from the loudspeakers at Fenway after the final out of every Red Sox win.

Beneath a bright moon that lit up the sky and ballpark below it, Springsteen showed his gratitude, causing the crowd to bare a collective smile when he said, "There's not many places where you can walk into an empty place and feel the soul of the city, but this is one." Erica Tarlin, a board member of the historic preservation group Save Fenway Park!, went to both shows and recalls that moment fondly, telling me that "he could have said a lot of things, but he said *that* about our ballpark and our city. 'The soul of the city,' and people wonder why we want to save it."

Even though the Springsteen concerts were considered a success by most of the parties involved, aside from complaints made by some residents in the surrounding neighborhood who would have liked the concert to have ended before its scheduled 11:00 p.m. stop time, the Red Sox do not plan to turn the ballpark into a regular concert venue. They have, however, started an annual concert tradition.

In early September 2004, about seventy thousand men, women, and children donning Hawaiian shirts, beach sandals, cheeseburger headwear, and faux coconut brassieres strolled into Boston for two Jimmy Buffett concerts at Fenway Park. Due to the ban on tailgating, which is a staple for Buffett concertgoers, the Parrotheads flocked to Fenway's local taverns and bars. Michael DeBiase, a bartender at Cask 'n' Flagon on Lansdowne Street (you can see a sign pointing to it above the Green Monster if you're sitting on the first-base side), said, "The bar was as packed and crazy as any night the Red Sox are in town, but instead of Bud Light–swilling baseball fans, it was frozen drinks and Coronas all around."[48]

In August 2005, the Rolling Stones took the stage beneath the Green Monster, continuing a newly minted Fenway Park tradition. As the *Boston Globe*'s Eileen McNamara wrote, "If Fenway is being recast as a once-a-year concert site, the appeal has everything to do with the novelty; the acoustics are terrible."[49] Novelty and acoustics aside, these annual events are unique opportunities for people to come together at Fenway Park and enjoy the ballpark in nuanced ways.

Philanthropic

The Red Sox currently host a number of philanthropic events at the ballpark. Some are holdovers from the Yawkey days, like the Jimmy Fund Fantasy Day discussed earlier. Another commitment that the Henry/Werner/Lucchino regime has inherited is the "Field of Dreams" fundraiser for Boston's only official antipoverty agency, Action for Boston Community Development (ABCD). ABCD serves more than eighty thousand people, and its list of services extends from housing to work programs to summer job employment to education for both children and adults.

In 1998, John Harrington, former Red Sox CEO and current executive director of the Yawkey Foundation, and the ABCD came up with the idea that local corporations would be willing to sponsor employee softball teams to play a few innings on Fenway's diamond as a daylong fundraiser. Some of the regular teams participating in the event have been from local companies such as John Hancock Financial Services Inc., Partners Health Care, and FleetBoston Financial Corp. and from local law firms Palmer & Dodge, Ropes & Gray, and Bingham Dana. Each company pays $12,000 to enter a team in the Field of Dreams tournament. The Red Sox and ABCD raised over $1 million in 2004.[50]

Another event that has been held at Fenway Park is not about raising money but about raising children, or at least connecting adults with parentless children. In 2001, about 180 children wearing Red Sox caps and jerseys stepped to home plate and had their image projected on the big screen above center field with the hope that one of the nearly fifteen hundred adults in attendance would bring them home with them. Although the idea of this type of "adoption party" may seem odd, and it has been criticized as a kind of merchandising of children, the Red Sox reportedly decided to lend Fenway Park for the event because of the ballpark's potential ability to ease both children's and adults' anxieties.[51]

Political

Since Boston Mayor John "Honey Fitz" Fitzgerald threw out the *first* first pitch at Fenway Park on April 20, 1912, in front of twenty-four thousand excited rain-soaked fans,[52] hundreds of local and national political leaders have thrown out first pitches at the beginning of Red Sox games. A few days before Massachusetts senator and 2004 presidential hopeful John Kerry was expected to receive his party's nomination in Boston at the Democratic National Convention, he made a surprise visit to the ol' ballpark. On the eve of the convention, a crowd filled with celebrities and politicians eagerly awaited the start of another Red Sox–Yankees battle. The evening already had a playoff atmosphere, not only because of the Yankees' visit but also because of the 8:05 p.m. game time, the nationwide broadcast on ESPN, and the network's daylong broadcasts from the third-base line. Heightening the emotion was Kerry's surprise arrival, the draping of the Green Monster with an American flag, and the roar of a Coast Guard Blackhawk helicopter that circled the ballpark after Kerry threw out the first pitch.

Fenway Park has also hosted a few overt political events. In 1964, Republican presidential candidate Barry Goldwater held a rally, and in 1968, Democrat Eugene McCarthy held his own rally to support his run for president. But both of those events were preceded, and forever upstaged, by one of the great non-sports-related events to occur at the ballpark. Three days before being elected to his fourth term as president, Franklin Delano Roosevelt made a fiery speech at Fenway Park. On November 4, 1944, after speaking in Worcester earlier in the day, Roosevelt arrived at the ballpark to speak to about forty-five thousand supporters. To get the crowed warmed up, Roosevelt enlisted a cast of superstars. Film star Orson Welles spoke to the crowd before a young singing sensation named Frank Sinatra performed the national anthem. After

A crowd of over sixty thousand people fill the stands, the infield, and the outfield to hear Eamon de Valera speak at a rally for Irish independence, 29 June 1919. (Photo courtesy of the Boston Public Library)

his car pulled onto the field through the center-field garage door, Roosevelt, wearing a light-gray topcoat and gray fedora, delivered an address on racial intolerance. "Here in New England," Roosevelt said, "you've been fighting bigotry and intolerance for centuries. You know that all of our people—except red-blooded Indians—are immigrants or descendants of immigrants, including even those who came over on the *Mayflower*."[53] Ironically, Red Sox officials seemed to have ignored Roosevelt's strong remarks. The Red Sox did not put a black player on their roster until 1959, the last major-league team to do so, choosing to ignore both Jackie Robinson and Willie Mays for no other reason than racism.[54]

Conventional Religious

Though many people describe Fenway Park as a sacred site in itself, the ballpark has also welcomed more conventional religious groups into its house of worship. Ceremonies have been held for various religious groups, though mostly Christian groups ranging from Catholics to Jehovah's Witnesses.

A Palm Sunday Mass at Fenway Park in the 1940s. The service was led by Archbishop Richard J. Cushing, who can be seen walking near home plate. (Photo courtesy of the Boston Public Library)

In 2000, Cardinal Bernard Law led up to twenty thousand young Roman Catholics into Fenway Park for Pilgrimage 2000, a "Celebration of Faith." Mixing Christian rock and reggae with a Mass beneath the Green Monster, the Fenway jubilee was the culmination of an eight-month-long effort to reconnect youth with the Catholic Church. The main stage was built over second base, with ramps leading up to it from both dugouts. A giant wooden cross was suspended above the stage, and a hot-tub-sized pool of "holy water" was placed behind home plate for baptisms. Giant letters spelling out "F-A-I-T-H" were arranged across the bleachers behind right field, and attendees could also go to confession booths set up in the park's luxury suites. Further mixing conventional religion and popular culture, Sixpence None the Richer, a Grammy-nominated Christian rock band that achieved crossover success with two Top-40 hits, serenaded the Catholic revelers throughout the festivities.[55]

Civil Religious

Although the case of Fenway Park compels us to take sociologist Robert Bellah's definition of "civil religion" seriously, we can also bring the term beyond the realm of presidential speeches and into the city and the ballpark.[56] Whereas Bellah and others have tended to equate civil religion with acts and ceremonies of national political figures,[57] the realm of popular culture today supplies even better civil religious fodder. In popular literature and films and in academic studies, baseball has long been deemed a civil religion or, as it was recently dubbed by two theology professors, the "faith of fifty million."[58] But baseball does not need to be the sole object of worship. Many activities at Fenway Park—from the singing of the "Star-Spangled Banner," as well as the recent addition of "God Bless America" in the post-9/11 era, to children trick-or-treating beneath the daunting stare of the Green Monster—demonstrate the various ways the ballpark is used to celebrate other civil religious rituals and holidays.

As Larry Lucchino's quotation at the beginning of this chapter attests, the new owners recognize their esteemed position in the community. Since 2002, the Red Sox have allowed people into the ballpark to

Closeup of Archbishop Richard J. Cushing before a Palm Sunday service at Fenway Park. (Photo courtesy of the Boston Public Library)

Altar set up on the pitcher's mound for a Catholic religious ceremony circa 1920. Notice how the pre – Green Monster left-field wall is covered with advertisements, showing that Fenway is being used here not for baseball but for marketing and religiosity. (Photo courtesy of the Boston Public Library)

celebrate civic holidays such as Mother's Day, Father's Day, and Halloween. These community-building practices have been well received and well attended.

The first two years that the Red Sox opened the ballpark on Father's Day, the team was away on a week-long road trip, which allowed enough time for the field to recover after twenty thousand fathers and sons throughout the day played catch across the outfield. "How many people in New England, for generations, have dreamed of stepping on that outfield grass—for just five minutes—and playing catch? That's a dream that can come true," said Charles Steinberg, the Red Sox's executive vice president of public affairs.[59] Tickets to enter the ballpark for non-season-ticket-holders (who got in free) were $10 for adults and $8 for children. After the team covers the expenses of opening the ballpark, it donates the rest of the money to the Red Sox Foundation.

The 2004 Father's Day event, like the 2003 and 2004 activities for Mother's Day, was a "walk in the park" rather than a "catch." The team was scheduled to begin a six-game homestand two days after the event, which did not give the field enough time to be rustled back into shape. Fans were still allowed to walk around the outfield warning track, touch the Green Monster, peer inside the booth that houses the people who manually operate the left-field scoreboard, and walk up to both the Green Monster seats and the Right Field Roof. Discussing the adapted arrangements for the event, Steinberg said,

It's an opportunity for a Sunday stroll on Father's Day. Because the team plays two days later, we of course could not use the outfield grass this year. Nevertheless, we did want to offer a special day at Fenway for families. . . . Many fans indicate they enjoy experiencing the ballpark at rest. It's unusual to be able to walk at your leisure to the Monster seats, catch the view, and then check out the new Rightfield Roof. As you look at the field, your imagination fills in the rest.[60]

The prohibition on tossing a ball on the grass did not keep people away, however. An estimated ten thousand participants showed up, some waiting for close to two hours in a line that circled the ballpark and stretched down Brookline Avenue.

A father and son duo took the two-hour trek down Interstate 93 from New Hampshire to take the Sunday stroll at Fenway. Joe, a carpenter in his late thirties, made the trip two years prior to attend the first Father's Day event with his father.

It was a real *Field of Dreams* moment. I felt like Kevin Costner. You know, having a catch with my father in the middle of Fenway like it was our backyard or something. Even though this year we can't go on the field, I still wanted to bring my kid here so he could touch the Monster and grab some dirt from the warning track. . . . I took him to his first game a few weeks ago. Lowe's pitching was shaky, but the Sox won.

By opening the ballpark for more than just baseball games, Fenway Park becomes a place to share and make personal memories in public. Although that can, and does, occur during games, the solitude of the empty ballpark allows a bit more space for reflection since fans are there and the team is not.

For Halloween, hay was strewn across the outfield, spooky music with howling sounds and creaking doors hissed from the loudspeakers, and the screen above center field attempted to startle onlookers with a digital "Boo." Though many people would say that Fenway Park has been a haunted house every single day since 1918, the Red Sox explicitly turned the ballpark into one for Halloween in 2002, 2003, and again in 2005. With the help of Stop & Shop, a local supermarket, the Red Sox provided candy, as well as toothbrushes and toothpaste, to trick-or-treaters who attended the free event.

As a smoke machine helped set an eerie mood throughout the ballpark, the Red Sox didn't miss an opportunity to poke fun at their New York rivals. The visitor's bullpen was transformed into a haunted pumpkin patch, and a cardboard cutout of Darth Vader stood tall and frightening in the visitor's dugout, denoting the pet name given to the Yankees by the Red Sox: the Evil Empire (a pop cultural reference to *Star Wars*, not a political reference to Communist Russia). Also, all the candy was placed in the Red Sox dugout.

CELEBRATING THEMSELVES AND THEIR PLACE

The Red Sox did not hold a Halloween event in 2004 because they were too busy celebrating their exorcism: a historic defeat against the Yankees (the Red Sox came back to win the seven-game series after losing the first three games) and then a World Series Championship sweep beneath a total lunar eclipse. And when the Red Sox came back home from St. Louis, the city smiled and celebrated together during a "Roaming Rally" that featured almost the entire Red Sox organization waddling through the rain-soaked streets of downtown Boston on the famed Boston tour Duck boats.

Recognizing themselves as a civic institution, the Red Sox give fans opportunities to celebrate themselves. And like all religious rituals, celebrating being a Red Sox fan is, in the true Durkheimian sense, a celebration of community.[61] Tours of Fenway Park are now given all year long as a way to "connect with our shrine without all the hoopla of the game," as one fan said as we made our way up to the new Right Field Roof seats during a tour on a typically humid August afternoon in Boston.

Along with the increased availability of the tours, the Red Sox established the "Fenway Ambassadors," a group of men and women whose sole goal is to accommodate the fans and make "Friendly Fenway" even friendlier. The gatekeepers of the sacred grounds, the Fenway Ambassadors are, according to Kasey Lindsey, "the living, breathing face of Fenway Park." Lindsey has worked as a tour guide, a ball girl during games, and as an Ambassador. "We are the public relations on the ground; we interact with fans on a regular basis." Despite the Red Sox's strong record of sellouts, the Red Sox executives believe that the Ambassadors are necessary to help sustain the loyalty of the fans and the community.

The loyalty and devotion of Red Sox fans is at no time more apparent than on Opening Day, when "hope springs eternal." Opening Day of the Red Sox season at Fenway Park is an example of an annual event that allows fans to celebrate and honor the team, the ballpark, and the city. This "civil religious" holiday is observed by many more than the thirty-five thousand or so fans allowed inside with their tickets. People fill the streets, some looking for tickets from scalpers, but most are just happy to be there among others reciting the Opening Day mantra: "This is the year."

A carnival-like atmosphere rings through Kenmore Square and encapsulates the ballpark as fans tumble in and out of local bars and vendors hawk peanuts, sausages, game programs, and T-shirts. Scott MacKay, a reporter for the *Providence Journal*, writes about Boston's special day,

> In a homogenized culture and global marketplace, Opening Day is an event that makes New England and its Hub distinctive. New Orleans has Mardi Gras, New York has Broadway openings and Washington, D.C., has presidential inaugurations. We have the ancient rhythms of a game played without a clock; time is measured in innings.[62]

And as local tradition dictates in Boston, Opening Day is the first day of spring.

Opening Day in 2005, however, broke with tradition, as the Red Sox were announced as World Series Champions for the first time since 1918. The World Championship flags from previous winning years—all from the first two decades of the twentieth century—were spread down along the Green Monster to Richard Strauss's *Also Sprach Zarathustra* (the opening music from Stanley Kubrick's *2001: A Space Odyssey*) played by the Boston Symphony Orchestra. As the music reached a high crescendo, a huge banner that read "2004 WORLD CHAMPIONS" descended from atop the Monster to cover the entire wall.

The Opening Day ceremony was more than just a celebration for the 2004 Red Sox. About thirty former Sox players were on hand, representing teams from 1946, 1967, 1975, and 1986, all the years that the team came within one game of winning it all. The gathering of vintage players included Charlie Wagner, Dom DiMaggio, Johnny Pesky, Bobby Doerr, Rico Petrocelli, Jim Lonborg, Luis Tiant, Carl Yastrzemski, Bill "Spaceman" Lee, Jim Rice, Dennis "Oil Can" Boyd, Fred Lynn, and Dwight Evans. Wagner, who was ninety-two years old, uttered the ceremonial pronouncement, "Play ball!"

As a civil religious event, the celebration was also about honoring the city. Past and present Boston champions representing the three other major sports (football, basketball, and hockey) were at the ballpark. New England Patriots Richard Seymour and Tedy Bruschi, former Celtics star Bill Russell, and former Bruins legend Bobby Orr shared in the Opening Day/Championship festivities by throwing out the first pitch. That day at Fenway Park, the city's sporting history was linked together in one moment, in one place. Charles Steinberg, the Red Sox executive vice president for public affairs and architect of the Opening Day agenda said,

> This is designed to bring together children, parents and grandparents to embrace memories of those who would have loved to have seen this day.... We want to do this in some kind of mood that elicits emotions. That could mean clapping or laughing or cheering, but you want them to feel emotionally spent from the experience. You don't do that giving a high-energy song and dance. You do that by nurturing their emotions.... *Opening Day is designed to be a somewhat spiritual day, a renewal, a rebirth.* This day has unusual elements to it that have the capacity to unleash the emotions that some people feel.[63]

Although Opening Day certainly has its "spiritual" overtones, the civic holiday has on occasion over the years been faced with opposition, or even competition, from other religious "firms."[64]

In 1998, Opening Day at Fenway Park fell on both Good Friday and the start of Passover. The Red Sox tried to show respect for these two conventional religious holidays by banning the sale of alcohol for the day, as well as by pushing the starting time back from 1:00 p.m. to 3:00 p.m. to accommodate those attending midday Good Friday services. The later time was purposefully not set too much later because they wanted to allow enough time for Jewish Red Sox fans to return home by sundown, when Passover begins. But such maneuvers did not sit well with those who treat Opening Day itself as a sacred holiday. Dan Cordella and Jim Gavin both attended the game and were unhappy with the Red Sox's decision to tone down Opening Day. "To me, Opening Day is sacred," said Cordella. "This is what people live for," added Gavin, "especially in the beginning of the season, when we have hope."[65]

Although neither Fenway Park nor the Red Sox can offer answers to this clash between organized, conventional religion and the somewhat sticky civil, "secular but sacred" religion of baseball, the ballpark does provide a medium for people to negotiate their own opinions and beliefs. The best thing that a ballpark can do is provide a wide enough canopy for a variety of people to rest beneath. Some of those people may bring other sacred objects with them, and others may worship and revere the "sacred canopy" itself.[66] In this sense, Fenway Park is a place that serves the public as both a place *of* and *for* reverence, devotion, loyalty, and faith.

CIVIC CULTURE, IDENTITY, AND THE AMERICAN URBAN LANDSCAPE

Many studies of the construction and use, or misuse, of public and private social spaces are either implicitly or explicitly about "civic culture," about the way that diverse groups and individuals manage to foster a shared sense of community in public. Historian Gunther Barth's study of nineteenth-century urban life was devoted to understanding the common culture that exists between segments of a population often divided by neighborhood, language, style, and ethnic ancestry. Barth found and depicted an emerging urban culture that was a hybrid of past beliefs and present practices. "City people," he writes, "forged the new culture from the elements that characterized their world."[67] Americans' new urban culture included a mixed work ethic/leisure ethic that was evident in both the building of urban ballparks and the droves of spectators who flocked to them.

When we want to find places where civic culture is displayed, celebrated, and negotiated, "third places" are the best places to look. The advantage of looking at *big* third places like Fenway Park, rather than at neighborhood bars and coffee shops, is that we can see a city's civic culture in action. We can see how such places, which are often called "civic arenas," are inclusive enough to allow for individual difference under the same civic umbrella. In this way, something akin to an urban community emerges, creating a connection between the often physically fragmented and segregated neighborhoods and enclaves that constitute the city.

In Boston, Fenway Park is a place not only to display one's allegiance to the Red Sox but also to display a multitude of other allegiances. Fans come to the ballpark with signs, clothing, and even flags to demonstrate their identities in an open public forum. Boston Latinos have embraced current players like David Ortiz and Manny Ramirez, a native Dominican. On May 12, 2004, Ramirez became a naturalized citizen. Later that day, he ran to his position in front of the Green Monster waving a miniature American flag.

After Pedro Martinez, who was born in the Dominican Republic, made his first start for the Red Sox at Fenway Park on April 11, 1998, pitching a two-hit, twelve-strikeout masterpiece, more Latinos, especially Dominicans, began attending games than ever before. While fans of different ethnicities are crammed into close quarters at Fenway, there is enough *cultural* space for the flag-waving Latinos at the ballpark to express both their ethnic and local pride.[68]

The Red Sox have extended that cultural space by instituting an annual Latino Night at Fenway Park. Instead of Dutch pretzels and Cracker Jacks, fans are treated to stewed beef, fried sweet plantains, and mango and passion-fruit smoothies. On the eve of the first Latino Night in 2001, Jose Masso, former director of the Center for the Study of Sport in Society at Northeastern University, remarked that "Fenway Park is finally going to look like the rest of the city, in terms of demographics."[69] At the time, Latinos made up about 14 percent of the Boston population, but that number is pushed higher when surrounding cities like Lawrence and Chelsea are included.

Hector Piña, owner of a Dominican-cuisine restaurant in Boston, was asked to cater some of the concession food for the "fiesta at Fenway" and was excited about the opportunity to share his Dominican delicacies with fellow Latinos and non-Latinos. Piña believed nights like this are a good sign that Boston's history of racial intolerance may finally be left in the past.

I remember when Tony Peña was a catcher here seven years ago [in 1993]. I would bring my Dominican flag, and people would ask me,

Displaying of multiple group allegiances is common at the ballpark. This young boy is wearing a navy-blue yarmulke with a red "B" on one side and a baseball with a red sock in the middle of it and "Boston Red Sox" around it. (Photo by the author)

> "Why do you have to pull the flag out?" Now, it's different. You go to a game and see white Americans waving Dominican flags. They even sell them at the park.[70]

Providing fans with foreign or ethnic paraphernalia does not stop at flags, however. The green Red Sox hat and jerseys that the team wears for St. Patrick's Day are available at Fenway Park, even though the Irish holiday falls during spring training. The green hats can be seen in the crowd throughout the season and not just in March and not just by the Irish.

During a game against the Cleveland Indians, I spent some time roving around the new Right Field Roof Deck. While trying to maneuver into position where I could see home plate between four shifting rows of shoulders and necks, a boy sitting at one of the home-plate-shaped tables caught my eye. Actually, he looked at me. The boy, who must have been about eight or nine years old, was taking in the scenery and the game with his mother. When he turned around to face the field rather than the deck where I was standing, I saw that he was wearing a yarmulke. It was a navy-blue yarmulke. It had a big red "B" on one side and a stitched-on baseball patch with the words "Boston Red Sox" on the other.

The Red Sox do not sell yarmulkes with team logos for their Jewish constituency. So either this boy made it himself or someone made it or bought it for him from somewhere else. Either way, the boy's yarmulke, physically demonstrating his dual allegiances to Yahweh and the Red Sox, provides another example of Fenway Park as an open space where one need not disavow one's other identities in order to be an active member of Red Sox Nation.

In a time when a common ground between the various populations of people who call themselves Americans has become less distinctive and thereby harder to find, many have asked if America is breaking apart. To that question, sociologist John Hall and anthropologist Charles Lindholm answer with an emphatic no. Their argument rests on Americans' "voluntary and overlapping nature of group member-ships," which has characterized civic life in the United States since Alexis de Tocqueville first observed the phenomenon in the early nine-teenth century.[71] The flexibility and permeability of these associations both constructs and is constructed by a culture that vacillates between the valorization of individual and community interests and powers. Hall and Lindholm conclude,

> In general, then, despite the high ideals Americans hold about groups as the locus of caring and sharing, the culture is held together not by cohesive associations but by the infinite dispersal of weak and flexible personal links between individuals, who move freely between one group and another, search for the elusive and often contradictory goals of loving community and personal self-satisfaction. These open group experiences give Americans practice at participating in community ac-tivism *when they want to* but permit detachment otherwise.[72]

When individuals move from one group to another, they do not leave the first group behind. As demonstrated in places like Fenway Park, they can take their allegiances to other groups with them and act on them simultaneously. These hybrid identities are the pragmatic answer to an urban culture made up of mixed beliefs, practices, and affiliations, rather than a simple nostalgic retreat to safe, exclusive enclaves.

Ethnicities, religious symbols and beliefs, and sports fandom are important tools for contemporary Americans to use as a means for constructing both collective and personal identities. An individual can cobble together these cultural resources, among other distinctive markers like gender, race, class, and lifestyle, to construct an identity that is relatively flexible. But that flexibility can either be tightened or loosened depending on the place in question. Civic cultures that offer high degrees of flexibility enable individuals to find symbolic and material common ground within the public realm as expressed in and through urban third places.

OBJECTS OF FAITH
AND CONSUMPTION
Souvenirs, Replicas, and Other
Representations of Fenway Park

You can go and take pictures of Fenway Park but to actually have a 3D model—well, people loved it. . . . we sold all twenty thousand copies. . . . if you find one, can you let me know?

> —Len Martin, engineer, Pittsburgh, PA,
> author of *Fenway Park: Build It Yourself*

Fenway Park is definitely a character in the play. The scenes take place in a bar, but Fenway is referred to a lot. The main character in the play, the title character, the "Savior of Fenway," everything in his life is falling apart, his personal relationships, his job. And some of the other characters are also in the same situation, on the edge. But yet they had this one thing in their lives that keeps them going, like religion; it's the Boston Red Sox. And the greatest symbol of the Boston Red Sox to these people is Fenway Park. . . . These four men in this play are definitely represented out here in the ballpark today.

> —Nate Meyer, producer and actor, *Savior of Fenway*

The day after the Red Sox won the World Series in 2004, fans flocked to the ballpark to buy mementos to celebrate an achievement many of them had anticipated since they were children, when they didn't know any better, never imagining they would have to wait so long. Like religious affiliations, many people inherit their sports fandom from their parents. And although some people do switch, convert, or change religions, most do not. The same can be said about sports allegiances. As such, fans often celebrate a team's achievement as their own, as well as suffer from losses, sometimes in starkly more dramatic ways than the players or organization do. This makes perfect sense in a time when players frequently move from team to team, leaving the team's fans behind and leaving the ballpark as the lasting cornerstone of fans' devotion. When people think of the "Red Sox" or "Fenway Park," they are thinking about a corporate entity that transcends the actual players on the field. They think about the team's history and, for devoted fans, their relationship to and with that history.

Red Sox fan Tom W. of Falmouth, Massachusetts, spent a few hours waiting in line outside the Souvenir Store on Yawkey Way to be one of the first people in eighty-six years to wear the words "Boston Red Sox" and "World Series Champions" on the same shirt. Wearing a Red Sox hat and a tie printed with baseballs, this forty-four-year-old Red Sox fan waited patiently to buy his souvenirs like the hundreds of others who stood in a line that stretched down the street and around the corner, continuing several hundred feet down Brookline Avenue. "I'm not going back until I get large quantities of shirts and hats, forty-eight caps, forty-eight shirts," Tom said. "I'm going to take a couple of items and put them on gravestones of people who didn't get to see this."

The purchasing of these items, which could only be found that day in the store across the street from Fenway Park, had very little to do with their aesthetic, functional, or economic value. Devoted to his city and his team, Tom's motivation for buying the items was for their connection to an important and iconic event. Whether the T-shirts are used in a creative manner like being draped over a gravesite or are, more conventionally, tacked to a wall, these acts of consumption are acts of cultural consecration. These objects took on sacred qualities as they helped Tom connect to friends, family, and fellow fans who witnessed the breaking of the Curse and to those who had passed away before that moment of redemption.

The timing (the day after the Red Sox won the World Series) and the place (outside Fenway Park) added to the mystique of the sought-after treasures. In order to acquire the most sacred souvenirs, "I needed to come to Fenway," said another fan waiting in the same line for the same mementos as Tom W. "We won last night, so I had to be here today to get some shirts and caps and pins and whatever else they have in there. I still can't believe it," he explained. Pointing to the ballpark, he continued, "I just wish it happened in there. That would've been great. Though it probably wouldn't be standing today if the Sox won the Series at Fenway. We would have torn the place down out of joy. . . . these emotions have been building for eighty-six friggin' years!"

The use of material objects and artifacts as objects of devotion was first recognized and explained by seminal sociologist Émile Durkheim in 1912. In his classic study of Australian Aboriginal totemic practices, Durkheim investigated the "sacralization" process of cultural objects. According to Durkheim, a clan's reverence for a particular object— whether a species of animal, a vegetable, or a land formation—follows a consistent pattern of religious behavior. "A rock, a tree, a spring, a pebble, a piece of wood, a house, in a word, anything can be sacred" because the sacred quality of an object cannot be found in the object itself.[1] Even though this means that the sacred object is arbitrary (i.e., it originally could have been something else), the socially constructed nature of the sacred does not detract from the totem's sanctity; rather, it constitutes it.

A totem is created through the veneration or worship of an object. It is attributed power or some other sacred capacity by a clan. Through this process of attribution, the object begins to manifest those qualities. That is, the reverence for the object is exactly what makes it special, sacred, and powerful. The object, in turn, influences the lives of those who worship it by helping them define and modify their beliefs. Yet reverence for an object by some people does not necessarily mean that others will treat it the same way. Despite a lack of consensus, the object, however, can still function as a medium for the negotiation of culture and individuals' place within it. Big objects, like Fenway Park, can become totems that help mediate cultural discourse, debate, and community-building practices.

A totem acts as a binding mechanism, linking people in the present together with one another, as well as with those from past and future generations. For Durkheim, this is the primary function of all religions and belief systems. Totems are in effect common references for people to rally behind and believe in together.

No one possesses it entirely and all participate in it. It is so completely independent of the particular subjects in whom it incarnates itself, that it precedes them and survives them. Individuals die, generations pass and are replaced by others; but this force always remains actual, lived, and the same. It animates the generations of today as it animates those of yesterday and as it will animate those of tomorrow.[2]

The potency of such symbols is rooted in social interaction and therefore has the potential to change. Because the meanings of symbols are inherently fluid, they can be altered. The power of the symbol to animate a "community of believers" can decrease over time. As such, the totem must be periodically "recharged" if it is going to last. The recharging of symbols is done through the enactment of culturally defined ritual practices that can range from communal events (like baseball games) to solitary acts (like buying a Fenway Park snow globe to put on your desk).

Many of the rituals that recharge Fenway Park can be interpreted as forms of consumption. In order to recognize consecrating practices as acts of consumption, and vice versa, we are bound to blur the traditional distinction between the sacred and the profane. On one hand, we can say that Fenway Park is sacred because it is extra-ordinary, or out of the ordinary, because it is physically unique and set aside from daily routines. This meaning of "sacred" certainly goes beyond the typical or stereotyped images of temples and cathedrals, because, "at the level of experience, sacred phenomena are those that stand out from the commonplace and interrupt routine."[3] Certain codes of behavior are suspended while at the ballpark, interrupting the normal routines of everyday life. The cheering and jeering of fans, as well as their attire (e.g., hats and jerseys) and eating habits (e.g., consuming large quantities of beer and hot dogs and littering the aisles with peanut shells), make sense in the ballpark, whereas they might be condemned on public streets, in classrooms, or in the workplace.

Despite the emphasis on hard work and accomplishment in American sports, there is still room allowed for some supernatural tinkering. It is common to see athletes pointing skyward as they round the bases or cross themselves as they reach home plate after hitting a homerun. In the stands, spectators hunch over in silent, or not so silent, prayer as the game comes to a close: *Just one more out, please, one more hit, please. All we need is one more run.*

On the other hand, Fenway Park is ordinary or, in Durkheim's sense, profane, as in *mundane* or *routine* (rather than, say, evil). Most startling to the notion of Fenway Park as a sacred site is that it is a place of business. A lot of money flows in and out of the hands of the fans, the organization, and other businesses that sell products or advertise at the ballpark. Traditionally, economics and commercial affairs have been viewed as profane activities. For Durkheim, the sacred and the profane constitute two different worlds that are not merely separate "but are even hostile and jealous rivals of each other. . . . The sacred thing is *par excellence* that which the profane should not touch, and cannot touch with impunity. . . . The two classes cannot even approach each other and keep their own nature at the same time."[4]

Because Durkheim used "profane" ambiguously to refer to *both* the emotionally charged realm of evil and the mundane routines of everyday life, Durkheim's dichotomy misses the merging of, or connections between, the sacred and the everyday. The ultimate and unyielding distinction between the sacred and the profane (and the routine) covers up the faint convergence between them. If we relied on such a model, we would miss many of the ways that people use, act toward, and consecrate places like Fenway Park through the representations of it on posters, in movies, and in some people's backyards. Purchasing tickets and memorabilia does not diminish the sacred reverence people feel toward the ballpark. If anything, such acts enhance its sanctity.

In her study of the material forms of contemporary American Christianity, religious studies scholar Colleen McDannell aptly describes the confusion that underlies many commentators' analyses of American culture and religion when they employ Durkheim's understanding of pure sacred and profane forms. "If we immediately assume that whenever money is exchanged religion is debased, then we will miss the subtle ways that people create and maintain spiritual ideals *through* the exchange of goods and the construction of spaces."[5] McDannell's study explores the connections between popular material culture and religious iconography, like nineteenth-century German lithographs of the crucified Jesus printed on paper that were swallowed to prevent or cure sickness, a practice that lasted into the 1940s.[6]

Certain traditionally religious images and objects have been adapted to fit in with contemporary American consumer culture. Many contemporary American Christians have tried to appeal to teenagers and young adults by using pop fashions as a medium for explicitly religious purposes. In the 1960s, religious sayings were printed on bumper stickers, and in the 1980s, they began appearing on T-shirts.[7] In the first decade of the twenty-first century, nondenominational Christian music festivals have moved Christianity fully into the consumer market of kitsch wear. For example, Dave Lula and ninety-one other vendors sold their religious merchandise (mostly Christian CDs, T-shirts, and hats) at the four-day Creation East festival in Mount Union, Pennsylvania. Many of the T-shirts mimicked the styles of commercial products' advertising logos (e.g., a faux Mountain Dew label that reads "Do the Jew," meaning "emulate the life of Jesus"). Other shirts had slogans such as "I Love Christian Boys," "I Mosh for Jesus," or "Body Piercing Saved My Life" above an image of Jesus's hand with a nail through it.[8] Are these T-shirts really that different from those that are sold on the streets outside Fenway Park that read "Reverse the Curse," "I Believe: In Theo We Trust," or "W.W.J.D.D.—What Would Johnny Damon Do"? No.

A selection of T-shirts for sale, including the somewhat infamous "W.W.J.D.D. — What Would Johnny Damon Do?" shirt, outside Fenway Park. (Photo by the author)

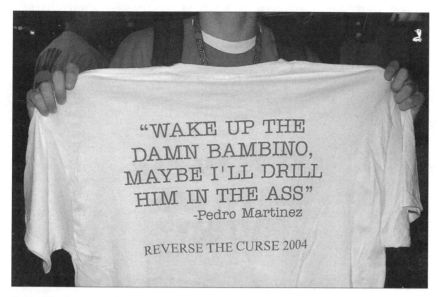

"WAKE UP THE DAMN BAMBINO, MAYBE I'LL DRILL HIM IN THE ASS"
-Pedro Martinez

REVERSE THE CURSE 2004

A fan displays a T-shirt that he recently purchased. This "article of faith" shows his allegiance and devotion to the Red Sox as they made their campaign to Reverse the Curse. (Photo by the author)

Even when the religious artifact is a traditional sacred site, the connection between consumption, commercialism, and religiosity is present in a way that Durkheim's structuralism could not account for or analyze. Consider the example of the Islamic sacred city of Mecca in Saudi Arabia. For Muslims, the pilgrimage to Mecca is not simply an act of religious devotion and obedience; it is a duty. The tenets, or pillars, of the Islamic faith require that every adult Muslim perform the pilgrimage to Mecca at least once in a lifetime. This pilgrimage—known as *hajj*—summons millions of people for a month's stay in the otherwise relatively small city. In recent years, upward of 2.25 million believers each year, for one month, flood the streets and surrounding towns of a city with a resident population of about 150,000 during the other eleven months.[9]

These mass pilgrimages to sacred sites like Mecca obviously involve the transportation of large collections of people and thereby have a significant economic impact on the local and neighboring areas. The Muslim *hajj* to Mecca "promotes secondary flows of trade."[10] Pilgrimages, as a distinct form of tourism, can have a major effect on local economies through the development of secondary sites, shops that sell devotional articles or related items (like the T-shirts discussed earlier), and overnight accommodations that range from hotels to hostels to camp sites for both RVs and tent-toting backpackers.[11]

When religious or socially revered objects and practices are presumed to be *too* wed to the market, they are said to lose their authenticity or to be devoid of spirit. Many people have bemoaned the "commercialization" of holidays, religious iconography, and sacred sites.[12] But evidence supports both the historical and contemporary connections between the sacred devotion of, and to, certain objects and the profane buying and selling of the same objects. Certainly, the money spent on airfare for a Muslim American to travel to Mecca does not compromise his or her spiritual pilgrimage, nor does it stop the millions who journey there each year from doing so. People regularly make pilgrimages to Fenway Park and buy and wear multiple combinations of red, blue, white, green, pink, and camouflage hats, T-shirts, sweatshirts, shorts, socks, jackets, and jerseys while they are there.[13] In fact, such items are often their most treasured items: "I'd never go to Fenway without my Sox hat. I've had it since I was seventeen," said twenty-four-year-old Red Sox fan Pete T. from Waltham, Massachusetts. "It's faded in all the right spots, and I like to think it's good luck, but it's hard to tell, you know, since they haven't really won anything. But this year looks pretty good. I'm going to the Saturday Sox-Yankees game, and I'll be wearing my hat and my V-Tek [Varitek] jersey."

The reverence for Fenway Park goes well beyond passive admiration and awe. Both locals and out-of-towners who make pilgrimages to what more than one interviewee called "the Mecca of baseball" actively *practice* their devotion. It is through their actions, which are eclectic, often eccentric, and occasionally esoteric, that Fenway Park becomes and remains an object of devotion, a sacred place, and a shining beacon amid Boston's symbolic landscape.

CONSUMING FENWAY PARK AND THE "FEEDBACK LOOP" OF MEANING

When Fenway Park is emulated by architects of other ballparks, when people turn their backyards into mini–Fenway Parks, when Fenway makes its way onto T-shirts, and when it becomes a character with its own personality in plays, stories, and movies, its symbolic worth is heightened and memorialized. Representations of Fenway Park are, of course, induced by the ballpark, but they too add to the mystique, importance, and power of the place. By looking at the ways that the ballpark is represented in souvenirs, like snow globes, T-shirts, and posters, or in movies, novels, or plays, we can empirically see how people actively make Fenway Park important.[14] These acts of consecration help establish and sustain the meaning and symbolism attached to the original place.

Focusing on the dynamic processes by which these representations are both produced and consumed shows how people act toward Fenway Park with reverence and adoration even when they are not at the ballpark. And those who produce or consume representations of Fenway Park are actively, though not necessarily intentionally, taking symbolic steps closer to the ballpark. In some cases, people literally build a connection between themselves and a place to display their allegiance to it and reenact their "rootedness" even when far away. Why else would the American soldiers of the 3rd Battalion 11th Marine Regiment build their own miniature replica of Fenway Park at Camp Ramadi in the sandy deserts of Iraq?[15]

The Red Sox organization is far from the only group that produces memorabilia and souvenirs of the ballpark. Many Fenway Park representations are private affairs, produced and consumed by one individual or by one small social group. Regardless of whether or not an individual builds a faux Fenway in his or her backyard, buys a "Green Monster" T-shirt, or sees the ballpark in a movie or on a television commercial for Dunkin Donuts, MasterCard, or Nike, these representations enhance the meaning and cultural capital of Fenway Park. They help people display and sustain the meaning of the ballpark even when they're outside or far away from Boston.

These visual, physical, and referential representations are part of a "feedback loop" in which they signify Fenway Park while also expanding its cultural significance. The meanings of these items are not inherently designated through their design or by their economic worth, but their very existence adds to the overall awareness that there is a place called Fenway Park and that that place fosters a special kind of reverence. Moreover, the adoration of Fenway Park is practiced through the consumption of its representations. In this way, material artifacts and objects provide physical and symbolic mediums for individuals to connect beliefs and actions.

Exploring the ways people actively consume material culture brings us closer to the ways they construct meaning. The process of production may be responsible for the availability of objects or places and for some of the meanings and values attached to them, but it does not account for the goods after the purchase, when other types of interactions happen between an individual, group, or community and the material objects. People consume goods both before and after the exchange of money at the point of purchase.[16]

Meaning is derived from persons' interactions with the product, regardless of whether it is a public, private, or shared object, from a monument to a water fountain to a coin to a ballpark. The meaning of the product emerges neither from the product alone nor from its functional or economic utility but, in part, from what it represents or mimics and from people's interaction with it.[17] Consumption can then be understood as a set of practices that involve noneconomic factors. Sociologist Pierre Bourdieu writes that consumption is "a stage in a process of communication, that is, an act of deciphering, decoding, which presupposes practical or explicit mastery of a cipher or code."[18] Following Bourdieu, I am concerned here with the cultural life of an object beyond the point of purchase, and I therefore focus on the uses of products as representations and expressions of culturally important allegiances, beliefs, and narratives.

Objects and places are endowed with meaning by individuals and groups in ways that tend to blur the line between traditional notions of the sacred and profane. The breakdown of traditional dichotomies is consistent with the paradoxical nature of urban culture. We would then expect to find consumption as both a secular practice and an act of "sacralization" or consecration in cities.[19] At Fenway, or through Fenway, a clear connection between consumption and spirituality has developed. I found two types of cultural consumption/consecration that persons employ as means for developing and declaring the importance of Fenway Park and their relationship to and with it. I call these practices *devotional consumerism* and *creative consumption*.

Devotional consumerism is an act of purchasing and consuming products not for their use or exchange value, nor for their aesthetic value, but for their connection to or allegiance with a community or group. This practice is based on beliefs that the product has significance beyond its economic worth or its beauty by aiding in the construction and maintenance of culture. *Creative consumption* is a practice of appropriating products in a way that goes beyond or outside its originally intended use or meaning. Some acts of creative consumption can be rebellious, like the manipulation of advertisements and billboards and other forms of "culture jamming" that appear regularly in magazines like *Adbusters*,[20] the erotic "slash fan fiction" adaptations of *Star Trek*, *Starsky and Hutch*, and *Miami Vice*,[21] or the playfully redefined roles of Mattel's Barbie as a prostitute, a heroin addict, a dominatrix, or a saint.[22] These acts do not require vandalism or radicalism but do require an active imagination and the desire to express something through the consumed object.

These two cultural practices—devotional consumerism and creative consumption—are two of the key ways people purchase, hope to purchase, use, adapt, and refashion material representations of Fenway Park. Souvenirs, memorabilia, and replicas of the ballpark consequently boost the visibility and significance of both Fenway Park and Boston's urban culture. Moreover, such acts help make the city less anonymous, less chaotic, and less "strange" not only by displaying individuals' and groups' attachments to places but also by constructing, refreshing, and recharging those attachments. Both types of consumption practices reveal the importance of place through the ways people appropriate it for communal and personal acts of reverence and possession.

DEVOTIONAL CONSUMERISM AND ARTICLES OF FAITH

The enculturation of particular beliefs and tastes is so powerful that we often describe our preferences for certain cultural objects as natural, inevitable, eternal, and sometimes universal. Although persons' cultural tastes have been repeatedly linked to social class,[23] Red Sox fans' "articles of faith" of personal adornment do not point to any clear class division. Though some distinctions are observable, and sometimes quite blatant, it is generally hard to tell how much money is in most fans' bank accounts. In other social contexts outside the ballpark, people have become very good at displaying a wealthy status by engaging in acts of "parallel play" and "conspicuous consumption."[24] Many have become very good at raising the *appearance* of their economic status by carrying a Gucci bag or driving a Mercedes. On closer inspection, the bag may be a knockoff or the car may be a rental. Through such means, the *display* of status is leveled, even if it is not so in actuality.

Whereas Americans once "dressed up" to go the ballpark in the pre–World War II era, today they "dress down" to cheer and root, root, root for the home team. These rituals lead to greater connections, at least visually, both to the players (e.g., when fans wear "authentic" jerseys of their favorite players) and to their fellow fans (e.g., wearing any sort of Red Sox gear as a sign of affiliation and allegiance). There is then a sense of social equality in the purchasing of similar goods and using or wearing them in the same setting.[25] It would not be surprising to see a working-class fan at a game or at a bar watching the game wearing an authentic Red Sox jersey, which can cost up to $200. These jerseys, like other articles of faith, may be a major economic indulgence for a fan. When asked about his Trot Nixon jersey, with a number 7 and the name "Nixon" on the back, Jon P. from Billerica, Massachusetts, replied,

> It cost me some money, but it's a small price to pay to cheer on my team and my favorite player. I wear it to the handful of games I go to each year at Fenway, when I go to the bar to watch the Sox, or even when I'm sitting at home watching the game. . . . I'm going to get Trot's away jersey soon so I can wear it when I watch away games.

Wearing his jersey is less about displaying wealth or keeping up with the Joneses and more about displaying his loyalty, devotion, and passion for his team and his city.

Arguing against common theories that deride consumers' purchases as narcissistic and superficial, sociologist Daniel Monti writes,

> Without denying the validity of these observations, we have seen that there is another way to look at all the investing and shopping which men and women, and to some extent even children, of modest means have been doing since the end of the nineteenth century. It is to see shopping and personal adornment as expressions of values and habits that are vital to the well-being of the whole community. The items we buy are much more than trinkets that make it easier to show off or to identify persons we would like to meet or become. They are the articles of faith we have in each other and particularly in the way we manage the ticklish business of accepting each other as equals in some setting and not in others.[26]

Purchasing and displaying articles of faith like a Red Sox jersey or cap —from the authentic game hats to the visors with two red socks patched to the front—is part of what Monti calls "consumer communalism." My idea of devotional consumerism, however, takes Monti's notion one step further or, in some ways, one step backward. Rather than looking at the role that the act of shopping plays in the construction and maintenance of urban culture, devotional consumerism accounts for the motivations and beliefs that are present *before* the actions that lead to community-building.

The following comment by a converted Red Sox fan, who grew up in Albany, New York, but now lives in Boston, reveals an important aspect of devotional consumerism: the belief that an object's or place's symbolic worth trumps or is independent of its monetary value. This fan demonstrates how the money spent at Fenway is qualitatively different from money spent elsewhere.

> Let me just note that prior to moving to Boston from New York four years ago, I actually hated baseball and thought it was boring. Never could it have the excitement and passion that football had. Since moving here and going to my first Red Sox game at Fenway four years ago, I consider myself a die-hard fan. I even put my beloved New York Giants [football], who I grew up with since birth thanks to my Dad, number two. At this point in my life, I'm considering moving to a more affordable state altogether to settle down, but I'm trying to delay that until the Sox win the Series so that I can be here for it. Yes, it's been eighty-six years, but I feel it's right around the corner. Anyway . . . I realize that these days it is hard financially for the organization to compete with a stadium that holds twenty thousand less than their rival [the Yankees], but *I'm willing to pay more than double the ticket price that other fans pay around the country to watch the game in a place that oozes history.* When you go to Fenway, it's like stepping back in time.

On average, tickets to Red Sox home games are the most expensive tickets in professional baseball, at nearly $45 a seat. Despite their ever increasing ticket prices, the Red Sox have had the most sell-outs in the past five years. Attendance has risen steadily each decade since the ballpark was built in 1912. Moreover, people have fought with ardent devotion to save the ol' ballpark in spite of the possibility that the additional ten thousand seats a new ballpark would provide would lower ticket prices by creating a larger quantity of "cheap" seats.

Paradoxically, some fans who would like to pay less for tickets so they could go to more games are still willing to pay the higher prices, perhaps as a form of sacrifice. Their devotion to the team and the ballpark supersede their economic situations and the economic value of the tickets. In 2004, Major League Baseball established the prices of World Series tickets available at both Fenway Park and the St. Louis Cardinals' Busch Stadium. The prices were $190 for box seats, $145 for grandstand seats, $70 for bleachers, and $50 for standing room. For fans desperate enough and/or wealthy enough, tickets were available through online auction sites like eBay and ticket agencies like StubHub for tickets ranging from $1,375 for bleacher seats to over $6,000 for a seat behind and above home plate in the .406 Club.[27]

A scalper stationed near the Kenmore Square T stop about an hour before the first pitch of Game 2 at Fenway told me that he sold four box-seat tickets for $3,500 each just ten minutes before he started talking to me. Although postseason games are worth more than regular-season games, if we concede that the goal of a baseball season is to win a championship, the seats are no different from the seats during the regular season. They are not more comfortable; they are not closer to the field. They are still wooden and too small, and most are behind one pole or another. Regardless of the money fans spend to sit in those seats, many of them leave with back and neck aches, but, of course, suffering has long played a significant role in Red Sox Nation, as it does in many religions.

In early December 2004 (barely a month after the Red Sox beat the Cardinals and became World Series champions), more than three thousand fans camped out on Yawkey Way, braving cold and wet winds, to buy tickets for Opening Day of the 2005 season. Kip Lamberg wore a plastic fluorescent-green wrist band with a number 1 on it, denoting his coveted position in line. He spent $1,440 on thirty-two tickets that he planned to share with friends and family. The tickets were for eight games, including Opening Day. "I know there are a lot of things in life that are much more profound than baseball," Lamberg said. "But life can be a rough ride and baseball provides relief and sanctuary for so many people. It's such a pure and simple gift."[28] As Lamberg made his way home, he passed a grounds-crew truck filled with dirt headed for Fenway's infield. With his bare hands, he scooped up a handful of the red dirt, a souvenir to be displayed and cherished through the upcoming season and afterward.

LOOKING TOWARD FENWAY FROM AFAR

The desire to be at Fenway Park, or even near it, to witness significant events like Opening Day, any Yankees game, and the postseason, and to show one's communal allegiance while there creates connections between the ballpark and its patrons. Even though such desires and actions help construct attachments to a place, they are not confined by geography. A similar dynamic is involved when Red Sox fans outside Boston go to, support, and convene in Red Sox–themed leisure sites. Places like the Riviera Café in New York City, Sonny McLean's in Santa Monica, California (the self-proclaimed home of Red Sox Nation West), and Humpy's Great Alaska Alehouse in Anchorage (located forty-six hundred miles from the ballpark, it is home base for the Far From Fenway Fan Club) provide environments for displaced New England "expatriots" and other members of the Fenway faithful to congregate, celebrate, and commiserate together. These "off-site" places help build a connection to Fenway Park, the center, the *axis mundi*, the site of origin for the Red Sox faith.[29]

The Riviera Café's sports bar, located in Greenwich Village, shows all Red Sox home and away games, including preseason spring-training games. The Riviera has gained a reputation in recent years as a safe haven for transplanted New Englanders and other Red Sox devotees who live in the heart of the Yankees' Evil Empire. According to the Riviera's general manager, Steve Serell,

> Over the years, there's been a considerable word of mouth that we're a place you can go in New York and watch the Red Sox without getting a beating. It's a place where Red Sox fans can be with other Red Sox fans. If you're from Boston and live in New York, the West Village is a lot closer than Lansdowne Street.[30]

A regular at the Riviera said that "being a Red Sox fan, and meeting others, I've discovered that it's like being part of a brotherhood."[31] When the Red Sox played the Yankees for the American League championship in 2004, the Riviera's usual occupancy limit of seventy persons easily tripled.[32]

At Sonny McLean's in Santa Monica, Foxboro, Massachusetts, native Jim Connors sells T-shirts with the slogan "Who says you're 3000 miles away?" And no one asks, "Away from what?" "Fenway Park, stupid," would be the likely response by any number of the not-so-Californian Red Sox fans who frequent the bar, many of whom have roots in places spanning the New England region. "You can take the fan out of Boston, but you can't take the Boston out of the fan," said one fan who left Medford, Massachusetts, for Southern California in 1983.[33]

FENWAY ON FILM

Sonny McLean's and its patrons gained local and national exposure by representing the geographical depth of Red Sox Nation in the documentary *Still We Believe: The Boston Red Sox Movie* (the name was supposedly chosen by fans through a team-sponsored contest). A film crew followed several fans through the pains and joys and pains again of the 2003 season from the first ticket sales to Yankee Aaron Boone's eleventh-inning home run that ended the season for the Sox in the seventh game of the American League Championship Series (ALCS). The first words of the film express the agony of "cursed" Red Sox fans when a voice off-camera explains, "Red Sox are like the woman who treats you so bad, you don't care," as the camera focuses on Fenway Park.

The film premiered in Boston at Loews Theatres Boston Common, just a few miles from the ballpark. A red carpet welcomed the filmmakers, the featured fans in the film, Red Sox players and executives, and a few hundred Red Sox fans. On his way into the showing, one fan summed up his and others' motivations for seeing the movie: "Being a Red Sox fan is like a religion. It's like faith." So going to see a movie that purportedly documents that faith is, in itself, an act of faith and devotion. The Fenway faithful who either saw *Still, We Believe* in the theater or rented or bought the DVD were practicing devotional consumerism. Their motivations for seeing the film were not about the quality of the film but about its subject matter, their object of devotion.

Another recent film that drew Red Sox fans to the theaters and exploited their thirst for all things Sox-related is the Farrelly brothers' *Fever Pitch*. Adapted from a Nick Hornby novel about English soccer fans, Rhode Island natives Peter and Bobby Farrelly translated

Hornby's tale into a Red Sox–infused love story about a man's passion for the Olde Town Team and for a girl he meets along the way. Although two popular Hollywood stars played the leading roles (Jimmy Fallon and Drew Barrymore), Fenway Park was the most important character. Some scenes were filmed during actual games, with many locals either playing minor roles or filling in as extras cheering on the hometown team at the ballpark. "Without sounding self-aggrandizing, we feel like Fenway Park is the star of the movie," said Chuck Steedman, Red Sox senior director of broadcast services.[34]

Fever Pitch simultaneously benefited from and was cursed by the Red Sox Curse being broken by the team's World Series win. It was easier for the film's producers and directors to adapt the script to include the unexpected win than to try to capture a real-life fairy tale in Hollywood fashion. The original screenplay assumed that the Red Sox would falter in September, as was their usual trend, so the Farrellys rearranged the ending and even filmed a scene, much to the chagrin of many diehard Red Sox fans, during the on-field postgame celebration with the Red Sox on the field in St. Louis. In what was certainly a strange mix of Hollywood and real life, those who saw the film saw, in Bill Simmons's words, "a brief shot of Curtis Leskanic turning away from the happy pig pile near the mound and *high-fiving Fallon*. I'm convinced that's why the team didn't ask him back this season."[35]

Taking center stage, Fenway Park hosted its own red-carpet premiere for *Fever Pitch*. The actors, directors, and screenwriters of the film, along with nearly a third of the Red Sox team and Larry Lucchino, addressed the invitation-only crowd after strolling along the red carpet draped down the first-base line. The festivities inside the ballpark showcased Boston by including past and present star members from the region's other sports teams (New England Patriots, Boston Celtics, and Boston Bruins, as well as former Boston College football hero Doug Flutie), Boston-bred Aerosmith bassist Tom Hamilton, and Boston's favorite ska band, the Dropkick Murphys. After the 2004 championship season, Red Sox fans have a special place in their heart for the Dropkick Murphys. Early in the 2004 season, the band remade an old local hymn called "Tessie" that Red Sox "Royal Rooters" sang during the 1903 World Series and was/is believed to have helped the Red Sox (then called the Pilgrims) beat the Pittsburgh Pirates. The Dropkick Murphys' updated version of "Tessie" became a favorite throughout the season and was, consequently, featured in the movie.[36]

Fever Pitch was not the first film in which Fenway Park was featured, but the occasions have been rare. After Larry Cancro, Red Sox senior vice president of Fenway affairs, joined the organization in 1985, he tried to get the Red Sox involved in other cultural spheres outside the sports world. "I made a concerted effort to get us into things in the mid-1980s," said Cancro.

The filming of *Field of Dreams* brought Kevin Costner and James Earl Jones to the ballpark in 1987. Their two characters meet in Boston in the middle of a cosmic trip down baseball's memory lane. At Fenway, they receive a message on the scoreboard to find Archie "Moonlight" Graham and bring him back to play in Costner's character's homemade ballpark in the middle of his Iowa cornfield. Cancro told me that if you look very closely at the Red Sox lineup that also appears on the scoreboard during that scene, you can see his name along with other Red Sox executives. "If you stop it at the right place," Cancro said through a poorly hidden laugh, "you can see that I'm batting cleanup."

A few other television shows, commercials, and movie productions have since used the Red Sox trademarked logo, showed the inside or outside of Fenway, or even simply made references to or about the team or ballpark. A few examples include *Wings* (a character tried to sing the national anthem before a game), *Spenser: For Hire* (Fenway's outside ramps were used for a chase scene), *The Practice* (two characters were married at home plate), *Average Joe II* (bachelor brings date to Fenway to introduce her to his home city), *Legally Blonde 2: Red, White, and Blonde* (main characters plan wedding at Fenway), and *Good Will Hunting* (shots of Carlton Fisk's famous homerun as well as aerial shots of Fenway). When the creators of these ads, movies, and television programs reference or show Fenway Park, they are trying both to represent local culture and to appeal to a devoted public.

When the devoted consumers of Red Sox Nation support the product, whether it's a movie or a new egg sandwich at Dunkin Donuts, they do so, at least in part, because of their loyalties to the Red Sox, Fenway Park, and the city of Boston. When a Red Sox fan who moved to Virginia from Boston claims that he only buys Citgo gas because it reminds him of Fenway, he is acknowledging the devotion behind his consumption of a particular product or brand. When this type of consumption is attached to Fenway Park the way the Citgo sign sits perched atop a building in Kenmore Square peering down on the Fenway faithful, it endows the place with meaning, to the point of consecration.

CREATIVE CONSUMPTION
AND THE APPROPRIATION OF MATERIAL CULTURE

By reappropriating materials, symbols, and images, fans begin to carve out their own ways of worshipping through acts of creative consumption. The ways that fans refashion and assimilate popular or mass cultural artifacts to the particulars of their lives can be empowering.[37] They provide practitioners with a greater sense of connection and a greater sense of ownership.

Len Martin, the engineer and author of *Fenway Park: Build It Yourself*, told me that he has heard from people that after they build the model, they use push pins to show where they have sat for particular games. By doing so, they display memories that give them a sense of ownership of their experience at Fenway Park. Martin's Fenway Park model includes very minute details of the ballpark, including the names of Tom and Jean Yawkey written in Morse code on the scoreboard. And as a part of his own creative consumption, the scores and names on the model's scoreboard are from a game that he attended while putting together plans for the miniature ballpark.

Along with Martin's build-it-yourself ballpark, miniature Fenway Parks come in snow globes, plastic blow-up tubes, and miniature models. Steve Wolf builds and sells handcrafted replicas that range from three and a half square feet (for $28,000) to six and a half square feet (for $80,000). Though the people who buy Wolf's replicas are practicing devotional consumerism, Wolf himself began building ballparks after his beloved old Comiskey Park in Chicago was demolished in 1990. Comiskey's cross-town rival, Wrigley Field, was his next project, followed by a replica of Fenway Park that included hand-airbrushed pewter seats, a working Green Monster scoreboard, and seven miniature light standards with a total of 650 bulbs. Wolf said that "the only thing missing is plumbing—and 33,420 Boston Red Sox fans."[38]

Although people are constrained by the primary subject matter of material and pictorial illustrations of Fenway Park, the variety of such illustrations shows the creative consumption of culture. Degrees of replication may vary depending on the objective, scope, and scale of the project. Like some heritage sites or reconstructed villages, producers of replicas and reproductions of Fenway Park try to create a likeness, verisimilitude, or "mimetic credibility" of the original. Yet, unlike some

Artist M-C Lamarre has painted custom murals of Fenway Park in both commercial and private residences. Here is Lamarre in front of one of her pieces in Bedford, New Hampshire. (Photo courtesy of M-C Lamarre, www.mclamarre.com)

heritage sites or reconstructed villages—like New Salem in Illinois, where Abraham Lincoln lived for six years in the 1830s; Colonial Williamsburg in Virginia, where people flock to "experience" the everyday life of the eighteenth century;[39] or Little Sweden, U.S.A., in Lindsborg, Kansas[40]—they do not have to worry about being exact or even structurally accurate.

Unlike postmodernist renderings that would conclude that the representation, or *simulacrum*, replaces the original,[41] I am making the argument that these representations supplement and even enhance the sentiment and value of the original. In the same way that no one would mistake a poster of Van Gogh's *Starry Night* that hangs in a college student's dorm room for the painting that hangs in the Museum of Modern Art in New York City, no one would ever mistake Bill Von Klack's backyard Fenway facsimile for the real thing. The intention is usually to create a "mnemonic" artifact that resembles the real ballpark.[42]

Fenway Park has been replicated for both private and public use from Massachusetts to California to Iraq to Australia. The art of replication is a form of creative consumption whereby individuals consume

Fenway Park via its replica, however miniature in form or reduced in scale. Replicas that are big enough for children and adults to play baseball, softball, Wiffle ball, or T-ball within it add to the intensity of both the builders' and players' devotion and consumption of Fenway Park. As players try to hit homeruns over their local Green Monsters and replay favorite Fenway moments in their backyards or town recreation fields, they are manipulating the symbolic boundaries of the original ol' ballpark.

BUILDING FENWAY AT HOME

Like the fictional character Ray Kinsella in *Field of Dreams*, some fans have substantiated the mantra "If you build it, they will come" in their own front- and backyards. These Fenway devotees try to "poach" the essence and aura of Fenway Park by including details that transform a nondescript space into their very own field of dreams. In 1998, Wayland, Massachusetts, native Kirk Carapezza built an eight-foot Green Monster in his family's front yard and continued to replicate many of Fenway's famed details. Carapezza converted a large piggy bank into the Coke bottle that sits atop his left-field wall. The Citgo sign is an enlarged photograph attached to the outfield wall. The scoreboard is a photo on cardboard of Fenway's left-field scoreboard, donated by Carapezza's high school history teacher, who bought it for a mere sixty-nine cents.[43] "There's such a passion for the Red Sox around here that the team and the ballpark have become a big part of the culture," said Carapezza.[44]

In Needham, Massachusetts, City of Von's Park (a play on the Red Sox's spring-training ballpark, City of *Palms* Park) is Bill Von Klack's prized possession and favorite toy. A ten-foot-high, thirty-two-foot-long wooden replica of Fenway Park's thirty-foot-high, thirty-thousand-pound left-field wall runs almost the full length of Von Klack's backyard. His own Green Monster stands complete with a net and Coke bottle perched atop it and a downsized but realistic left-field scoreboard across it, and a small Citgo sign he bought for $25 at an antique store hangs just above and behind the wall. Von Klack has continually been adding details to his Fenway facsimile for eight years. Across from the wall stands a large yellow pole marking the foul line from home plate, which sits a few feet away from the Von Klacks' porch, to the end of right field. At Fenway, that pole is the famed Pesky's Pole. In Von Klack's backyard, it goes by the same name.[45]

Batter's boxes made out of real ballpark-grade infield dirt lay on each side of home plate, and a bank of twelve floodlights peer down onto the field for nighttime Wiffle-ball games. The Red Sox's retired numbers (including Jackie Robinson's "42," which hangs in all major-league ballparks in honor of the first black major-leaguer)[46] are painted at the top of the right-field wall, and a red square is etched out on the roof of the garage with a small "9" painted on it, imitating the lone red seat in the Fenway bleachers, 502 feet away from home plate, in which a man reportedly sat when Red Sox legend Ted Williams's homerun went through his straw hat.

Known in his hometown of Needham as Mr. Fenway Park for his dedication to his backyard faux Fenway, Von Klack's practice of creative consumption transplants *something* of the real Fenway Park into and onto his lush green lawn. By constructing his ballpark and tending to it with care, he is engaging in an activity similar to those of the people Laura Chester documented in her study of personally designed private sacred places.[47] From Michael Dowling's "Root Cellar Chapel" in Boston to Margaret and Hermon Dennis's "All Is Welcome Temple" in Mississippi to Jerry Wenstrom and Marilyn Strong's "Flaming Stupa" in Washington, Chester found people stationed across the United States who have carved out their own sacred sites. "Though we may not have to create our own underground chapels because of persecution any-more," writes Chester, "there is still a yearning for religious privacy, a deep desire to create for oneself a holy chamber, *a place where creative expression joins hands with devotion.*"[48]

PLAYING TOGETHER AT FAUX FENWAY

Creative expressions of Fenway Park are not confined to exclusively private acts of devotion. Carapezza opens up his backyard ballpark in Wayland for an annual fundraising Wiffle-ball tournament. Although admission is free for the five hundred to one thousand fans, all donations ($10 is requested) are forwarded to the Jimmy Fund, the Red Sox's official charity, at Boston's Dana-Farber Cancer Institute. The tournament raises nearly $15,000 each year. Carapezza also rents out the field for "corporate outings and birthday parties with the money going to the

Jimmy Fund. No matter what your age, standing with a bat in your hand at Pupque Park [named after his pet poodle] makes everybody feel like a kid dreaming of hitting a home run at Fenway."[49]

Creative consumption can be practiced together as a collective and communal affair. Town and camp recreation fields across the United States have been transformed into mini–Fenway Parks where kids can be seen, in Carapezza's word, "dreaming of hitting a home run in Fenway." "Little Fenway," a 1:4 scale replica of its namesake, is located in Essex, Vermont, and was built by a former Boston-area resident, Pat O'Connor. With an eye for detail, O'Connor placed a Citgo sign in the trees that stand just behind his park's Green Monster. His left-field wall is painted the identical shade of green as the real Monster in Boston. A friend of O'Connor's scraped a chip off Fenway's left-field wall and matched it after Red Sox officials refused to reveal their color formula. He uses his Fenway for charity and community Wiffle-ball games that are so popular that three hundred spectators were on hand for its grand opening in April 2003.[50]

There is a similar Wiffle-ball mini–Fenway Park in Winslow, Maine. One of the key attractions at Camp Caribou, a popular boys' overnight summer camp, is its state-of-the-art Wiffle-ball diamond. Lars Jonassen, an unabashed Red Sox fan who has been the camp's head counselor for nineteen years, estimates that he spent 150 hours on his plywood version of Fenway. Jonassen's Green Monster was re-created down to the smallest detail, including an out-of-town scoreboard that shows each game's score, inning, and pitchers by number. During the 2002 and 2003 seasons, Jonassen had the Red Sox beating the Yankees and Roger Clemens, with Nomar Garciaparra at bat and the scoreboard still showing a recent error by New York's Derek Jeter. "We think we can save this for ten or fifteen years and improve on it a little bit," Jonassen said. "At some point in time, we want to put in a bullpen, the right-field stands. We'd like to add the Prudential building behind it."[51]

Former Red Sox third-baseman Tim Naehring built a $700,000 mini-Fenway, which is 90 percent the size of the real Fenway, in Cincinnati on the Little League field where he played as a boy. He paid for the construction through his charity Athletes Reaching Out and then donated the park to the city. "I never thought it would have the impact it's had on that community," Naehring said after discussing plans with acting governor Paul Cellucci in 1998 to build a "Little Fenway" just a short drive south of Boston in Quincy. "I can only imagine what it would be like building a Fenway Park here when the real Fenway Park has been a part of people's lives here."[52] Cellucci filed legislation in 1998 giving Naehring's Athletes Reaching Out Foundation the option to lease nearly twelve acres of state-owned Metropolitan District Commission land in Quincy for the project. The bill, approved by lawmakers and signed by Cellucci, envisioned a twenty-five-hundred-seat park with lights and a detailed replica scoreboard. Naehring hoped to raise the money needed to build the mini-ballpark in large part through corporate donations. Naehring's time with the Red Sox, however, ended abruptly after he sustained a career-ending elbow injury. After his release, he returned to Cincinnati to work in the Reds' front office, and his replica-Fenway project floundered.

In 2000, Rick Iacobucci brought Naehring's project back to life. Iacobucci's group picked up the ball and filed a bill so that his nonprofit group, Mini-Fenway Park Inc., could continue the project. Iacobucci's group is planning to build a $7.5 million, two-thousand-seat ballpark that he promises will deliver all the charm and character of Major League Baseball's oldest park. "Carl Yastrzemski summed it up best when he said, 'Fenway is the best place to play baseball in the world,'" said Iacobucci after finalizing a lease agreement with the state for an eleven-acre site next to the Blue Hills Reservation. "We wanted to recreate that experience for kids and give them a chance to feel what it's like to play day in and day out at a Fenway that's suitable for their size."[53]

Mini-Fenway Parks have also been constructed outside New England. In fact, they have popped up all over the United States and in other countries as well. A municipal park and recreation construction group called "Big League Dreams" has either built or plans to build more then ten replicas of Fenway Park for youth softball games and leagues. These faux Fenways are primarily scattered throughout the state of California, though the group opened a new ballpark in May 2005 in League City, Texas.

Perhaps the most ironic mini-Fenway is a Little League ballpark in Delray Beach, Florida, that is part of the town's Miller Park. Miller Park is home to the Bucky Dent Baseball School and to "Little Fenway." In "Little Fenway," time has stood still since that famous (or infamous) afternoon of October 2, 1978, when the Yankees' Bucky "Bleeping" Dent (as he will forever be known to Red Sox fans) hit a seventh-inning three-run homerun off Mike Torrez that propelled the Yankees over the Red Sox by one run in a one-game playoff for the American League Eastern

Division Championship. The scoreboard on the mini-Fenway's left-field Green Monster consistently shows a big yellow "3" in the top of the seventh.

All of these replicas, from backyards to town recreation fields, are examples of creative consumption. For a variety of reasons, people have chosen to build ballparks that emulate Fenway Park and, through their replication of the original, have put their own imprint on it.

THE POWER OF REPRESENTATIONS

Rather than simply replacing the original and seeping its aura or authenticity, replicas can enhance the cultural significance of the original that they were designed to emulate. By owning, building, or using replicas, souvenirs, and memorabilia of a place like Fenway Park, individuals and groups engage in complex forms of consumption. In the same way that "collective representations persist for reasons other than those that brought them into existence,"[54] replicas of places can take on a life of their own but are always connected to the original, often in a deferential way. The consumption of places and other material objects goes beyond the production process and the point of purchase and is often about how people choose to recall and re-create their past experiences with and of those places and objects.

Devotional consumerism and creative consumption are two ways that people show their community allegiances through the use of replicas, souvenirs, and memorabilia. These practices also reconstruct and reappropriate the meanings of both the representations and, more importantly, the original place itself. When such practices are motivated by the cultural value of an object, rather than its monetary value, consumption is more than an economic activity and moves into the realm of cultural consecration. This type of consecration is prevalent in Boston and throughout American cities and has become an important way that individuals and groups can refresh, recharge, and express their allegiance and devotion to a place and the beliefs, values, and experiences that they believe that place signifies.

SOME DIAMONDS ARE NOT FOREVER
Debating the Future of Fenway Park

There's nothing wrong with hanging on to history; you just can't hang on to it with your chin forever and ever and ever. It's just time. The ballpark's tired. Fenway's definitely unique, but it's tired.
— Bob Montgomery, former Red Sox catcher (1970–79)

Places of the heart, even impure ones, are worth the effort. Your home, your neighborhood, your city—you have to defend your piece of ground. Manufactured, mediated experience is ubiquitous. Battling to preserve a special place is not quaint provincialism. It is defiance against the relentless obliteration of memory and community.
—Michael Betzold, ballpark advocate, Detroit

March 23, 2005, would have been just like any other day in Boston if Fenway Park didn't exist. More to the point, it was a significant day in Boston *because* Fenway Park exists. Despite a number of attempts to knock it down, Fenway remains standing as the oldest active ballpark in Major League Baseball. And on that fateful day in the spring of 2005, a few weeks before the Red Sox would take the field at Fenway as World Series Champions, the Red Sox made the announcement that many people, though not all, were happy to hear. Under the previous ownership, the Sox had argued that they would need a new, larger ballpark in

133

order to pay for escalating player salaries and other expenses. When John Henry and his group of limited partners bought the team in 2002, however, they tried to look for ways to save Fenway first. In the process, the new ownership group adopted a number of proposals from preservation groups in the neighborhood, who had been fighting against a host of alternative new ballpark plans, all of which included the demolition of Fenway.

Then the Red Sox announced that they were committed to staying at Fenway, even though it is a "no strings attached" commitment. "We're establishing ourselves as long-term residents, and we share with other residents a desire for improvements to this area," said Larry Lucchino, the chief executive officer of the Red Sox.[1] "This is a historic day for baseball, and a historic day for Boston," Henry exclaimed. "Today is a great victory for all of us who love this park."[2]

Many people certainly do "love this park." It is telling that Fenway Park's features have been emulated in the newer retro ballparks across the country from Baltimore to San Diego. Apparently, there is something special about Fenway Park, something that is worth replicating. And if you already have Fenway Park, the original and not an ersatz version of it, then there must be something about it that makes it worth keeping. As I was told repeatedly, that something, call it an "aura" if you like, is tied up with the ballpark's history, the generations who have cheered and jeered there, the players that have swung their bats and made diving catches, and the seating bowl that situates the fan and player into rare close proximity. Fans sit so close to the field that, as the former Red Sox outfielder Ellis Burks put it during my interview with him, "someone might yell 'Hey Ellis, how 'bout a picture?' and I'll come over and smile and then get back to the game. We're that close to the fans."

According to Red Sox fan Paul L. from Nashua, New Hampshire, the proximity of the fans to the players on the field and in the dugouts makes him feel like he's going back in time every time he enters the ballpark.

> Everyone is so packed in at Fenway; we're right on top of the players. It's great; it's like old baseball, like in the fifties, or earlier, you know, the way it should be. *Fenway is real. You know, it's unique; it's authentic.* I couldn't imagine coming down [to Boston] and watching the Sox anywhere else. You know, there's just something so special about this

place. Would I like it if the seats were more comfortable? Sure. But there's something real about sitting in those seats. . . . with a few beers and a win, I'd sit on concrete bleachers if I had to.

The "authenticity" associated with the ballpark is a key concern for both folks who want a new ballpark and for those who want to save the original. Recent additions and renovations to Fenway have been lauded for their ability to maintain the authenticity and integrity of the original plan.

The Green Monster seats, built for the 2003 season, look as if they have been atop the great wall since its original construction. Gazing at those newly planted seats from across the field above Section 16 on the first-base side, Andy B., a Red Sox fan since the early 1970s, spoke positively about the new addition:

It's funny. I see pictures of Fenway from even just a few years ago, and it seems like something's missing. It usually takes me a couple seconds until I realize that there are no seats on the Monster. It's kind of strange; they've only been up there for a year now, right? And it seems like they've always been there. I know they haven't been, so why would I expect to see them in old pictures? Funny, right? I guess the Sox are doing something right with those seats.

Comments like these made me pause to question whether authenticity can be constructed into a place or whether conscious construction depletes any "real" sense of authenticity.

The "New Fenway Park" plan of 1999 was supposed to be a larger replica of the ol' ballpark, advertised as a way to retain the "Fenway experience." But can the physical confines of a place determine or at least influence the type of experiences people have in and with that place? Can authenticity be purposely constructed into a place? Some would say that constructing authenticity or even purposely seeking out authentic places is, in effect, inauthentic.[3] In order to recognize authenticity, or the search for authenticity, as a social phenomenon, I understand it primarily as a matter of practice and experience rather than as an essentialist *sui generis* quality. That is, no thing is inherently authentic; it is only deemed to be so by people based on certain cultural beliefs and experiences. The ways that people define and adjudicate what is and is not authentic are "strategies of action" that make up their overall cultural "tool-kit."[4] Tools such as stories and habits reinforce taken-for-granted understandings of how things should be done. Beliefs about authenticity, then, are part of people's "strategies of action" when it comes to their understanding of the past, present, and future of Fenway Park. Such strategies are neither purely rational nor totally built from scratch.[5] At Fenway, they are connected to a person's relationship to the ballpark's history and its supposed authenticity, however defined.

Opinions about the future of Fenway Park can be located along a continuum from the most rigid and conservative to the most flexible and liberal.[6] I have placed responses to the Fenway Park debate into four categories: Orthodox, Conservative, Reform, and Radical (see table 5.1). Each category reflects a distinctive "strategy of action" or "frame" for practicing culture and commemorating that culture's past, present, and future. The term "frame" is useful for understanding the different ways that people see Fenway Park. Sociologist Erving Goffman wrote that "frames" are "schemata of interpretation" that help individuals "locate, perceive, identify, and label" occurrences and experiences in their lives and about the world they live in.[7] Frames allow people to view an issue, form an opinion, and then determine a strategy of action.

Those who adopt an Orthodox frame see Fenway Park as an artifact of the past that should be preserved without additions or renovations. Instead of trying to change Fenway Park and make it fit into today's culture, people in the present and in the future should adapt to Fenway Park. From this point of view, the building doesn't need to change; people do. Authenticity is viewed as a quality that transcends the present by being fully connected to the past, a lost past perhaps that can only be touched by entering an edifice like Fenway Park in its presumably purest form.

Like the Orthodox frame, the Conservative frame also holds a great deal of reverence for history. Looking through the Conservative frame, however, allows more flexibility when trying to preserve the past. That is, Fenway Conservatives want to maintain the ballpark but are willing to add to it if it will help it last, both structurally and financially. More to the point, they want Fenway Park to last as a marker that connects generations from the past to those in the present and future, as long as the integrity and authenticity of the original design in preserved.

Preserving history is also important for those who view Fenway from a Reform frame. History for them, however, is less about maintaining the physicality of the old ballpark and more about creating something new that reminds them of the past. History, then, should be remembered, but people shouldn't live in the past. A new ballpark that

TABLE 5.1. TYPOLOGY OF CULTURAL FRAMES AND THE FUTURE OF FENWAY PARK

Frame (approx. %)	Old vs. New	Action	Location	Examples
Orthodox (<5%)	Save old ballpark	No renovation; keep all old features; no additions	Current footprint	"Creature comforts and amenities are for yuppies and wussies. . . . be a man, whizz in the horse trough."[a]
Conservative (45–50%)	Save old ballpark	Renovate or "improve"; make additions but preserve integrity of the original design	Current footprint	"Don't throw out something good. Take what you've got and build on it."[b] "Replace Fenway with a McStadium and you've lost more than a ballpark. You've lost a part of Boston's history that no 'mallpark' can replace."[c] "We're just looking for new ways for fans to enjoy Fenway. When you can add seats, add space, and add comfort, then you're helping everybody."[d]
Reform (35–40%)	Build new ballpark	New ballpark should be replica of the original; should include old features like the Green Monster, Pesky's Pole, and idiosyncratic field dimensions	Expand current footprint; South Boston (waterfront); Assembly Square/Somerville, MA	"[The plan] is a new Fenway Park, just like the old Fenway Park. The difference is that outside the baselines, we'll have 40 percent more space and all the comfort of a modern facility."[e] "The green wall is the magic thing, though. You gotta bring the wall. If the wall goes (to the new stadium), it's all good."[f]
Radical (<10%)	Build new ballpark	New ballpark should *not* be a replica; should have its own unique characteristics related to its new location	South Boston (waterfront); Assembly Square/Somerville, MA; Foxboro, MA; Salem, NH; Hartford, CT	"You break completely, and you do something new."[g] "The history that has occurred at Fenway will always be history, but it's not necessary to continue to have Fenway per se factored into the new ballpark."[h] "Once you replicate the Monster on a different site, you've transformed it from reality to stage set. Instead of being a real place with a real game, the park will feel like a planned amusement-park ride. When image becomes more important than reality, architecture and baseball are in big trouble."[i]

[a] Anonymous Red Sox fan, quoted in Dan Shaughnessy, *At Fenway: Dispatches from Red Sox Nation* (New York: Three Rivers Press, 1996), 226.

[b] Patrick Pinnell, quoted in "No Need for New Fenway," by Tom Condon, *Hartford Courant*, 17 September 2000.

[c] Erika Tarlin, member on the board of directors for Save Fenway Park!, "Letter to the Editor," *Boston Globe*, 25 June 2001.

[d] Charles Steinberg, Red Sox vice president for public affairs, quoted in "From 'Monster' Seats to Right-Field Party," Corey Dade, *Boston Globe*, 8 November 2003.

[e] Anonymous Red Sox executive, quoted in "New Ballyard Would Look Like an Updated Fenway Park," Scott Farmelant, *Boston Herald*, 4 January 1999.

[f] Emmanuel Paine, quoted in "Park's Design Impresses Many," Lynnley Browning and Steven Wilmsen, *Boston Globe*, 16 May 1999.

[g] Richard Johnson, curator of the Sports Museum of New England in Boston, interview with author, December 2004.

[h] Jim Lonborg, former Red Sox player (1965–71), interview with author, February 2004.

[i] Robert Campbell, "If We Build It Right," *Boston Globe*, 30 July 2000.

was designed to look like the original but included more amenities like comfortable seating and easier parking is desired, when looking through this frame, because it preserves the authenticity of the present while still being reminded of the past.

But can a replica be authentic? Those who adopt a Radical frame would say no. They believe that a new ballpark should have its own idiosyncrasies that emerge from the new footprint, wherever that may be. The Green Monster had a functional genesis. Fenway Park was squeezed into a plot of land that didn't allow for a long enough left-field foul line. Because the Red Sox couldn't build out into an already existing street, they built a thirty-foot-high wall. For Fenway Radicals, a Green Monster in a new ballpark with a different footprint would be totally contrived and inauthentic. History, then, does not exist in the physical places of the past but through the stories we tell about our experiences in that place.

Despite these different "strategies of action" that range from total preservation to completely starting over, there is nonetheless a common thread woven into and through the positions of the varying camps. All express concerns for preserving the authenticity of Fenway Park. And regardless of their conclusions—renovate or remove or something else —all identify Fenway Park as hallowed ground, a symbol of their city and themselves. As such, level of emotional attachment to a place is not a good indicator of an individual's or group's hopes or plans for the future of that place. How they construct narratives about history and authenticity may prove to be better predictors.

The built environment and the places within it that make it special, interesting, authentic, and important provide a medium for negotiating the meanings and values that people hold near and dear. Many of the people I interviewed and spent time with at the ballpark wondered aloud what Boston would be like without Fenway Park.

PLAYING WITH TRADITION

Before 2002, with only a few exceptions, Fenway Park had remained relatively unchanged following Tom Yawkey's 1933–34 renovations after a fire burned down the center-field bleachers. Both the visiting team and the Red Sox shared the same runway from their dugouts to their locker rooms until 1953. During the 1952 season, Red Sox shortstop

Jimmy Piersall exchanged blows with Yankee second-baseman Billy Martin on their way to their respective clubhouses. Separate passage-ways were constructed the next year.

The next minor change to the ballpark came over the winter before the start of the 1976 season. During the 1975 World Series against the Cincinnati Reds, a.k.a. the "Big Red Machine," Red Sox outfielder Fred Lynn was knocked out after barreling into the outfield wall while try-ing to get under a deep fly ball. Lynn's scary crash forced the Red Sox to add padding to Fenway's outfield walls.

The only other things to change at Fenway Park are its billboards and advertisements, which are themselves, quite literally, signs of the times. And they are not without their own controversies. For in-stance, in 1995, the Justice Department announced an agreement with Philip Morris Co. to move its cigarette billboards from the view of television cameras at sports stadiums. According to Justice De-partment officials, the placement of Philip Morris's Marlboro bill-board above the right-field bleachers at Fenway Park violated the ban on cigarette ads being shown on television. The billboard could be seen in camera shots of homeruns or plays in the outfield.[8] The Marlboro ad, featuring the rugged Marlboro Man, had long been a source of frustration for antismoking advocates, particularly because of its position near a billboard for the pediatric-cancer-fighting Jimmy Fund. Local Boston WEEI sports-radio host Eddie Andelman expressed these sentiments:

> The Red Sox are deeply associated with the Jimmy Fund, which has saved thousands of lives, and the Marlboro sign is incongruous with what they stand for. You can't have the Jimmy Fund and Marlboro signs in the same focus. Covering the Marlboro sign is doing the right thing. And this comes from a guy who smoked three packs a day for twenty-five years.[9]

The trajectory of the change in advertising signs in ballparks reveals so-cial changes in American culture. The first urban ballparks of the early twentieth century had advertisements on their walls, as well as on the walls of adjacent buildings, for products for working-class men, such as whiskey, beer, and tobacco.[10] The ban on ads for Marlboro cigarettes in sports arenas was consistent with the widespread bourgeois, health-conscious, middle-class culture of the 1990s.[11]

Fenway Park's left-field wall contained commercial messages until 1947, when it was painted completely green and, in effect, became the "Green Monster." During the 1950s and 1960s, the Jimmy Fund billboard in the outfield was the only billboard allowed in the ballpark. It stayed that way until the current ownership group took over the team in early 2002 and changed that policy. On Opening Day of the 2003 season, fans were greeted by new advertising on the scoreboard on the left-field wall and a pair of new information boards (sponsored by Fleet Bank, now Bank of America) in left center field. Baseball purists and the Fenway Orthodox might cringe at the ads that have sprouted along the left-field wall (W. B. Mason, Bob's Stores), the center-field triangle (Stop & Shop, Giant Glass, Verizon Wireless), the walls along the visiting and home bullpens in right field (Bud Light, Delta PC Connection, Comcast/NESN, MasterCard), and, beginning in 2004, the glaring red Budweiser sign above the new right-field roof seats. Yet many of the people I spoke with believe it is the only way the new Sox ownership can remain competitive without building a new ballpark. From that point of view, they are willing to sacrifice some of the presumed authenticity of Fenway in order for the team to keep the ballpark and generate enough revenue to put on the field the best team that money can buy. In an oddly similar way, many Red Sox fans would have liked the Red Sox ownership in the late 1950s to have sacrificed their racism for a World Series ring by signing either Jackie Robinson or Willie Mays, or both.[12]

Major League Baseball, and its fans, has maintained self-imposed limits on the amount of advertising and the areas where advertisements can be placed. Columbia Pictures and Major League Baseball were very close to implementing their collaborative plan to place the *Spider-Man 2* name and logo on bases during games from June 11 to 13 during the 2004 season. Due to an overwhelming outcry of fan disapproval, Spider-Man did not show his face on the base pads at Fenway. When asked about this incident, one fan at Fenway cried, "Ads on the bases? What's next, Budweiser logos on the jerseys? This ain't friggin' NASCAR!"

There is one advertisement, however, that fans have fought not only to save but also to restore and venerate. The iconic Citgo sign is the most famous and continuous advertisement in Boston. Used by many people as a landmark, for both practical and sentimental reasons, the Citgo sign, perched atop a building in Kenmore Square owned by

Boston University, is visible in the ballpark from most seats on the first-base side. *Boston Globe* correspondent Sam Allis writes,

> The CITGO sign must always be spectacular. It is, hands down, the most absorbing confection in our night sky. (Granted, that's not saying much.) And as installation art, it is surpassed only by the sinewy grace of the Zakim Bridge. Since 1965, when it acquired its current look, the sign has been distinguished for its simple elegance and mesmerizing kinetics.[13]

In late September 2004, Citgo began repairing the side of the sign that faces the ballpark. The company wanted to ensure that the sign would not go out the way it did the year before during the American League playoffs, leading some superstitious Red Sox fans to blame the darkened sign for the team's loss. "It appears [Citgo] understand[s] the significance and importance to keep the sign lit," said Thomas Tinlin, deputy commissioner of the Boston Transportation Department. "Finally, this is the year the Sox will reverse the curse. . . . I'm just hoping they keep it illuminated until after the victory parade. We need all the help we can get."[14]

Tinkering with the Citgo sign, which is intimately connected to the ambiance of Fenway Park, is seen by the people of Boston as a way of playing with tradition. The Citgo sign is a good example of the way an advertisement can be appropriated by the public so that its original meanings have changed. Here, the Citgo sign is no longer about gasoline. Instead, it advertises and locates Fenway Park.

When it comes to the actual ballpark and its future, however, we enter a far more contentious ground than debates about ads and other such decorations. The various approaches to the debate about Fenway Park—from the "New Fenway Park" plan that was designed in 1999, to the Save Fenway Park! group that was created to combat the Red Sox's plan for a new ballpark, to the John Henry–led new ownership group and its recent "improvements," to other proposals that include moving the Red Sox to New Hampshire—reveal the multiple interpretations and consequent actions people take toward the material products that symbolically express their way of life. In turn, we can see that culture is neither a matter of consensus nor a static entity but, rather, a set of beliefs that are continually negotiated, tended, and practiced.[15]

This is a rendering of the "New Fenway Park" as seen from outside the ball-park on Boylston Street. (Graphic courtesy of HOK Sport)

NEW MILLENNIUM, NEW BALLPARK:
THE "NEW FENWAY PARK" PLAN

Jim Healy, vice president of programs and administration for the Yawkey Foundation, has spent the majority of his adult life, and a good portion of his adolescence, at Fenway Park. A New Englander by birth, clocking in time at the ballpark for thirty-two years, doing everything from field maintenance with local groundskeeping legend Joe Mooney to installing Fenway's first video monitor, he is well versed in both Red Sox lore and the culture of Boston. Healy started working for the Red Sox while he was a student about four miles west of the Fens at Boston College.

From the mid-1990s until he submitted his resignation in 2002, Healy not only oversaw the design and construction of the City of Palms Park, the Red Sox's spring-training facility in Ft. Myers, Florida, he was the Red Sox vice president and project manager for the proposed new ballpark in Boston. He was former CEO John Harrington's point man and worked closely with HOK Architects of Kansas City, the brain trust behind Camden Yards, Jacobs Field, and other retro ballparks. He also spent a great deal of time discussing community issues with local civic associations, community-development corporations, and other in-terested parties like Save Fenway Park!

In the Red Sox's 1999 "New Ballpark" press release, Healy justified the advantages of replacing Fenway Park:

> We all love Fenway Park, but at eighty-seven years old, it cannot be renovated further. We believe the design we are proposing honors the grand history of Fenway Park by preserving parts of the original ballpark as public space with a new educational center that creates a wonderful, historic entrance to a modern facility. The new ballpark will feature many conveniences—wide aisles, modern restrooms, great concessions, and all the key elements that enable fans to experience the intimacy that is unique to Fenway Park.[16]

A new ballpark with comfy seats, and more of them, does not sound too bad and could be a nice alternative to the elderly edifice. But would Red Sox Nation choose the comfort of seats and concessions over their distress of losing the Fenway experience?

A sentiment-driven slogan and a picture of Ted Williams midswing adorned the cover of the informational and promotional pamphlet for the "New Fenway Park" that accompanied the press release and was made available to the public by the Red Sox. "Preserving the Red Sox Experience" was printed atop a black-and-white photograph of Williams, one of Boston's favorite sons and arguably the best hitter to ever swing a baseball bat.

The language and tone of the appeals made by Healy and his associates who promoted building the new ballpark was undoubtedly civic-minded; at least that is how it was supposed to sound. Those who are opposed to the new ballpark might say that the overt appeal to community sentiment is nothing more than a manipulative marketing ploy. Sociologists Rick Eckstein and Kevin Delaney argue that the "power elite," which includes the team's administration, local politicians, and affiliated businesses, purposely manipulate the public by constructing beliefs that new stadiums will increase "community self-esteem" and "community collective conscience" in their respective cities.[17]

Although there is growing evidence that publicly financed stadiums have not been as economically beneficial as boosters touted them to be, occurrences of calculated public deceit remain unfounded, at least regarding Boston and the Red Sox.[18] Boston is, however, somewhat notorious for political cronyism and "old school" hobnobbing. But such generalizations occlude the possibility that even members of the "power elite" may have emotional attachments to people, places, and, in Healy's case, prospective plans.

When I spoke with Healy in February of 2004, he was not lamenting the loss of the ol' ballpark but the loss of the plans for a new ballpark. Just like every other interview I conducted, I asked Healy why Fenway Park is important to the people and City of Boston. He leaned back in his chair, cocked his head a bit to the side, raised his eyebrows, and said with a grin, "It's where we all grew up."

After sharing a few personal memories about the ballpark, he told the following story. Around the same time that the new ballpark plans had been announced, former Red Sox catcher Carlton Fisk was hired by the Red Sox to be general manager Dan Duquette's special assistant. At a press conference announcing Fisk's return to the organization, a sportswriter asked him whether he would be upset if Fenway Park was replaced. He said, "No."

Fisk's opinion carries a good deal of weight in Boston. Fisk is a native New Englander who grew up dreaming of playing for the Red Sox. He has made his mark on local folklore, most recently, by being inducted into baseball's Hall of Fame in the summer of 2002 wearing a Red Sox cap (despite the fact that he played more seasons with the Chicago White Sox). Most significantly, Fisk became a local and national icon after hitting a twelfth-inning homerun that won Game 6 of the 1975 World Series (despite the fact that Fisk would have never had a chance to win the game if Bernie Carbo had not hit a pinch-hit homerun in the bottom of the eighth inning to tie the game).

Fisk's homerun is one of those memories that people not only talk about but can easily picture in their minds. The shot of Fisk leaping down the first-base foul line, waving his hands in unison, and trying to direct the flight of the ball he just hit to keep it in fair territory is easy to recall. And the image of the ball soaring through the air, propelled by Fisk's bat, guided by his prayers, arching high in the air toward the Green Monster, and finally hitting the left-field foul pole, winning the game and sending the series to a Game 7 tiebreak, is a classic and iconic sports moment. This scene has been replayed over and again on television, in popular films like *Good Will Hunting,* and on Little League ballparks and faux-Fenway backyard Wiffle-ball fields.[19] Moreover, Fisk's shot is one of the most memorable events in all of baseball history, and not just Boston sports history. It is one of the events in the mid-1970s that helped restore Americans' faith in their national pastime.[20] And it happened at Fenway Park.

As shown in this rendering, the "New Fenway Park" plan would have retained the original field dimensions. Notice how the Citgo sign would still be visible from the first-base side just beyond the Green Monster and the foul pole that made Carlton Fisk a legend in Boston. (Graphic courtesy of HOK Sport)

Fisk provided one of the most memorable moments in popular culture for Sox fans and even for folks who either were not born yet or are not from Boston or both (like myself). In 1998, *TV Guide* named Fisk's homerun the top televised sports moment in history. It was a play that displayed Fenway Park in all its glory and grandeur. So, when Fisk is asked if he will miss the place when it's gone, when they tear down the Green Monster and the foul pole that kept his homerun in play, and he says "No," it is significant.

Fisk tells the crowd that he loved playing baseball at Fenway Park, but his memories of the ballpark will outlast the physical structure. He said, if they build a new ballpark and have similar dimensions and have a high left-field wall, "I will make new memories, my children will have new memories, and my grandkids will have new memories. That's what we'll cherish. We won't cherish the bricks, and the mortar, and the seats, we'll cherish the memories we have." "You wouldn't drive a car that's a hundred years old," Fisk continued, "because it wouldn't work very well. And you don't want to continue to play in a ballpark that doesn't work very well. Bring the memories with you to think about."[21]

Fisk's comments aptly underscore one of the most important issues related to the future of the ballpark: memory. The type of memory that he spoke of was not only about personal remembrances but shared memories, collective memories. For a family, these memories provide the connective tissue between members and generations. Told and re-told at holidays and other gatherings, these stories help define the fam-ily unit. The same phenomenon occurs at a wider level and on a greater scale, at the cultural and community level, where such memories can become defining markers of a generation.[22] These stories are important for the construction and maintenance of a city's identity, as well as in-dividuals' identities. But the question remains, Where are these memo-ries stored? Are they in the bricks and mortar of buildings? Or in the stories we tell about those buildings and what happened inside them? Do those stories need "the bricks and mortar of buildings" to survive? That is, do they need some sort of physical manifestation to retain their importance and meaning?

Places can provide an anchor, a foundation, a mnemonic device, for shared experiences between people in the present, past, and future. Mnemonic devices, either as ideas or objects, help individuals retrieve or preserve memories. Public places as public symbols can do the same for communities. They can act as reminders to people in the present about people, events, or ideas from the past. Sociologist Eviatar Zerubavel makes that point clear:

> The preservation of social memories need not depend on either oral or written transmission. After all, material culture plays a very similar role in helping us retain them. Consider, for example, the mnemonic role of ruins, old buildings, souvenirs, antiques, and museums. . . . A visit to the National Museum of Anthropology in Mexico City clearly "connects" present-day Mexicans with their Olmec, Mayan, Toltec, and Aztec ancestors. A walk around the old neighborhoods of Jerusalem likewise allows modern Jews a quasi-personal contact with their collective past.[23]

Places endowed with meaning by one generation, whether implicitly or explicitly, provide meaning for the next, thereby constructing a bridge between past and future that binds people together.

According to historian Bruce Kuklick, a place like Philadelphia's Shibe Park, which was built in 1909 (three years before Fenway) and razed in 1976, functioned as a medium for collective memories. He writes,

> Meaning and the items that bear it are fragile. The meanings accrue over time in their visible embodiments, artifacts like Shibe Park. Memories do not exist in the mind's isolation but are connected to objects and stored in them. The destruction of artifacts can thus sever the present from the past and the accumulated significance the past embodies. We do not create the legacy of the city but find it in our memories, because in cooperation with others we locate this legacy in the world around us and make it salient in our lives.[24]

Because memories are often incomplete and fade as time persists, material objects are often helpful reminders of past events. Commemorative monuments are purposely built to prevent cultural amnesia and keep the past from becoming so remote that it drifts into irrelevance.

As Philadelphia spectators moved from watching games at Shibe Park to Veterans Stadium, cultural amnesia set in. Outside of Philadelphia fans and sports-history buffs, generations born after Shibe Park's leveling are hardly aware of the old ballpark's existence or the ballclub that played there, the Philadelphia Athletics. Persons born in the early 1970s and after grew up watching the Phillies play at Veterans Stadium, a nondescript multisport, oval-shaped facility capable of seating over sixty-two thousand spectators. When three thousand explosives took down "the Vet" on March 21, 2003, team announcer Dan Baker told the cheering crowd of several hundred people, "Ladies and gentlemen, you just witnessed history."[25]

The Phillies started the 2004 season in the newly built Citizens Bank Park, which purportedly was inspired by elements from Shibe Park, such as its field dimensions and seating bowl. As nice as Philly's new ballpark may be, the connections to the past are tenuous at best because of its location on the periphery of the city. Rather than being nuzzled into a neighborhood, Citizens Bank Park is surrounded by a large parking lot that connects to a few other large parking lots that serve the nearby football and basketball arenas. Behind center field, however, stands a "Memory Lane" that chronicles the important moments in Philadelphia's baseball history.

The red brick wall of Memory Lane at Citizens Bank Park in Philadelphia is located behind center field and faces Ashburn Alley, an open-air concessions concourse. Memory Lane is an attempt to connect the new ballpark and its players to the history of baseball in Philadelphia. (Photo by the author)

Can a place that reminds you of the past thwart cultural amnesia as much as a place that's actually from the past? Maybe.

Bob Montgomery was drafted by the Red Sox in 1962 and played at Fenway Park from 1970 to 1979. He told me that he would love to see a ballpark like Citizens Bank Park or San Francisco's SBC Park built in Boston, believing firmly that the Red Sox fans, "the best fans in the world," deserve a new ballpark. Montgomery was once Carlton Fisk's backup. Years later, he, like Fisk, supported the "New Fenway Park" plan and hopes that someday they will build it, either in the same footprint or somewhere else like the South Boston waterfront.

Even though he thinks that "the new ownership and [architect] Janet Marie Smith are doing a very good job of making a Cadillac out of a model T," he still believes that the time has come for the wrecking ball to have its way with Fenway Park and that plans should be made now to figure out what of the ol' ballpark to keep and what to discard.

History runs rampant through New England, and New England traditionally doesn't like change. History is a wonderful thing, . . . but I
think progress needs to take over a little bit around Fenway Park. The
park is very old, it is very costly to maintain. And by today's standards,
financial standards in the sports industry, a thirty-five-thousand- or
even a thirty-eight-thousand-seat stadium just doesn't get it done.

Montgomery's comments clearly represent the Reform disposition toward culture: don't forget the past, but don't live in it either.

About 35 percent of the people I spoke with supported the building of a new ballpark that would essentially be a replica of the old one
or that even includes parts from the original, like Pesky's Pole or the
Green Monster. Red Sox fan Emmanuel P. said, "The green wall is the
magic thing, though. You gotta bring the wall. If the wall goes (to the
new stadium), it's all good."[26] Another fan from Woburn, Massachusetts, told me that you could not have a Fenway Park without the
Green Monster, "and they shouldn't replicate it; they should bring it
with them." For fans like these, the characteristics that make Fenway
unique can be transferred to another site. The previous Red Sox ownership, the Phillies organization that built Citizens Bank Park (who
used the same architect group), players like Fisk and Montgomery,
and fans like those quoted here all take a Reformist position. They
want to keep elements of the past but want to make them work in a
contemporary context.

SAVE FENWAY PARK! AND THE WILL TO PRESERVE

If the connective tissue of a culture is threatened, then that culture and
the way of life it fosters is in danger of collapsing. The entire practice
and industry of historic preservation is predicated on the belief that
places are valuable symbolic bridges between the past, present, and future.[27] A fan-based nonprofit group called Save Fenway Park! (SFP) has
had the loudest and strongest collective voice in the fight to preserve
the original ballpark. They want the Red Sox organization and local
government officials to preserve Fenway Park and not build a new ballpark that merely looks like the old one. For most of the group's members, preservation does not mean keeping the ballpark the same. That
is, they advocate "touch-ups" and piecemeal renovations.

There are, however, a few "purist" or Orthodox members of SFP who have been skeptical about *any* renovations to the ballpark. But as a group, they support the renovations that have been made to the ballpark, some of which they claim were their ideas (like the Green Monster seats and the new right-field roof seating and concessions area). In fact, they have had considerably more contact with the new ownership group than with the last owners. The new owners have even solicited SFP, as well as season-ticket holders, for ideas about future additions to or renovations of the ballpark.

The dialogue between the two groups exists and has been fruitful, in part, because the new owners and SFP have constructed similar narratives about the importance of retaining the ballpark for both the team and the city. According to John Valianti, one of the founding members of SFP,

> Fenway is important to us as Bostonians. If we get rid of Fenway, we'll be just like any of the other cities who have knocked down their great old ballpark. They already got rid of the [Boston] Garden here. What's next? Faneuil Hall? The Old North Church? You gotta save things like that. That's why people come to Boston.

By comparing Fenway Park to other well-known and revered local historical landmarks and by referencing the 1997 demolition of the Boston Garden, the former home of the Boston Celtics where sixteen championship banners once hung, the members of SFP have tried to summon emotional and nostalgic attachments. Nostalgia is called on to help solidify a collective history and identity in Boston that would, or should, include Fenway Park.

"Some things are constants in cities," said Erica Tarlin, a six-year SFP veteran and a current member of the group's board of directors. "Architecture and places that pull people together help identify a place. . . . I believe that you just don't destroy things that are unique. *Those who don't see Fenway Park as unique see it as archaic. . . . But it's real, authentic; Boston needs this place to be Boston.*"

Like Tarlin, Valianti fears that Boston without Fenway Park, *the* Fenway Park and not some "cheap knock-off," would diminish what he deems as special about the city. "Take all things away that are important to Boston," warns Valianti, "and we'll be just like any other yahoo city." Valianti became interested in the future of Fenway Park shortly after the wrecking balls permanently splintered and cut up the Boston Garden's parquet floor. Save Fenway Park! was started by a group of historic preservationists affiliated with the Boston Preservation Alliance who also happened to be baseball fans. There were about twenty-five people at the first meeting, and the group was continued by a core of about ten people. The inaugural edition of their newsletter was published in January 1999 at the height of the debate. Later that same year, the nonprofit group Historic Massachusetts put Fenway Park at the top of its annual "Ten Most Endangered Historic Resources" list. According to Historic Massachusetts, the list includes landmarks that "represent the history and culture of the Commonwealth and are seriously threatened by neglect, insufficient funding, inappropriate development insensitive to public policy, or vandalism."[28]

Members of Save Fenway Park! supported the ballpark's designation as "endangered" in 1999. Today, Fenway is in far less trouble then it was then. Because Fenway is still standing, the directors and members of SFP believe that they've won the battle, they've fought the good fight. Because of such progress, SFP's green "Save Fenway Park!" stickers are far less prevalent around the city than they were prior to the sale of the ballpark in late 2001–early 2002. There are probably more "Ortiz Has a Posse" stickers than there are SFP stickers on billboards, street signs, and lampposts in and around Boston these days.[29] But in the early days of the group, when they would meet weekly and hold frequent rallies outside the ballpark during home games, those stickers could be found around most corners in the Fenway/Kenmore Square area. Between 1997 and 2001, SFP distributed more than one hundred thousand bumper stickers at rallies and through the group's website. It has become harder to find the stickers on cars, but there are still a few in and around the city on street signs and T stops, reminding those who thought the issue was resolved that the survival of Fenway Park is still not secure.

The big green SFP bumper stickers attracted Tarlin, not for their aesthetics but for their cause. A Boston native, Tarlin describes herself not only as a lifelong Red Sox fan but also as a lifelong fan of the ballpark. For her, there is no real way to separate the team from the ballpark or the ballpark from the city. So, being a fan and a Bostonian meant that she felt obligated to "save" Fenway Park.

> I stumbled upon the group coming out of a game in 1998, the last game
> of the season, and I saw a guy at a table handing out those bumper

stickers and I said "What do you mean 'Save Fenway Park'? Where's it going?" Bostonians have a sense of what our city is, what our home is; we have feelings for it. It's not just that it's familiar, but it has certain qualities. Boston is certainly cosmopolitan, but it's small. It has great architecture, but it's not overpowering. It has immigrants from all over the world, but it's not teeming. There are a lot of blends. There are a lot of old things as well. Boston has always seemed to me to be a place that holds certain, different standards whether it be in culture, education, architecture, behavior. This is the right way to get things done, the appropriate way to get things done, the thorough way to get things done.

In these few words, we begin to see how the "will to preserve" Fenway Park can be understood as a conservative response to culture. Conservatives believe in consistency, in the unchanged, and they want to see things remain the same. In the classification scheme I presented in table 5.1, SFP members are Conservative rather than Orthodox because they allow for a minimal degree of change, evident both in their own proposals for additions to Fenway Park and in those implemented by the Red Sox since 2002.

Calling a preservationist group like SFP conservative is counterintuitive. Many of them are politically liberal, expressing deep concerns about "big business" and the "corporatization" of sports. But I am interested here in the ways that they approach and practice culture. Their way of life can be described as conservative because of their piety toward the past and the rules of preservation.[30] They also expressed dissatisfaction with certain changes at Fenway and other ballparks across the United States (like the inclusion of arcades, batting cages, and other games at ballparks) and with the people who fill those ballparks. The members I spoke with frequently talked about Americans' obsession with entertainment and creature comforts. Fighting against the past ownership of the Red Sox, they feared that the "New Fenway Park" would be a "mallpark" with big comfy seating, waitress service, and other accoutrements that provide distractions and spectacles that take away from both the game being played on the field and the history that they feel connected to through the ol' ballpark.

Regardless of the merits of their argument, this nostalgic reaction can be understood as a conservative disposition toward one's culture and its past. Sociologist Fred Davis recognized the connection between nostalgia and conservatism, noting that "in its distaste for or alienation from the present [conservatism] still envisions a better time, . . . a time we have already known."[31]

Members of SFP discussed the opposition they faced not only from the Red Sox ownership that pushed the "New Fenway Park" plan but also from their fellow fans and Bostonians. Valianti mentioned that people have thrown things at him while he handed out stickers. Adopting a mix of passion and sarcasm, Tarlin talked about her experience during SFP rallies outside the ballpark:

> When we're handing out stickers, we usually can't get our hands moving fast enough. But there's that guy who walks by and says, "Blow it up." Then you get the well-dressed [guy] in golf clothes who think he knows everything about the situation because he's in business and thinks he's a better sports fan because he's a man and believes you can't save this thing. Then I start talking to him and showing him the numbers and he says, "Oh, I never saw it that way." If you actually break the argument down rather than thinking that it's about a grungy old park versus a new, shiny stadium with cushy seats, you see that that's not the argument at all; it's about saving a place that means something other than just feeling good. . . . I don't hand out stickers in the stadium; we're not subversive. But if you're sitting there or walking around with a "Save Fenway Park!" T-shirt, I'll talk to people about it. We don't go out to try to convert people. Sometimes, we automatically get stereotyped as Birkenstock-wearing, kumbaya-singing, tree-hugging hippy dippies. . . . We even discussed changing our name because we knew the verb "save" was a turn-off.

"Like 'save the whales'?" I ask.

> Exactly, that's what they've yelled at us. It's like a junior-high cafeteria fight. It's embarrassing. But also the word "save" gives the connotation that we don't want to touch it—wrap it up in bubble wrap and it's a museum. But, no, that's not what we want to do; look at the mission statement. We want to modernize the ballpark even though we don't want to change it too much because it really is a neat place.

Tarlin believes that people who have been hostile toward the group think that building a new ballpark is the only way the Red Sox could bring a championship to Boston. Both Tarlin and Valianti think that fans' views about these issues have been obscured by the local sports media, especially talk radio, a notorious bastion of vitriol and conceit.

Valianti blames the sports-radio hosts that were busy banging the drum for a new ballpark from 1998 through 2001 and that can still be heard some today. "There's a weakness in some sportswriters in that they're afraid to show that they might care about something," says Tarlin. "And they gotta be the tough guy. Gee, we'd like to save Fenway, but let's be practical. Well, we are being practical; here are the facts, so shut up." She particularly points the finger at local celebrity sportswriters like the *Boston Globe*'s Dan Shaughnessy.

Shaughnessy's two books about Fenway Park, *At Fenway: Dispatches from Red Sox Nation* (1996) and *Fenway: A Biography in Words and Pictures* (1999), can be read as preobituaries, swan songs for a place he admittedly loves but refuses to try to salvage. "I won't be one of those thousands of Save Fenway zealots, hugging the brick walls and lying down in front of bulldozers," writes Shaughnessy, "but before Fenway is gone I plan to spend some time in the empty yard, remembering all the things that happened there and contemplating what it has meant to my life."[32] Shaughnessy obviously has a different take on his own nostalgia than the SFP "zealots" he demeans. Maybe he's just preparing himself for the worst. Maybe he has a bunker underneath his backyard with a stockpile of baseball cards next to the maroon cardigan he got when he "lettered in baseball as a sophomore at Groton High School."[33] Maybe he's ahead of the game. Maybe he's right.

But who is right and who is wrong is beside the point. The SFP group occupies a unique, albeit wavering, position in social space in relation to Fenway Park. Their position wavers not because their motivations or beliefs have changed. The world around them, the debate that has admittedly obsessed them day in and day out, has changed. They are no longer a fringe group trying to throw pebbles at the organization's windows to get someone to listen to them. Though they are not part of the Red Sox organization, they now have much more in common, in terms of their goals and methods, with it and its current renovation schemes.

Using sociologist Japonica Brown-Saracino's differentiation between *gentrification* and *social preservation*,[34] we can see that Jim Healy and the past ownership's "New Fenway Park" plan falls into the former category and that the SFP group engages in the latter. Even though

Brown-Saracino discusses these as ideologies and practices employed as ways of investing in one's local *residential* neighborhood, they can also be applied to persons' approaches to common civic places like Fenway Park. Gentrification usually finds supporters among predominantly young, affluent professionals, constituents of what economist Richard Florida calls the "creative class,"[35] who aim to find affordable housing in older and often run-down neighborhoods. This practice often leads to the physical displacement of old-timers due to the increase in housing costs associated with the act of neighborhood revitalization.

Social preservation, on the other hand, abides by the goal of keeping things as they are and disrupting, or displacing, neither the traditions of the past nor the people who helped build those traditions. These members of the "creative class" are "drawn to more organic and indigenous street-level culture."[36] Even though such scenes are usually associated with smaller cultural places like Oldenburg's "third places" (e.g., bookstores, cafes, taverns),[37] the same approach to a city's culture can be directed toward big third places, especially when they serve as symbolic representations of the city as a whole. Gentrifiers often try to sequester such symbols as their own. As Brown-Saracino defines the distinction between these two different dispositions, "while gentrification is an investment in the social, economic, and cultural future of space, social preservation is an investment of economic, political, and cultural resources in the past and present social attributes of a place. Gentrifiers seek to tame the 'frontier,' while social preservationists work to preserve the wilderness."[38]

The former ownership group that supported and sought to implement the "New Fenway Park" plan can be considered gentrifiers because they wanted to refine, or tame, and drastically remodel the current ballpark by creating it anew, even while they were trying to pay proper homage to the original ballpark. And although their plan sought to preserve and honor the history and aesthetics of the original ballpark, it was dependent on displacing some of the local businesses, and residents, that align the surrounding area. As discussed earlier, the plan revolved around taking the land on the other side of Yawkey Way by eminent domain as exercised by Mayor Thomas Menino and the Boston Redevelopment Authority. The government is only allowed to take an area by eminent domain if it is declared to be blighted. Those opposed to the "New Fenway Park" plan have gone as far as saying that the Red

Sox organization had purposely not taken care of the ballpark so it would appear more decrepit than it was in actuality. They would thereby be able to elicit the $200–300 million needed from the city and the state (i.e., Massachusetts taxpayers) to subsidize the construction of a new stadium.

Making a critical and sardonic gesture, the April/May 2000 edition of the *Save Fenway Park! Newsletter* asked readers and supporters to suggest names for the new stadium. Some of the most purposely horrid submissions included "Taxpayer Stadium," "Megaplex Field at Former Neighborhood," "Red Sox Stadium at Fenway Pork," "Wally World," "Menino's MoneyPit," and "Eminent Dome."

SFP members and their supporters oppose the use of taxpayers' money as the "New Fenway Park" plan suggests, and they fear the devastation of the local neighborhood that could ensue if the new stadium is built in or relocated to either another part of the city or one of Boston's surrounding suburbs. "Baseball may be the American game, but property is a fundamental American right," says Liane Newton, an owner of one of the businesses that the "New Fenway Park" plan would need to push out. "Not only do they have the gall to demand that private owners be forced to give up their property, but they want the taxpayers of the city and state to pay for it. There's no charity work that justifies that." Speaking about the issue in 2000, Kimberly Konrad, the president of SFP at the time, made the following observation:

> Having the community and local officials on board is a tremendous plus for our efforts to keep the Red Sox in their historic home. Renovation is good for the team, good for the fans, and good for the neighborhood. We look forward to continuing to work with all affected parties to develop a plan which is good for everyone and preserves the number one tourist draw in the Commonwealth.[39]

Again, a word like "historic" is used less as a descriptive adjective that might mean "old" and more as one that means "good" and "authentic." Moreover, Konrad uses "historic" to modify "home," which invokes warm feelings for and emotional attachments to "the number one tourist draw" in Massachusetts.

As social preservationists, supporters of Fenway renovations also value, and even enjoy, the grittiness and inconveniences that are part of the Fenway Park experience. One local fan that I interviewed during a cold and rainy game in late September 2004 said that a polished place "like some of those new parks wouldn't make sense here. We, the fans, we're not so polished. Our team? They're the most disheveled bunch in the league. And we love 'em for that. Have you seen Pedro's hair?"[40] He looks around, points to the gray skies, and continues, "This is Boston weather, and this is Boston's place. Those new parks might fly in California, but not here."

Most Fenway Conservatives would begrudgingly go to watch the Red Sox wherever and however the ballpark was built, despite their insistence that both Red Sox and Boston would not be the same without the original Fenway Park. "You could put a bunch of lawn chairs around a cow pasture, and people would probably still come see the Red Sox play," said one fan. "But we wouldn't be happy about it, . . . and we wouldn't be happy if they called it Fenway even if it wasn't the real thing." Fortunately for persons in the Conservative camp, the new ownership has tried to ensure continuity between the Fenway of old and the "improved" one not by knocking it down but by adding to it and making it more comfortable for the Fenway faithful.

THE NEW OWNERSHIP, THE "WOMAN OF STEEL," AND FENWAY'S "IMPROVEMENTS"

Following a long and drawn-out negotiation process and bidding war, which was steeped in controversy concerning tribal turf battles and local cronyism, the Red Sox accepted a bid from a group headed by then Florida Marlins owner John Henry. The spring 2002 sale of the Red Sox has turned out to be a blessing for Fenway "renovationists" like the members of SFP. The record-setting $700 million purchase included the ballpark, as well as a large share of the New England Sports Network cable station.

After taking over the franchise, the new ownership immediately recognized that Fenway Park, the place and not just the name, was and should continue to be its greatest asset. As such, it did not take Henry & Co. too long to cozy up to the Red Sox fan base and the Fenway faithful. They had to make nice right away because of their outsider status in Boston.[41] In one of his first public statements after it was announced that his crew would take over the Red Sox, Henry referred to Boston as "the Mecca of baseball. Everywhere you go, people are talking about the Red Sox, watching the Red Sox. I go to Nantucket in the summer and in every bar and restaurant, the TV is turned to the Red Sox."[42] Even though he was telling Red Sox fans what they already knew, validation goes a long way, especially for devotees of a perpetually second-place team, at best.

On the day after the group's bid was accepted, though still pending Major League Baseball's approval, the Red Sox held a press conference to introduce the prospective owners. Larry Lucchino, the former CEO of the Baltimore Orioles (he helped Camden Yards come to life) and the San Diego Padres (who recently built their own new ballpark: Petco Park), was announced and continues to serve as the chief executive officer of the Sox. Lucchino, along with Tom Werner, famed TV producer (the *Cosby Show* and *Roseanne* are on his résumé) and former Padres owner, pledged that their new ownership group intended to renovate the ballpark, hoping to add a new deck to the existing structure if possible. But Lucchino made it clear that they were still open to possibilities and would not close the door on building a new ballpark if their renovation ideas were unrealistic or too costly. "Our plan is to renovate and expand Fenway," he said. "If we find that it is unworkable, obviously we will have to make adjustments."[43]

Two years after taking the wheel of one of baseball's oldest and most interesting franchises, the new ownership has made some considerable additions to the ballpark, yet the Red Sox purposely delayed announcing their decision about the ballpark's ultimate fate. On Opening Day 2004, Red Sox fans and followers expected the new ownership and administration to make an official decision about their plans. But at that time, no such announcement was made, nor would it be throughout the year. With a new season about to begin, with new hopes and old dreams waiting to be fulfilled, Red Sox fans were eager to begin the season. As Paul C., who traveled to Fenway Park from Scranton, Pennsylvania, to attend his third Opening Day in a row, remarked,

> It would be great to know what they're going to do, but maybe they've just been thinking about other things right now, like breaking the Curse [i.e., winning the World Series]. . . . I love Opening Day in Boston. I've made the trip here every year since 2002. Look at all the people; it's great. This could be the year, you know. They're going to be tough. . . . I hope they win it before they get rid of this place. You know, *if* they get rid of it.

The Red Sox had made some important and what would turn out to be crucial off-season acquisitions, namely, Curt Schilling and Keith Foulke, who both played integral roles throughout that magical year in Red Sox history. So the fans were pleased and were willing to follow the new ownership's lead.

As important as the ballpark is, however, winning a World Series is the team's first and foremost objective. Even though the Red Sox won the World Series in 2004, they do not want to stop there. "There's no reason why it has to be only one in eighty-six years; why not two in eighty-seven years?" Larry Lucchino said during my interview with him. As Red Sox historians Glenn Stout and Richard Johnson write, "if Fenway Park ever becomes the sole focus of this franchise—as Chicago has done with Wrigley Field—then the future risks looking an awful lot like the past."[44] The Chicago Cubs have been dealing with their own "curse" that has kept them out of the World Series since 1945 and without a ring since 1908.[45] Here in Boston, if people think the Red Sox are spending more money on fixing the old ballpark or building a new one rather than trying to put the best team on the field, the new ownership's popularity will decline quickly. One need only look at the attendance numbers prior to 1967 to understand that filling the ballpark is hardly inevitable.[46]

Still, the Red Sox have put a lot of time, effort, and money into "saving" Fenway Park. Their commitment to renovation was pronounced when Janet Marie Smith was hired as the Red Sox vice president of planning and development in 2002. Initially, this looked like a very bad move for those who wanted to keep Fenway Park. Smith is largely credited with implementing the retro-style of Camden Yards, the ballpark that started the third wave of baseball stadium construction.

In his detailed history of the rise of Camden Yards, author Peter Richmond refers to Smith as the "woman of steel" and quotes an Orioles official who said that "Baseball should kiss her feet. She's responsible for them being able to build stadiums for the next twenty years."[47] But her work on Camden Yards was not just about style; it was also about what that style means. For her, the "Golden Age" ballparks offered a better experience for fans and spectators than did the multisport cookie-cutter arenas that replaced them.

Smith recognized that Fenway Park and its "Golden Age" cousins had an "authentic quirkiness" that made the game more interesting because of the odd angles and asymmetry of the confines that enclosed the playing field. The fair territories between the foul lines shoot out from home plate and diverge *ad infinitum*, theoretically, so the physical confines of the seating bowl and the outfield wall define the space where the game is played. Because the early ballparks were fitted into already existing city blocks, these "quirks" were not contrived. They were necessary.

Discussing her use of Fenway as a muse for Camden Yards, Smith remarks,

> What we thought was important about Fenway Park was its quirky angles, and their authenticity—they weren't quirky to be cute or they weren't quirky because it was popular to say that baseball is more interesting in an asymmetrical ballpark. It was quirky because of the necessity because of the block it sits on.

Smith told me that she paid particular attention to the intimacy of the ballpark. She talked about intimacy in relation to the fans and the players inside the ballpark, as well as the way the ballpark is nestled into the neighborhood. Smith noted that "there isn't another place, except for Wrigley [the only other surviving "Golden Age" ballpark], where a homeowner lives thirty feet away from the façade of the ballpark. Even the new ballparks aren't that confrontational; there's usually some sort of buffer." Fenway is so squeezed into the city block that the Red Sox had to build the Green Monster, "the quirkiest quirk of them all," as Smith called it, to offset the shortened length of left field. Similarly, in Baltimore, they used the warehouse and Eutaw Street to constrain the dimensions of Camden Yards.

Smith owes a good deal of her interest in the olden ballparks to Larry Lucchino. An architect and urban planner by training, she had worked in New York City on Battery Park and in Los Angeles on public park renovations, but Camden Yards would be her entry into the world of baseball. Clearly she had spent many years thinking about and dealing with issues of urban civic space. Building a fan-friendly downtown ballpark seems like a logical next step.

In 1988, Lucchino received an unsolicited letter from Smith. The Orioles had not advertised any job openings. But in her letter, Smith was not asking if they had any jobs or if they needed any help. She told them they needed her. After an initial "standard kiss-off letter," Lucchino reconsidered. Looking back at that time, Lucchino says "she

Baltimore's Camden Yards, the first of the retro-style major-league ballparks, was the first project that Smith and Lucchino worked on together, about ten years before they began "improving" Fenway Park. (Photo by the author)

was the best off-season acquisition the Orioles made that year." Lucchino, the current president and CEO of the Red Sox, was a minority owner and team president of the Orioles during the planning, building, and honeymoon stages of Camden Yards. In fact, building a baseball-only stadium was his idea. On her first real day on the job in early February 1989, Smith was approached by Lucchino.

"What makes you think you can do a stadium?" Lucchino challenged.

"As I understand it, you don't want a stadium," Smith replied. "You want a ballpark."

At the moment, Lucchino's ears could hear no sweeter sound. He had been thinking about the old and mostly extinct ballparks for a while before Smith came on board. His vision was starting to take shape; it was going to become a reality. He admits that even in those years well before he would have an office that overlooks Yawkey Way, Fenway Park had made an indelible impression on him and would, through a few strange twists of fate, be wed to Camden Yards and the ballpark-building frenzy it would unleash. When I asked Lucchino about the relationship between the two parks, it was obvious he had mulled over that question many times over the course of the past twenty years.

> Fenway Park was one of the models, one of the inspirations for Camden Yards conceptually as well as for some of the specific details. Conceptually, because we looked at other ballparks and franchises that were successful, that were among the most admired, the most storied franchises in baseball. When I say "we" I mean Edward Bennett Williams and I in the early '80s shortly after he bought the Orioles. The Orioles were playing in an antiquated, albeit charming, football/baseball facility [Memorial Stadium]. There was a movement afoot to build a new stadium in or around Baltimore that could serve both a baseball team and potentially a football team. I suggested to him that we consider building a baseball-only facility. I pointed to Fenway Park as the classic example of the success that could accrue to a baseball team if it had the right kind of facility, with the right kind of charm, the right kind of appeal, and without the compromises inevitable in a multipurpose football/baseball stadium. I pointed also to the Yankee Stadium and Wrigley Field, and I said that we in Baltimore will never get to be one of these tier-one franchises or cities unless we have the kind of facility that mirrors or is at least comparable to those top-notch facilities.

Williams thought that building a stadium for baseball exclusively was a bit "off the wall." He told Lucchino that he should float the idea out to other baseball folks and the media to see what their reactions were but to make sure not mention his name because, Williams predicted, Lucchino would be crucified.

To even Lucchino's surprise, the people he talked to agreed that a baseball-only ballpark could do some things that the symmetrical cookie-cutter stadium could not. When he showed a model to Bart Giamatti, the commissioner of baseball at the time and former president of Yale University, he told Lucchino that if they added some more "quirks" to the model he would give it an "A+." One of the features he added was a garage door in play in right field where a ball could bounce around, mirroring the one in Fenway's left field.

Despite the fact that no team that plays in one of the new retro ballparks has won the World Series, not to mention issues regarding the overuse of public funds to build them,[48] the ballparks are generally deemed a success, at least in terms of moving the ballparks back into the cities from the suburbs. So how could they not build a new ballpark in Boston, especially since Lucchino had been through the process in Baltimore and, more recently, with the San Diego Padres' Petco Park? And with Smith on board, it seems like they have the perfect team to right all of the imperfections the previous ownership saw in Fenway.

So I asked Lucchino, "Why keep the old one?" My supposed irreverence made him smile. Then he replied,

> Because this is not just any old one. It's a very special, distinctive, historic, and beloved old one. Those things aren't easy to duplicate or replicate. And we think that if it didn't have this special and beloved history, it would be a lot easier to toss aside. . . . Fenway Park works as a ballpark, as a fixture in a community where it's been for a long time, where it's been accepted. It works in the ecosystem in terms of transportation and other things. You'd take a lot of risk by building a new ballpark. . . . I think the past ownership was caught up in the wave of enthusiasms for the new ballparks that was sweeping the country. . . . We came in here predisposed to save Fenway.

Lucchino had been through the process of building a new ballpark twice before, in Baltimore and San Diego. He knew how hard it would be to get a project like that completed in Boston. But it was not hard work that stopped him and the Red Sox's new top brass from bulldozing the ol' ballpark. This was about something else, as indicated by his goal to "save" Fenway Park.

The only way to "save" the ballpark, from the point of view of Lucchino, Henry, and Werner, is to add to it, to play with its physical structure and amenities, to give it a facelift rather than major reconstructive surgery. All the recent additions to the ballpark since the ownership group took the reigns of the Red Sox have, according to Lucchino, been done "always with the intent of not damaging the essential nature of Fenway Park." Anyone who works on the ballpark must take the "Fenway Hippocratic Oath"—*do no harm.* Lucchino explained:

We do not want to destroy the village in order to save it. The point is to improve it, to make it even better. And be very mindful of its core, the energy, the electricity that's generated here by the intimacy of the place, the quirkiness and the irregularities of it. Don't tell me you can put in another ten or twelve thousand seats and retain what we're talking about. I say you cannot. You will forever change it. So our plan is much more modest, more focused, and, I hope, much more likely to preserve the essence of Fenway's charm.

In an effort to uphold the "oath," Lucchino decided to bring Smith aboard. She would be, and has been, an integral part of Fenway Park's present and future. Soon after arriving in Boston, she began hunting down parts of the ballpark that were underutilized or poorly laid out. She sought ways to make the smallest ballpark in baseball a little bit more comfortable, a little bit more manageable, and a little bit more modern.

Toward the end of the 2002 season, Smith and the Red Sox put turnstiles on Yawkey Way during games, giving fans an additional ten thousand square feet on which to walk around and get a wider variety of concessions (such as former Red Sox pitcher Luis Tiant's Cuban barbeque stand, El Tiante's). This move was met with a fair amount of controversy and disapproval, mainly by the sausage vendors who used to park their carts on what once was an open public street. Now, the city allows the Red Sox to close off Yawkey Way for ticket holders and Aramark concessions vendors only. Most of the fans I spoke with, however, liked the new Yawkey Way, where they could leave their small cramped seats and mull around outside to stretch their legs, drink a beer, and have a smoke. Televisions were placed behind the vendors so the fans would not have to miss a single pitch. During the Red Sox's 2004 playoff hunt, a large television screen was placed alongside the building on the other side of Yawkey Way. During the last Red Sox–Yankees series of the regular season, a large crowd gathered around the big screen to celebrate after the Red Sox scored seven runs in the bottom of the eighth inning, stealing a come-from-behind victory, foreshadowing things to come.

In 2003, Smith executed plans that turned a poorly used parking and storage area into what is now called "The Big Concourse," which provides another place for spectators to gather between innings, to get "Fenway Franks" and expensive cheap beer, or simply to take a break

The view from the Right Field Roof gives spectators a clear shot of the playing field. To the left, Pesky's Pole is in clear view. Notice that the tables are shaped like home plate. (Photo by the author)

from the sometimes oppressive sun that lurks over the bleachers during weekend day games. The next biggest "improvement" was the addition of seats atop the venerable Green Monster for the 2003 season. "As sacred an icon as it is," said Smith, "we didn't want to treat it like a relic." The iconic Wall is now a thriving new destination for those attending games or taking tours of the ballpark. With seating for 274 spectators, the Green Monster seats offer spectacular views of the field and the city. After receiving great public approval, the Red Sox, unfortunately, increased the price of these tickets dramatically, making them highly coveted and practically unattainable for the average fan. (Even if you can only sneak up there for just an out or two, it's worth it.)

Riding on the coattails of the Green Monster seats' success, Smith fashioned a new seating plan on top of the right-field roof. The right-field roof expansion added fourteen thousand square feet of space, accommodating almost two hundred fans at tables shaped like home plate. There is enough room behind and above the seats for another two hundred standing fans. A sixty-foot-six-inch-long bar (the distance from the mound to home plate) was made from a lane from the old bowling alley beneath Fenway Park, home to some new Red Sox executive offices. Though the bar provides shade and drink, the view of the field is poor, so standing fans have to jockey for position if they want to see more than the backs of people's heads.

Smith also made a point of beautifying Fenway's exterior. Collaborating with the city, both creatively and financially, the Red Sox widened the Van Ness Street sidewalks, planted cherry trees, installed new ticket offices and lights, and erected a bronze statue of Ted Williams. With every addition, Smith tries to stay faithful to the "Fenway Hippocratic Oath" that Lucchino mentioned. She sees their collective goal as one of renovation rather than restoration. She explained that "Restoration implies a literal fix-up, back to its original birth form, whereas renovation acknowledges that things change, but it is the spirit or character that you want to keep." And renovation, to Smith, does not mean that it should be perfect, because some of the things that are "a bit off" are part of Fenway's charm.

> When do you lose the charm that comes from Fenway being like a gritty, bearded, salt-swept sailor, and when does it become too clean and perfect? So you have to be disciplined to know when to stop. . . . I would say that at least one out of every three people say, "I don't care about a gritty or authentic ballpark, damn it. Why can't we be as comfortable as everybody else in the major leagues." But I personally don't subscribe to that at all. I think when you have something special it ought to be worth a little inconvenience to be able to retain it. So that doesn't scare me away from thinking that we're doing the right thing. There's nothing wrong in my mind about a ballpark that has endeared itself so much to people that they come to see the ballpark.

Like the members of SFP, Smith and the new ownership are Conservative social preservationists concerned with maintaining the core aspects, the "authentic" qualities, the gritty charm of old-time buildings and communities. They too have constructed a narrative about Fenway Park where such physical and symbolic characteristics are as much a part of the ballpark as the team that plays there.

TABLE 5.2. FENWAY PARK'S MAJOR "IMPROVEMENTS" FROM 2002 TO 2004

"Improvement"	Year	Explanation
Yawkey Way	2002	Closed off street two hours prior to game for fans, creating additional concourse area. Turnstiles set up at both ends of street, adding ease of entry to ballpark. Addition of full-service cooking concession stands, offering wide array of food and beverage options.
"Dugout Seats"	2002	Addition of 160 "premium" seats in the first two rows located inside the dugouts.
Green Monster Seats	2003	Addition of 280 seats (three rows) plus standing room and wheelchair positions atop the Green Monster ("Monster Seats"). Addition of two full-service cooking concession stands, featuring the "Monster Dog." Addition of wheelchair-accessible restrooms.
"Big Concourse"	2003	Addition of twenty-five thousand square feet under center field and right field, between Gate B and Gate C, all wheelchair accessible. New cooking concession stands with eighteen new points of sale, providing wide variety of new menu items. New picnic area with tables, umbrellas, and televisions. Existing restrooms replaced with newer, larger ones (one hundred additional restroom fixtures). Addition of a family restroom and new water fountains. Addition of two new ticket booths. Addition of fan services stand. Addition of three new ATMs.
On-Field Seats	2003	Addition of eighty-seven "premium" seats in the first two rows located directly behind home plate ("Home Plate Seats"). Addition of 145 "premium" seats in the first two rows located between the dugouts and the right-field and left-field foul poles ("Extended Dugout Seats"), including wheelchair and companion seats.
Scoreboards	2003	Restored National League scores to manual scoreboard located at the base of the Green Monster. Addition of pair of scoreboards above left-center-field bleachers, sponsored by Fleet Bank (now Bank of America). One provides type of pitch, speed, pitch count, and other information ("Pitchers Board"), and the other provides "inside baseball" information, such as line-ups and how a hitter has fared against a particular club or pitcher or in a particular baseball situation ("Hitters Board").
Right Field Roof	2004	Addition of 194 seats arranged in groups of four, each with table and in-seat service on the original Right Field Roof, including tables that can accommodate wheelchairs. Standing-room positions for up to 250 fans. Addition of "open-air pavilion" with new concessions area, bar, numerous food and drink options, restrooms, televisions, barstools, and stand-up tables. Addition of new elevator to roof, grandstand, and private suites.
"Third Base Concourse"	2004	Addition of new concessions stands with wide array of food and drink options. Two additional gates for entry, more turnstiles, and a new ticket booth. Entire concourse now wheelchair accessible. New stairwell connects concourse to the Grandstand level and the Green Monster seats. Existing restrooms replaced with newer, larger ones, and addition of a family restroom. Addition of fan services stand. Addition of new ATMs. New water fountains.
"Crown Royal Club"	2004	Former Lansdowne shop renovated to become a new VIP lounge for Premium Seat ticket holders. Twins Enterprises store located on Yawkey Way becomes the club's official souvenir store.
Baseball Operations Office	2004	Created new office space for baseball operations staff in the basement of the Jeano Building (space previously occupied by the billiards room of the bowling alley).

Part of the new ownership's current narrative is about "improving" the ballpark, rather than, say, renovating or restoring it. This rhetorical move is not unlike the former ownership's insistence on its ability to "transfer the Fenway experience" from the old ballpark to the proposed new one. Smith said that describing the work on the ballpark as "improvements" was "a carefully thought-out semantic move."

> "Improvements" is a less intense term than "renovation." And in the city of Boston, where the future of Fenway Park has been under such scrutiny, it has been so debated, we felt that it was presumptuous to come in here and say "Eureka, we have the answer! All those people who were here before us just didn't see it; it was under their nose." We're just not that presumptuous. Part of what might allow us to succeed is a change in criteria. Ten years ago they were talking about a ballpark that had forty-five thousand to fifty thousand seats. I think today our thinking is that we probably don't want to be bigger than forty thousand, partially because we don't want to change the character of Fenway and partially because most of the new ballparks that were built with forty-five or forty-eight thousand seats are having a hard time filling them. Part of what believe people love about Fenway is its intimacy, but it also benefits the club because of supply and demand. Having fewer seats may well be working for us.

Here, Smith is talking about "saving" Fenway Park for emotional or sentimental reasons *and* as good business. The lack of seats makes them more coveted, helping the team draw fans to the ballpark in droves and allowing them to continually raise ticket prices. But as Smith continued to discuss the use of the term "improvements," she discussed the potential effects of the changes to the ballpark on the local neighborhood.

> We have always been cautioned that this neighborhood has had fifteen years of psychological beating-up over whether or not the Red Sox are going to leave Fenway, move elsewhere, build elsewhere. We didn't want to pretend that we could come in here and have a "renovation plan." What that would mean to most people is that we would have some sort of unveiling. So we've said, don't get nervous, and don't get too excited. Whether you love it or hate it, we're just going to peel this off layer by layer until we've extinguished all the possibilities. I hope that doesn't sound like a timid approach; we think it's a realistic one.

This piecemeal approach is intended to retain both Fenway's character and its authenticity. Smith has purposely tried to instigate an approach that does not feel too preplanned or too fabricated. In some ways they are granting the ballpark a certain degree of agency, letting it dictate its own facelifts.

RADICAL FENWAY: THINKING OUTSIDE THE BANDBOX

Alternative proposals for the future of Fenway Park have been offered since the debate became a part of public discourse in the mid-1990s. Although most people support the current renovations at the ballpark, many are skeptical about how much life the ballpark has left. And some are ready for something totally different from Fenway Park and want something completely new.

"There's no parking, not enough seats [at Fenway]. And even when you can buy seats, tickets are so expensive and they hurt your ass if you sit and watch the whole damn game," said Sean L., a Red Sox fan from Jamaica Plain (a section of Boston that borders the Fens). "I mean," he continued, "I thought they were talking about building a new park in Somerville?"

The lack of concern for Fenway to stay in its current and original footprint moves Sean L. into the Radical camp. Others who have adopted the Radical approach believe that the new site, wherever it may be, should dictate the physical contours of the building. This would lead to a more authentic and more original design than a replica of Fenway, which, as Dan Wilson of SFP fears, might end up looking like "the fourteenth reproduction of Camden Yards" and thereby losing any amount of noncontrived distinctiveness.

It is ironic that the retro-style ballpark movement, the "third wave" of ballpark construction that was supposed to counter and upend the stale, formulaic symmetry of the "second wave" cookie-cutter stadiums, has led to a series of ballparks in different cities across the United States that all tend to mirror one another.

Part of the uniformity of the new ballparks is due to the construction of these new ballparks by HOK Sports+Event+Venue of Kansas City, whose portfolio includes Camden Yards, Cleveland's Jacob's Field, San Francisco's SBC Park, Detroit's Comerica Park, and Cincinnati's Great American Ballpark, as well as a host of other major-league, minor-league, and college ballparks. They were behind the "New Fenway Park" plan and built City of Palms Park, the Red Sox's spring-training facility. But to be fair, when I visited both Camden Yards in Baltimore (the first major-league retro park, opened in 1992) and Citizens Bank Park in Philadelphia (opened for the 2004 season) during the same weekend in 2004, there were noticeable differences. During that twelve-year span, the HOK team had learned how to make the seating bowl even steeper. From my upper-deck seat in Philadelphia on the first-base side, it felt like I was looking down on top of the pitcher's mound. This sloping of the seats affords most fans a better and unobstructed view of the game.

Fenway Radicals have lodged complaints about replicating Fenway either at a new location or if they expanded the current footprint, like the "New Fenway Park" plan proposed. In response to the "New Fenway Park" plan and its inclusion of Fenway's most famed and fabled attribute, *Boston Globe* correspondent Robert Campbell lashed out in print:

> Perhaps . . . nostalgia would help sell the taxpayers on the idea of footing a chunk of the bill. But the Green Monster, like many things, is wonderful only so long as it is real. It exists today for a logical reason: because a city street sliced off a corner of the lot the park was built on. Once you replicate the Monster on a different site, you've transformed it from reality to stage set. Instead of being a real place with a real game, the park will feel like a planned amusement-park ride. When image becomes more important than reality, architecture and baseball are in big trouble. . . . I'm not asking for anything disruptive—not some architect's show-off masterpiece, not some monument that would clash with its surroundings. But something fresh and alive, expressing hope for the future, not pining for the past.[49]

The concern about authenticity is one of the motivating factors for not letting either a renovated, reconstructed, or replaced Fenway Park become a lifeless facsimile of its real self. For Campbell, a contrived ballpark with a contrived image automatically eliminates the prospect of an authentic place. From this point of view, a new ballpark must have its own idiosyncrasies that emerge from the ballpark itself rather than from an architect's ersatz reconstruction of the past.

Former Red Sox pitcher Jim Lonborg loved Fenway Park as a player but now as a spectator is fed up with skinning his knees on the seats in front of him. His 6'4" frame does not fit well into Fenway's narrow aisles and cramped seats. Though he understands the importance of the memories of and at Fenway for both fans and players, he supports the idea of building a totally new ballpark. Lonborg believes that "the history that has occurred at Fenway will always be history. It will always be wonderful for the people that have enjoyed it, but it's not necessary to continue to have Fenway per se factored into the design of the new ballpark." Thus, for Lonborg, the new ballpark should be its own entity; it should have its own unique special qualities, with bigger seats and with about forty-five thousand of them.

Ian Browne, a lifetime Red Sox fan and current sports reporter for mlb.com and redsox.com, loves Fenway Park, though he blames it for turning him into a "baseball junkie." He believes that the Red Sox will have to build a new ballpark at some point in the near future. According to Browne, the new ballpark should not "be a carbon copy of Fenway. They're not going to be able to duplicate what Fenway was, so the new ballpark should have its own character and its own distinct features."

As the curator of the Sports Museum of New England in Boston, Richard Johnson has a unique understanding of Boston's past that comprises one part nostalgia and two parts disdain. Like Browne, Johnson believes that if the Red Sox were to build an economically viable and aesthetically interesting ballpark, "you break completely [with the past] and you do something new." Johnson criticizes the dimensions of Fenway, including the Green Monster and the lack of foul territory, as being out-dated because the ballpark was built before the "live" ball was integrated into the professional game in 1920.

> I think people would still love their memories of Fenway Park; they'd continue to cherish them. But at some point you need a new car, you need new house, something breaks here, something falls off there. *Right now, what they're doing with Fenway is they're putting red lipstick on it, putting a new outfit on. They're doing a makeover, but what they need is a full religious conversion.*

Even if a new ballpark was built that looked radically different from Fenway Park, the issue of location still persists. Should it remain in the Fenway/Kenmore Square area or should they build a new ballpark elsewhere in Boston or, for that matter, outside Boston? I asked each interviewee about possible locations for a new ballpark. Many were aware of and therefore mentioned a few of the proposals that had become subjects of public dialogue. Some refused to even entertain the thought. Erika Tarlin, who goes to about thirty games a year at Fenway, said it did not matter to her because she would not attend any Red Sox home games outside Fenway Park. "I wouldn't go, so I wouldn't care, period, over, done."

According to Johnson, the Fenway location made sense in 1912, but not anymore. Therefore, he believes that the Fenway/Kenmore Square area of Boston should continue to grow as a center of other types of important urban cultural institutions, such as medical centers, museums, and universities. Right now, along with Fenway Park, that area lying beneath the watchful eye of the Citgo sign is home to the Longwood Medical Center, the Isabella Gardener Museum, the Museum of Fine Arts, Symphony Hall, the Harvard School of Public Health, Boston University, Northeastern University, and the Berklee College of Music, among other institutions.

Instead of building a replica of the original Fenway or a newly designed ballpark in an expanded version of the original footprint, a few other locations were suggested during the five-year span between 1998 and 2003, when the debate was the most heated. The proposals ranged from the intriguing to the embarrassing to the insulting. One interviewee even suggested that they should make the Green Monster transparent and let people watch the game from outside the park on Lansdowne Street. As crazy as that might seem, many of the new retro ballparks have areas for non-ticket-holders. I have seen this firsthand at both SBC Park in San Francisco and Jacob's Field in Cleveland. Anyone can walk up to the outfield wall from outside the ballpark and watch the game for free (though the regulated time for free viewing in San Francisco is limited to fifteen minutes). These ballparks took their cue from places like Fenway before the Green Monster replaced a constraining rope atop Duffy's Cliff, a ten-foot hill in left field that once bordered Landsdowne Street.

Critics of the "New Fenway Park" plan as well as of speculative renovation plans (prior to the recent "improvements" at the ballpark), including some city councilors and would-be owners, actively promoted alternative sites. These sites included a parcel near the South Boston waterfront, a site near the Suffolk Downs track on the East Boston–Revere border, one adjacent to the Assembly Square Mall in

Somerville, and another near the border of Charlestown and Everett. Other suggestions include moving the Red Sox out to Foxboro, Massachusetts (where the NFL's Patriots play their home games), Hartford, Connecticut (a city that lost its only professional sports team, the NHL's Whalers, in 1997—it then became a possible location for a combined Red Sox/Patriots stadium), and Salem, New Hampshire.

The Salem site was proposed by Chuck Geshilder, secretary of the libertarian Free Town Project Organization, and supported by New Hampshire state representative Henry McElroy (R-Nashua). The crux of this plan was generating greater revenue for the Red Sox because of the absence of an income tax or sales tax in the "Live Free or Die" Granite State. This extra revenue, which would be enhanced by building a fifty-thousand-plus-capacity stadium, could be used to attract the best players in the league, who would, so the argument went, beat the New York Yankees and their enormous-payrolled team. The plan even included letting the Red Sox and their fans keep Fenway Park, allowing the team to play twenty games a year at the ol' ballpark for sentimental reasons.

Though he did not have New Hampshire in mind, at the end of 2000, city council president James Kelly urged the Red Sox to look outside Boston for a new ballpark site. "We would like very much for the Red Sox to stay right here in the city, but the cost of land is making a new ballpark look like something that won't happen," Kelly said in an interview with the *Boston Herald*'s Cosmo Macero. "What the Red Sox may have to do is look outside the city of Boston." Kelly's analysis was in reaction to the former Sox ownership's struggle to assemble private financing and public assistance from City Hall and possibly the state for the $665 million "New Fenway Park" project. "I think that this proposal for the 'new' Fenway is dead. I've felt that for a long time," Kelly said, adding that "the Red Sox should look elsewhere."[50]

In 2001, Stephan J. Mackey, president and CEO of the Somerville Chamber of Commerce, looked elsewhere. He looked at a single square block of patchy grass enclosed by a chain-link fence and saw a ballpark with a home plate where a batter can stand and take aim at the Mystic River while a sold-out crowd cheers the Red Sox, eats hot dogs, and does not have to worry about public transportation or parking before and after the game. Mackey's proposal was entitled "Gateway Park: A Concept Paper," outlining a plan to build the Red Sox a new stadium on the other side of the Charles River in the Somerville/Charlestown Gateway area, within walking distance from Sullivan and Assembly Squares and within viewing distance of the Mystic River. A broadcast blimp would be able to project a view of the Boston skyline, of Bunker Hill, of Beacon Hill, of the USS *Constitution,* of the Old North Church. As Mackey sees it,

> This area right here has tremendous infrastructure. Outside of North and South Stations, this is the most multi-modal intersection in New England. If you built a stadium here, you'd be within a two-minute walk of a water shuttle, the Orange Line, a possible commuter stop at Assembly Square. You'd have yourself a rightfield T station and a left-field T station. I love Fenway Park just like everyone else. I grew up loving the Sox. But if it's going to move, this is the place it should move to. For one, it's cheaper than any other site—only a million dollars an acre. The team should, after all, put more money into getting a pitcher than into land acquisition.[51]

At another time, Mackey's plan would have been nothing more than a daydreamer's fantasy. In the summer of 2000, the state legislature, at the Red Sox's behest, passed a bill granting the team $100 million for building a new Fenway Park. But a few months later the Red Sox went up for sale, and the bill fell. Although the new ownership openly opposed the "New Fenway Park" plan from the beginning, it was open to hearing "interesting alternatives" (a phrase Lucchino used in my discussions with him). As such, all proposals were open for discussion when Henry & Co. bought the Red Sox. Even though they have invested a good deal of time and money into the ol' ballpark, their collective ear still remains open.

Mackey's proposal faced the stiffest competition from Boston land developer Frank McCourt and his twenty-five acres off South Boston's waterfront, where he was itching to build a state-of-the-art ballpark. McCourt, who made a late November 2001 bid on the Red Sox, told the Red Sox leaders in late October 2003 that he wanted the team to have first dibs on the site before he pursued other options, and before his deal to buy the Los Angeles Dodgers for $430 million was finalized.

McCourt's "waterfront" proposal intrigued many of the people I interviewed; even some of the fans who support the current ongoing "improvements" of Fenway thought a downtown ballpark on the water nestled beneath Boston's skyline could be attractive. Of all the various proposals, this was the one that most of the people I spoke with would support if the demolition of Fenway Park was inevitable. McCourt's land, along Northern Avenue, straddling Seaport Boulevard near Boston Harbor, is located across the Fort Point Channel near the heart of downtown. It is adjacent to several other major developments, including Fan Pier, the John Joseph Moakley Federal Courthouse, the World Trade Center, the Fidelity office towers, and the new Boston Convention and Exhibition Center.

Not only would a waterfront ballpark connect the South Boston area to both tourists and everyday Bostonians, it would connect the new ballpark to the ghosts of Boston's baseball past. The Boston Braves, who played at Fenway Park from August 11, 1914, until Braves Field (which is now Boston University's Nickerson Field) was completed on August 18, 1915, played on that parcel of land for a few months during the summer of 1894 at the Congress Street Grounds.

The case for a ballpark on the water in Boston becomes more attractive as more and more people hear about or visit SBC Park in San Francisco. Originally called Pacific Bell Park (the name changed in 2004), this retro-style ballpark, the first privately financed major-league ballpark since Dodger Stadium opened in 1962 in Los Angeles, was inspired by Fenway Park and its early-twentieth-century cousins. SBC Park is located on the edge of San Francisco Bay. The outfield stands rise above the water, where docked boats and kayakers wade in what is called "McCovey's Cove." Named after Giants legend Willie McCovey, the water, barely ten yards behind SBC Park's short right-field wall (only 309 feet down the line), has become famous, or infamous, because of the now familiar scenes of fans, many sitting in kayaks, diving in the water after slugger Barry Bonds's record-breaking homeruns. In April 2004, Larry Ellison, a Giants fan from the Bay Area, retrieved both Bonds's 660th homerun ball, which tied Bonds with his godfather, Willie Mays, for third place on the all-time career homerun list, and 661st homerun ball, which put Bonds alone in third place behind Babe Ruth and Hank Aaron. Since then, Ellison is often shown on television during Giants games paddling around the Cove in his kayak waiting for another souvenir.[52]

The success of SBC Park adds to the attractiveness of the idea of building a ballpark on the waterfront. After visiting SBC Park a few times, Richard Johnson, the curator of the New England Sports Museum, found the ballpark so alluring that he now thinks something similar to it would be a valuable addition to Boston.

> A park built like SBC, which is spectacular, would give life to that area. It's in a part of San Francisco that is very comparable to that area in South Boston. . . . It's not hard to visualize when you look at that space at night in, say, June, where the stadium lights are glowing, Custom House Towers are sparkling, the downtown skyscrapers are forming a nice outline in the sky, the smell of food, the sounds of people. You're talking about a vibrant, vital component to a landscape. I have no doubt that a ballpark in that area would shoot two hundred volts through the convention center and make it bigger, better, and more attractive. Baseball means so much to Boston; why not have the park be right in that part of town that has so much history? Everything that's happened in this town historically has been connected to the waterfront.

Even though Johnson takes a Radical position, he still refers to the history of Boston as a valued entity. Although he would like the new ballpark to be styled like those from the "Golden Age," he believes that an exact replica would not honor the history of Fenway Park, nor would a renovated Fenway Park. For Johnson, as well as others who are in the small minority of persons who take a Radical approach to the future of Fenway Park, the passion of Boston fans would make a new place as powerful an icon as the ol' ballpark by infusing it with a new type of intensity and authenticity.

BUILDING AUTHENTICITY?

The different cultural frames or dispositions that persons employ when responding to potential changes in their surrounding physical environments provide clues about the way they act on and negotiate their culture and their place in it.[53] The stories that are told about a place reveal these frames. Just as stories can change over time, so too can persons' responses to or opinions about the preservation, reconstruction, or demolition of culturally revered places, objects, and ideas. Because places in cities are used by many different groups and individuals for a range of intended and unintended purposes, urban culture does not derive from consensus but is rather a medium for constructive conflict.

The rhetoric of authenticity emerged as a means for distinguishing the varying positions about the future of Fenway Park. From the most Orthodox to the most Radical dispositions, believing in the value of an "authentic" place as a signifier of an "authentic," and thereby real or genuine, culture brings the different camps together. But the ways that they viewed authenticity and determined what constitutes the authentic is what separates them.

The small minority of individuals who adopt an Orthodox disposition want to keep Fenway Park the way it is, as it has always been. They cringed, for instance, when the Red Sox decided to add seats atop the Green Monster. Authenticity lies in the purity of an unadulterated ballpark that does not try to keep up with modern technologies and creature comforts. These neo-Luddites resist the modernization of the ballpark and believe that the only changes to the ballpark should come at the hands of Mother Nature and Father Time. "My grandfather had to deal with the same poles and obstructed views that I do, and I like that," one fan told me as we both tried to position ourselves so that we could see most of the infield, minus second base, behind one of Fenway Park's infamous steel supports.

Authenticity for those in the Conservative camp is about maintaining the integrity and character of the original design. The new ownership group, architect Janet Marie Smith, and members of Save Fenway Park! take this position, aiming to "improve" the ballpark but not devalue or dilute its meaningful content. Recall Larry Lucchino's comments about the "Fenway Hippocratic Oath": *do no harm*.

Those who take a Reform perspective supported the "New Fenway Park" plan or something similar to it. Basically, they would like to see a new ballpark built for the Red Sox that looks, acts, and feels like the old one. They want a new ballpark that replicates the meaningful features of Fenway Park (like the Green Monster, Pesky's Pole, and the manual scoreboard) but eliminates the nuisances (like small seats, small aisles, small seating capacity, and lack of parking). As one fan remarked, "We still want to be unique; we don't want to be like some other stadiums, with their electronic boom-box scoreboards [e.g., Atlanta's Turner Field], with Big Brother in charge of when we should cheer or when the two clapping hands tell us to clap." With this disposition, authenticity is about allowing the Fenway experience to change as the culture it is a part of changes. Authenticity, from this perspective, is about constructing a livable and comfortable present rather than trying to emulate a past that is fueled by nostalgia.

Viewed from the Radical frame, Fenway Park should be knocked down, and a new ballpark should be built outside the congested Fens/Kenmore Square area in a more convenient location. Moreover, the new ballpark should not be a replica of Fenway Park but should have its own unique characteristics dictated by the new plot of land. Authenticity, from this point of view, links function and form. The way that the short left-field foul line and the Green Monster grew out of necessity, so too should the new ballpark's features.

The motivation to renovate rather than remove Fenway Park is not about changing Boston's image. For people on that side of the debate, it is about keeping the image the same. Yet this can also be said about the people who want a new ballpark to look like the old one. Many people in Boston maintain a great degree of reverence for the past, a past that is both symbolized by and actively practiced at Fenway Park. Yet those in the Radical camp want a new ballpark that better reflects the city of today, rather than the city of yesterday.

Fenway Park's irregularities aptly match Boston's often hard to follow topography and traditionally hard-nosed people. Because Boston is arguably the oldest and most historical American city, it makes sense that it would be the home of professional baseball's oldest ballpark. But the same idea motivated the designers of and believers in the "New Fenway Park" plan, which sought to emulate and replicate the ol' ballpark's idiosyncratic characteristics. The connection between the park, old or new, and the city goes beyond their spatial, structural, and temporal similarities. It is about a culture that makes the city and the ballpark what they are and makes, or tries to make, them fit well together.

BELIEVE IN BOSTON
Red Sox Nation and the Cultural Power of Place

A baseball crowd in Boston is just like going to a play in the West End of London. People know when to clap, they know when a performance is great, and they plug right into it. It's kind of like Shakespeare's Globe Theatre. The groundlings are the bleacher people; the people rattling their jewelry are the people in the box seats. But one thing that they all have in common is their love for Fenway and that they know something about this game being played.

—Richard Johnson, curator of the Sports
Museum of New England in Boston

Every time I go to Fenway, I feel a sense of going home. I think the popular poster that refers to it as "The Chapel" captures some of those feelings. . . . My favorite memory of Fenway is of watching my son, when he was two and a half, have his first Coke, ice cream, and hot dog at the ballpark, and transform from a kid into a fan.

—Donald R., Red Sox fan, Bangor, Maine

After following the Fenway faithful into and around Boston's ol' ballpark, it is easy to see why baseball was promoted by social reformers, politicians, journalists, and ticket holders as a national communitarian pastime in the cities where it emerged, grew, and flourished. Baseball's distinctive style of play that in one sense is confining (runners cannot run outside the lines) and in another sense is free flowing (there is no time limit), embodies the paradoxes of yesterday's and today's urban culture. The distinctive iconography and playing grounds of urban ballparks became and remain fertile places *of* and *for* reverence, devotion, and collective prayer for people in and near cities. "Like a church, with its orthodoxy and heresies, its canonical myths and professions of faith, its rites of communion and excommunication," writes anthropologist David Chidester, "baseball appears in these terms as the functional religion of America."[1]

Throughout the 2004 season, it was easy to find signs and banners in the stands at Fenway Park that read "We Believe." People held them high above their heads, proclaiming their faith without apology or argument. A billboard stood outside the ballpark with the smiling Red Sox designated hitter and MVP candidate David Ortiz looming over Brookline Avenue, demanding Red Sox fans to "Keep the Faith." The same sentiment adorns the top of the 2004 Red Sox schedule, an artifact that many of the fans I spoke with carried in their wallets like sacred charms.

But what type of faith were Red Sox fans supposed to be keeping? Was it a faith in the team, the organization, the ballpark, the city, themselves? The short answer is "Yes." It was about keeping faith in something that was larger than each individual member of Red Sox Nation. It was about believing in something that transcends the here and now. It was about having and keeping faith in a collective consciousness that is defined by an allegiance and devotion to a particular cultural identity. And, like much of Red Sox folklore and mythology, that identity is intricately and intimately tied to a reverence for the past, even if that past is honored more for its pains than for its pleasures.

Waiting in line for a beer and a Fenway Frank between innings, I met a Vermont native and current resident of New Hampshire who tries to "make it down to Fenway" at least three or four times a year. This was his first game of the season. Even though he had not been up to the Green Monster seats or the Right Field Roof seats that he saw for the first time earlier that day, he supports the "improvements" at Fenway Park. Displaying what I have referred to as a Conservative disposition toward the preservation of Fenway Park, he passionately discussed the importance of the ballpark for the city's identity and its storied history:

Fenway is rooted deep into New England culture and is one of the biggest and most well known landmarks in Boston. My great-grandfather, grandfather, father, and myself have all seen games there, and probably sat behind the same beam! I hope to take my children (when I have children), as well as my grandchildren, to the ballpark someday so that they can *experience the history of baseball and the history of Boston.*

I emphasize that last phrase because it shows the connection that people make between the rise and growth of both the sport and the city. Those connections in Boston are strong. Baseball in Boston is never just about sports. Furthermore, it demonstrates that people want to experience the past in order to understand something about themselves and the world around them. Places provide more than simply the setting for those experiences. They also affect individuals' and groups' experiences within them. Those experiences may be interpreted in multiple ways for different individuals and groups within and outside cities, but common themes exist that transcend traditional exclusionary boundaries by providing a common language for making those inter-

This fan from California "needed" to stop at Fenway on his way through Boston, even though the Red Sox were out of town. On seeing the ballpark for the first time with his own eyes, he parked his car on Yawkey Way and then he dropped to his knees and raised his hand in reverence to Fenway. (Photo by the author)

pretations. A big "third place" like Fenway Park that is "rooted deep" into a culture as a character in stories and local tales, as a landmark, and as an identity marker easily fosters symbolic attachments to it. For almost one hundred years, Fenway Park has been revered to the point of consecration.

Sports teams offer a common referent for the urban community within city limits. Today, however, the Red Sox's and Fenway Park's reach stretches farther than Boston's borders, flooding New England and spilling over across the country and the U.S borders. Red Sox fans occupy territories well beyond both Boston and New England. For example, there is a group that calls itself the "Tennessee Hillbilly Division" (of Red Sox Nation). They stay in contact through fan websites and Internet message boards and try to schedule trips to Fenway Park at least once a year. And the citizens of Red Sox Nation reside in even more far-off lands than Tennessee, like Slovenia and Australia.

Two weeks after the Red Sox won the 2004 World Series, the *Boston Globe* asked "readers on Boston.com to tell [them] about passionate Sox fans who may live far from the Hub and may not get to Fenway often but still 'Keep the Faith.'"[2] A fan from London wrote the following:

> For eight years I worked for [a company] and came to Boston seven or eight times a year. I worked with a couple of diehard Sox fans who rapidly indoctrinated me into Fenway Park folklore and took me to games. Amazingly, a huge cricket fan became a huge baseball fan (there are key essential parallels), steeped in the bittersweet culture of the Red Sox. I left [the company] in '96, and worked for a couple of U.S. companies thereafter, enduring the usual jibes when U.S. colleagues learned of my baseball affiliation. If anything, this adversity hardened my loyalty. Years came and went, but every year my wife and I still came to Boston for our anniversary, to meet up with old friends, have dinner in the North End, and wonder when the Curse would end. . . . The games were shown live over here, with the small complication of being from 1 a.m. U.K. time to whenever they finished. By the end of ALCS Game Three I was a wreck; sleep-deprived, sullen, snarling at loved ones, and brain-dead. The comeback took me to the other extreme of the roller-coaster still sleep-deprived and brain-dead, but prone to embracing complete strangers and smiling all the time. So,

Boston, I have paid my dues. My loyalty for the Sox has never wavered even in the darkest times, I have accepted the derision from the unenlightened, and I have suffered with you and now rejoice with you, albeit from a few thousand miles away. Do I qualify as an honorary Bostonian? Please say "yes."[3]

This "honorary Bostonian" displays his devotion to a place, a culture, and a lifestyle that he could only take part in from afar. But through creative means, he has remained loyal to a baseball team and a city, even though he rarely experiences the place in person. Regardless of his geographical distance, he demonstrates the power and allure of important places that, through continued devotion and reverence, shortens the cultural distance between a person and a place.

While still riding the huge wave of joy that swept over Boston and the rest of Red Sox Nation after their World Series victory, the Red Sox, and Major League Baseball executives, planned a national ad campaign to sell Red Sox Nation citizenship cards to the Fenway faithful across the United States and, subsequently, beyond U.S. borders. Although the wallet-sized cards won't get you into a seat at Fenway Park, they can provide discounts on special Sox merchandise and memento offerings like caps, T-shirts, and desk calendars. Most important, the citizenship cards are a way of gauging how many fans there are beyond the Sox hotbed of New England. According to Red Sox vice president of public affairs Charles Steinberg, internal team estimates range from thousands to "outlandish" projections that range into the tens of millions. "We want to identify all the citizens," Steinberg said. "We (already) know how to find fans in New England—open up Fenway Park and they will come."[4]

A month or so after Red Sox Nation "citizenship cards" became available, the Red Sox and MLB executives realized that they set their sights too low. Declaring one's citizenship to Red Sox Nation apparently has a global appeal. More than twenty thousand Sox fans across the United States and also in several different countries bought the cards. Red Sox fans have declared their citizenship to the Nation in an array of overseas locales, including Australia, Scotland, Holland, Japan, and the Philippines. Michael Dee, the Red Sox's chief operating officer, said he was not surprised that the team's appeal has stretched across the Atlantic and Pacific oceans. Team executives and officials often open mail to find pictures from eager fans wearing Boston hats in front of various global landmarks.[5]

"We get mail from all over the world," Dick G., a Fenway ambassador, told me as he stood in the lobby of 4 Yawkey Way scooping bits of Fenway infield into little baggies to give to tour-takers.

I opened a letter a few weeks ago from a bunch of Japanese guys. They sent a picture of themselves in Tokyo; they all had Sox caps on. The letter asked if we could send them something from Fenway Park. So, I'm gonna throw a few of these [holds up a plastic bag the size of an Oreo cookie filled with the treasured reddish brown dirt] in an envelope and send it to them with a program or something.

Even fans outside a commutable distance look toward the city and the ballpark. This phenomenon points to the fact that urban culture is not only a matter of geography but also a matter of cultural confluence.

FENWAY PARK AND URBAN CULTURE

How well a building works functionally can be evaluated by looking at such things as the number of people it can hold, if it is structurally sound, or where it is located in regard to mass transportation, parking, and pedestrian traffic. A portion of the debate about Fenway Park concerns its structural safety and its location, as well as the location of a potential new ballpark, both of which are politically heated issues. But consideration of engineering and political disputes only provides a piece of the puzzle. It tells us little about the way the ballpark is used as an urban civic space and cultural symbol.

There is a difference between the financial value of a building and its symbolic worth. How well a building works symbolically yields questions that are more difficult to answer. This difficulty arises because such presumably subjective attributes as sentimentality, emotional attachment, nostalgia, and taste are not easily quantifiable. The dominant models in urban sociology have not provided useful ways for analyzing the symbolic and cultural worth of places.[6] The urban culturalist perspective offers a step forward for the study of urbanism by providing a way of looking at places in cities to learn how people make sense of the world they live in. Thus, we can see how people use places (like Fenway Park) as part of their

Fans will do almost anything to get into Fenway. Here, a fan holds a sign above a dense crowd outside the ballpark that reads, "Will Donate Semi-Healthy Liver 4 Tickets — No Guarantee." (Photo by the author)

cultural repertoires and how those repertoires can affect symbolic attachments to a city's social and physical environment (like the debate about Fenway Park's future).

IMAGES AND REPRESENTATIONS OF FENWAY PARK

Important places help represent a city to its citizens and to outsiders. Because cities are so large, these representations are necessary for urban living and become the foundation for a common language within the city and between other cities and regions. Individually and collectively, people attach these representations to both natural and artificial objects and artifacts located throughout the city. Trees, rivers, parks, buildings, street corners, and neighborhoods all can potentially become symbolic markers. Some of these, in fact, become synonymous with the city itself.

And these symbols and representations of the urban community help sustain local sentiments and beliefs beyond the lifetime of any given member or generation.

Sociologist Gerald Suttles called attention to various cities' respective "urban iconography" by clarifying the physical and spatial objects that are deemed meaningful in cities. He sought to make the analysis of cultural meanings objectively accessible and empirically observable by focusing on urbanites' "collective representations." In order to detect the "cumulative texture of local culture," Suttles directs our attention toward the things that people put in museums (i.e., high culture) and what they put on their car bumpers and T-shirts (i.e., popular culture) "because these objective artifacts give local culture much of its stability and continuing appeal."[7]

Although each social group, taste culture, or subculture may possess its own image of the city's texture, Suttles's approach recognizes the existence of overarching and inclusive place-specific urban symbols. These symbols and their meanings are both given and passed down by "expert" culture makers and workers (e.g., novelists, journalists, architects, museum curators, and archivists) *and* acted on and reworked by both residents and visitors.

Consider New York as the "Big Apple" or the "city that never sleeps" with its "city slickers," Boston as "the Hub of the Universe" or "Beantown" with its "proper Bostonians," and Los Angeles as "Tinsel Town," the City of Angels with its "stars" and "Valley girls."[8] As stereotypical as these impressions may be, they are the common and shared reference points that help define the texture of the urban community. Most of all, they are the representations that people use to identify the city and their relation to it.

Claiming that the symbolic expressions of the city are extrinsic or "out there," rather than merely subjective or personal expressions, Suttles showed how a city's texture is grounded in its history, architecture, street names, accents, and quirky sayings. These cultural products are evidence of and for the existence a common urban culture, common within the city in question and possibly between cities as well.

He tells us that "expert" culture makers and workers maintain such a culture through their creation and reformulation of the city's "urban iconography," though often based on "a selective reading of the present in the light of a believable past."[9] It is important to recognize that these

At dusk, the lights shine bright above the Green Monster, the ballpark, and the surrounding neighborhood, calling attention to the ol' ballpark. (Photo by the author)

"experts" do not create or select the city's images out of thin air. As members of the urban community, they are affected and influenced by the rituals and experiences that are played throughout the city, some of which they are involved in themselves. Moreover, the images and ideas they explore or exploit, or both, were a part of the city's cultural milieu before any of them attained their positions as cultural producers.

By situating culture producers within a particular context and recognizing that their interpretations of the city are never wholly their own, we can further elaborate the microstructural conditions that influence certain types of meaning-making.[10] As sociologist Barry Schwartz contends, "to focus exclusively on the use of [images] by a dominant class or dominant institution is to offer a supply-side theory that attends to the production of images and ignores how the images are used."[11]

While images of Fenway Park are used in corporate and tourism advertisements, they are also used as a symbol of Boston by everyday people in and outside the city. Even though certain meanings of Fenway Park and its relationship to the city vary between and within groups, there are certain features that remain constant, such as the outer red brick façade, the towering left-field wall (a.k.a., the Green Monster), and bright lights that shine during home games and other events.

Therefore, the debate about Fenway Park's future is not simply about the future of a ballpark. It is about the present state of Boston's urban culture and how the ballpark (old, new, or renovated) symbolizes that culture. And although people have responded to the debate in ways that range from absolute preservation (an Orthodox disposition) to starting over and building a completely new ballpark (a Radical disposition), all the arguments about Fenway's potential future(s) recognize the importance of the ballpark as a symbol of the city and its urban culture.

BOSTON'S URBAN COMMUNITY AND CIVIC CULTURE

Ever since the first studies of American urban life by the Chicago School of urban sociology in the early decades of the twentieth century, "community" has been most often talked about as a positive social phenomenon that was dangerously absent in the alienating, culturally corrosive cities.[12] The work of a number of urban sociologists challenged the generally accepted assumption that cities foster only superficial interactions that create destructive social pathologies.[13] Collectively, these findings suggest that community has not disappeared but may have changed. The ways of practicing community have multiplied along with the number of people and types of people that both live in and visit cities.[14]

"Community" can still remain a useful concept for understanding cities only insofar as its contours and complexities are not only acknowledged but explored. Rather than viewing communities, especially *urban* communities, as unitary, singular, consensual, or totally cohesive, they are better depicted as multidimensional and, perhaps inherently, paradoxical. Communities harbor within them a diversity of interests and dispositions, but that should not detract from the idea that an urban community can exist that stretches beyond the borders of neighborhood while still being rooted in a place.

Big "third places" like Fenway Park are important sites for the construction, maintenance, and reconstruction of urban civic cultures because they act as "not only models *of* what they believe, but models *for* the believing of it."[15] By taking part in both formalized and everyday rituals, people become members of the urban community through their acts of portraying and displaying their membership at places like Fenway Park.

The Red Sox organization under the helm of the Henry-Werner-Lucchino regime has recognized its role as an important social institution for the city of Boston. Thus, the ownership has opened up the ballpark for nonbaseball events including "civic holidays" for Father's and Mother's Day baseball catches on Fenway's hallowed playing grounds. But individuals and groups have found ways to express their community allegiances and civic "ownership" of the ballpark that go beyond officially sanctioned activities. These practices range from trick-or-treating around the dugouts at Fenway on Halloween to wearing a Red Sox yarmulke to games to waving a Dominican flag in the stands to building mini–Fenway Park replicas in backyards and town recreation fields. In all these instances, Fenway Park is the medium for the negotiation of cultural identities and the practice of urban community and civic culture. Following political scientist Norton Long's depiction of a city as an "ecology of games," the ballpark is a place where the players and rules of many of the "games" that compose the local community—"a political game, a banking game, a contracting game, a newspaper game, a civic organization game, an ecclesiastical game, and many others"—overlap, intermingle, and work together.[16]

The type of civic culture that has been built and continues to be built in American cities is neither liberal nor conservative but is a hybrid culture made up of a diverse collection of individuals and groups. And even though communities are collective accomplishments, not everyone plays an equal role in making those decisions or practices them exactly the same way all the time. As such, urban culture is continually changing, bouncing between liberalism and conservatism, and sometimes leaning more one way than the other. Urban dwellers can change their ways of thinking and acting but only tend do so within tolerable limits. This hybrid mixing is at the heart of the "paradoxical community" at Fenway Park, where the ballpark is *both* a place for people to escape from the city *and* a place to become fully immersed in it.

FENWAY PARK'S MYTHS, NARRATIVES, AND COLLECTIVE MEMORIES

People begin to recognize that they are attached to a place when they start noticing things missing. You either have or had lived in a place long enough or visited enough times to be able to get a feel for it, to know your way around, to get from here to there. And then stores declare bankruptcy, go out of business, and close. People move, people die, new roads are constructed, old buildings go down, and new buildings go up. But these missing persons and places do not stand alone; they are part of a shared urban culture, often becoming the fodder for local myths, narratives, legends, and stories—the stuff that a city's collective memory is constructed from and helps nurture.

A foundational cornerstone for this domain of the urban culturalist perspective is the notion that social, public, collective memories are "stored and transmitted" in and through places. Thus, narratives about past occurrences in particular places help shape the identity of the place and the people who use it, care about it, or are affected by the decisions made about it.

Place narratives are never filled with complete, unadulterated facts. Varying emphases on certain characters and plot lines offer multiple interpretations of similar events that affect the telling and retelling of stories about places. Even though place narratives are selective history, it would be a mistake to assume that the dominant narrative about a place is the only narrative that exists or the only one that counts. As sociologist John Walton writes, "multiple historical narratives are the rule, sometimes as oppositional positions and other times in complementary relation."[17]

Regardless of persons' feelings about the future of Fenway Park—preserve it, renovate it, rebuild it, or start over—anyone who has heard of the ballpark knows that it is full of history. As the oldest active major-league ballpark, its ninety-plus-year tenure as the Red Sox's home playing ground has given it plenty of opportunities to host a wealth of big and little moments. The big moments are the obvious ones, like World Series and playoff games. But the little moments are more discreet but also more frequent. A father taking his son to his first game, a caught foul ball, a marriage proposal, or just a Thursday night with some friends—these are the moments that connect individual memories to collective memories. Even though individuals have their own experiences with the ballpark from their own point of view, many people have experienced the same, or at least similar, feelings at the ballpark. These feelings become routinized as common cultural narratives.

So many of the stories I heard seemed like I had heard them before. Stories often started with a common theme, like "I remember walking up the ramp for the first time and seeing the Green wall" or

"One of my most memorable moments was being outside Fenway Park during the 1999 All-Star game" or "I'd love to see them break the Curse at Fenway" or "Fenway Park is important because of its history." The idea that Fenway Park has an important history is a popular cultural trope and speaks to the use of history as collective memory. As noted earlier, history is only one part of collective memory; commemoration is the other.[18] So when people talk about Fenway Park's history in a positive way, for example, they are rarely, if ever, thinking about the racial discrimination over the years by the organization and the fans themselves.

There is, however, a mystical, magical, mythological side to the collective memory of Fenway Park. Just as churches have statues and placards honoring heroes and saints, so too does the ballpark. Think of the retired numbers that adorn the right-field roof, the statue of Ted Williams just outside Fenway on Van Ness Street, or the "red seat" located at Section 42, Row 37, Seat 21 in the bleachers that commemorates Ted Williams's 502-foot homerun, the longest blast in Fenway Park history. There's Pesky's Pole in right field and the famous and fabled Green Monster in left. Knowing what these objects are and what they mean to Red Sox Nation, in and outside Boston, is less about historical accuracy and more about local cultural literacy. Collective memory is the end product of narratives, stories, and legends that the culturally literate tell themselves and outsiders to show who they are and *why* who they are is important.

SENTIMENT AND MEANING OF AND FOR FENWAY PARK

In some respects, we can say that any space that a human being encounters is necessarily given some sort of meaning.[19] But, here, we are interested in the meaning*ful* places that people hold attachments to and endow with value.[20] The reasons why people create attachments to places are varied, but they all point to the importance of people's relationship to the natural and built material environment around them. Making connections to a place is one of the essential ways that people try to make sense of the world they live in. As the number of people who become attached to a place increases, the meanings of that place multiply and tend to congeal, rather than separate and fragment, creating and maintaining shared meanings with the place and bonds with community.

Like people, locations have certain ascribed statuses or levels of prestige. So in some ways, "place" can also refer to social position, often reflected by the types of people allowed in and kept out of certain places. Even if the owners, employees, or patrons of a certain place make the decisions about who should or should not be included or excluded, "outsiders" also make judgments about which places are "better" than others.[21] Of course, what is meant by "better" depends on the people making the judgments and on what they want from or do at that place. It does not matter whether we know this because our friends told us, we read it in *Zagat's* or some other cultural guidebook, or we figured it out ourselves. What matters is that we make these judgments about places because we must. Being able to make or recognize the distinctions between places helps people avoid embarrassment and rejection.[22] Judgments about places are often connected to our perceived connections to that place, so that person's cold and dangerous slum may be another's warm and welcoming home.

Judgments about places can either lead to or be the result of sentiments and emotions. The emotional attachments that some people in Boston and throughout Red Sox Nation had for Fenway Park were strong enough to hold back the wrecking ball before it smashed through the ballpark's 1912 red-brick façade. In 1999, the Save Fenway Park! group was formed to thwart the Red Sox's plans to knock down the ol' ballpark and build a bigger, more modernized replica of the original in essentially the same footprint. The passion that the members of Save Fenway Park! have for the ballpark is extreme nearly to the point of fanaticism. Their passion did not constrain them; it propelled them. They worked effectively, spread their message throughout the city with bumper stickers, newsletters, and a website, and made suggestions to the new Red Sox ownership, which listened and subsequently announced in the spring of 2005 that it was going to commit to Fenway Park and continue to add "improvements" to the ballpark.

The SFP members' passion, however, is not unique. Other people often speak about Fenway Park the way most people talk about their favorite uncle. People often include Fenway Park in the most significant moments of their lives, from civic holidays to personal events like birthdays, wedding proposals, weddings, anniversaries, and funerals. People *make* Fenway Park meaningful by treating it with awe and reverence, consecrating it by dispersing loved ones' ashes on the field and throughout the ballpark, proposing marriage atop the Green Monster, and writing a realistic play with characters who threaten to shoot any Red Sox owner who decides to tear down Fenway Park. These are acts of meaning-making that are important for the continued attachment to and support for culturally meaningful places.

URBAN IDENTITIES AND LIFESTYLES AT FENWAY PARK

The notion of Fenway Park and the Red Sox as a subculture seems contradictory to the claim that Fenway Park functions as an overarching symbol of Boston's urban culture. And Red Sox Nation is certainly different than the "alternative" groups that are typically designated as subcultures.[23] People in cities, and near cities, have multiple group allegiances whereby each "scene," to use sociologist John Irwin's language, or "game" in Long's model, has its own conditions, practices, and forms of membership.[24] In this way, each "scene" or "game" functions like a subculture. Red Sox fans have their own "subcultural capital" in the form of memorabilia, number of games attended, which games were seen in person, location of seats, and sometimes even how many beers were consumed.[25]

Despite the flexibility of individuals' group allegiances and memberships, cities provide places for people both to try out new ideas and to practice the old ways that have been handed down. Fenway Park has been used in many different ways by its patrons and devotees. The members and practitioners who compose Fenway Park's "community of believers" "share speech-habits, folklore, ways of proceeding, frames of value, a collective self-image."[26]

People can, and often do, internalize the meaning, character, or status of the places they patronize.[27] Therefore, the debate about the future of Fenway Park is about not only the identity of the city but also the identity of its consumers. Individual and collective identities are constructed through acts of "devotional consumerism" such as buying, wearing, and using replicas, souvenirs, and memorabilia. These acts are defined by the motivations behind them that endow the place, team, and the city with cultural value and importance through the personal adornment and display of "articles of faith."

For sociologist Herbert Blumer, fashion is not driven by class distinction but by a "collective groping for the proximate future."[28] He suggests that the individual's engagement with personal adornments is not so much the desire to explore new ideas or to express opposition but the "wish to be in fashion, to be abreast of what has good standing, to express new tastes which are emerging in a changing world."[29] At Fenway Park, "in fashion" is not about *haute couture* but about wearing objects like a blue, blue-and-red, pink, or green Red Sox cap when at the ballpark or walking through the streets of downtown Boston.

SOCIAL INTERACTION AT THE BALLPARK

The 1960s media theorist Marshall McLuhan famously said that the "medium is the message because it is the medium that shapes and controls the scale and form of human association and action."[30] Although we generally think of mediating objects as televisions, newspapers, books, and the like, in an important cultural sense all objects, including places, are media. A mediating object carries information, emotions, ideas, and impressions between people, and it does so across space or time, or both—between people who are not necessarily present in the same place at the same time. The new seats atop the Green Monster convey the same message—the message of the new ownership's attempts to "improve" the ballpark—for the fans who saw yesterday, are seeing it today, and will see it tomorrow. As cultural artifacts, places carry messages about the culture they originate from and symbolize. They also affect the types of interactions that lead to the construction of their meanings.

Ballparks present interesting cases for studying the urban "esthetic" and "interactional pleasures" outlined by sociologist Lyn Lofland.[31] The spatial dimensions of a ballpark include the field of play and the stands for spectators, as well as its surrounding neighborhood or parking lot. The proximity of the spectators to the playing grounds affects the quality of the experience of the game. Because most of the action takes place between the bases and, even more so, between the pitcher's mound and home plate, patrons try to get as close as they can to the infield. Obviously, the closer seats are more expensive and more coveted than the Upper Deck seats I used to sit in at Shea Stadium, passing binoculars back and forth with my grandfather. The small, cozy, intimate size of Fenway Park is one of its most talked about attributes by the organization, its patrons, and the designers and developers of the Fenway-inspired retro-style ballparks that have been constructed in many cities since Baltimore's Camden Yards was erected in 1992. One of the goals of these new ballparks was to bring the fans closer to the field by constructing asymmetrical seating bowls that are steeper and smaller than those in the oversized cookie-cutter, multisport stadiums that the retro ballparks have been replacing.

Ballparks can also be evaluated based on the availability and accessibility of civic spaces within and outside them. These places, then, can be analyzed with regard to the quality of sociability of the ballpark. It was such an idea that propelled the Red Sox to close off Yawkey Way with turnstiles for ticket-holders to use before and during games. Along with major "improvements" like the Green Monster seats and the Right Field Roof seats, the Big Concourse beneath and behind the outfield bleachers was added, as the Red Sox's chief architect, Janet Marie Smith, said, "to create more places for people to mull around." Such open areas create more interaction between people at Fenway Park, enhancing both the feelings of solidarity and the cultural power of the place.

BOTTOM OF THE NINTH

As the oldest active ballpark in professional baseball, Fenway Park has motivated a following to urge for its preservation. Like the religious reverence of totems that Durkheim studied, Fenway's sacred quality veers outside the lines of modern economic, instrumental rationality. But far from being irrational, such adoration speaks to the need for communal traditions in cities, motivating Bostonians, implicitly and explicitly, to fight against the presumed fragmentation and disappearance of American civic life.

During the course of my research and writing, colleagues, friends, and interviewees would often ask me to answer my own questions about Fenway Park. When they wanted to know my opinion about the future of the ballpark, I would balk and stay silent. From the beginning of this project, I purposely didn't allow myself to make a definitive judgment in order to be able to hear the different arguments on their own terms. But when all is said and done, I have to get off the fence: Save Fenway Park!

Communities are hard to build from scratch. Tradition helps. Important places are, in effect, pedagogical tools for the transmission of cultural knowledge from one generation to the next. As one commentator remarks, Fenway Park "should be preserved . . . so that our children and their children can go to the park and say: 'That's the mound where Babe Ruth pitched. That's the box where Ted Williams swung his bat. That's the foul pole Carlton Fisk homered off. That's the Wall that Bucky &*%&ing Dent homered over.'"[32] Telling stories about both joys and pains helps generations define themselves and connects them both to their predecessors and to future generations.[33] One of the measures of how well a culture works is how well one generation passes its stories on to the next. Places help people tell their stories. Fenway Park helps Boston tell its story.

APPENDIX
Making the Familiar Strange
Urban Sociology at the Ballpark

The city . . . sets problems of meaning. The streets, the people, the buildings, and the changing scenes do not come already labeled. They require explanation and interpretation.
—Anselm L. Strauss, sociologist/theorist[1]

I am convinced that part of the marginalization of social science in contemporary public debates relates precisely to our lost capacity for storytelling. It is up to the reader to judge how much further an understanding of this social space is advanced by these narratives and how much might be distorted in their telling.
—Sherri Grasmuck, sociologist/ethnographer[2]

In 1956, the *American Anthropologist* published an article by Horace Miner about an "exotic" culture that was allegedly defined by its magical beliefs and practices. According to Miner, these men and women engaged in tortuous body rituals in front of their sacred charm boxes, each morning inserting "a small bundle of hog hairs into their mouth, along with magical powders, and then moving the bundle in a highly formalized series of gestures."[3] Writing as if he were describing an indigenous "primitive" tribe, Miner used his position as an anthropologist to deceive his readership, employing creative word play to disrupt

197

the reader's perspective. Not only did he spell "American" backward to come up with "Nacirema," the supposed name of the "tribe" he was writing about; he also noted that the nation was "originated by a cultural hero" called Notgnihsaw, known for two great feats: "the throwing of a piece of wampum across the river Pa-To-Mac and the chopping down of a cherry tree in which the Spirit of Truth resided."[4] Miner described other such common American cultural narratives and practices in "exoticized" terms, whereby mundane visits to the doctor in the hospital became sacred encounters that required undressing in front of the "medicine man" at the *latipso*.

Miner's article about the Nacirema was a tongue-in-cheek piece about the perils of ethnocentrism and the tendency of anthropologists, sociologists, and lay persons at the time to be overly critical of non-Western practices and beliefs and, in effect, to place Western "civilization" above and beyond "primitive" cultures. These are lessons that remain important today. But, for sociologists, especially cultural sociologists, who study the myths, symbols, and rituals of contemporary Americans, there is another important lesson that solidifies Miner's text as profoundly important rather than merely witty and amusing. Whereas anthropologists, or anyone who studies or tries to live in a foreign culture, seek to make the strange familiar in order to understand it and not become totally overwhelmed by culture shock, the sociologist's task is to *make the familiar strange*. Making the familiar strange is, perhaps, the only way to account for the things that people, including ourselves, take for granted. And studying the taken-for-granted is the basis of all sociological inquiry, regardless of whether the purpose of the study is to explicate a social practice or expose a social injustice.

Employing a certain, though wavering, degree of cognitive distance from one's subject matter is a necessary step toward a rich account of one's intended subject matter. This cognitive distance must waver along the continuum, the slippery slope, between the "native's point of view" and the "dispassionate researcher" in a way that does not view the "insider" and the "outsider" as mutually exclusive categorical identities. To hear our informants' and interviewees' stories, we must be able to empathetically understand what they mean, all for the sake of getting the story right—which, of course, is another lesson passed down from Miner, who purposely got the story wrong. So it helps to be close to one's subject, but not so close that the researcher's voice takes the place of his or her informants' and interviewees' stories.

Opposing the retreat to subjectivity embraced by postmodern ethnographers that "has reduced the epistemological status of the ethnographer and turned him or her more and more to stories in, rather than of, the field,"[5] I have attempted to identify the patterns and practices that help shape and give life to the stories about Fenway Park, which are accordingly about the people who endear it, are near it, or hope to be someday. In Boston, the significance of Fenway Park is even more taken for granted than, say, the difficulty of finding *pahking faw yawh cah*. And by studying Fenway Park, an object of devotion that is so near and dear to so many people's hearts (and wallets), we can learn something about the ways that people form relationships with places as a means of practicing the art and politics of social reality. Moreover, the ways that people use, act in, and act toward an important place like Fenway Park reveal some of the most skillful ways that people care about, and for, the culture of their respective cities.

In order to recognize the taken-for-granted aspects of Fenway Park and then connect those insights to a broader rationale about person-place relationships and the culture of cities, I combined the goals of "grounded theory" (e.g., inductive theory construction) and "interpretive case method" (e.g., the parts of culture can tell us something about the whole). Like anthropologist Clifford Geertz, who claimed to locate the essential features of Balinese society within a village cockfight, I sought to uncover the logic of urban culture as it is manifested through persons' uses of and attachments to Fenway Park.[6] Therefore, I chose to investigate a place that is used by people from many of the different communities and subcultures inside and outside Boston. In this way, I was able to study something that we can refer to as an urban community rather than investigating a collection of presumably disparate and isolated urban neighborhoods or ethnic populations.

Employing a "grounded theory" approach allowed me to uncover, rather than discover, the varied and various nuances of persons' relationships to and with Fenway Park. Barney Glaser and Anselm Strauss developed the idea of "grounded theory" in the 1960s as an alternative to deductive approaches associated with survey research, large data sets, and hypothesis-testing.[7] Whereas deductive approaches are concerned with establishing a relation between a few key predefined and predetermined variables, the grounded theory approach, in contrast, views data collection and analysis as procedures for generating and elaborating complex theoretical propositions through close, systematic investigation of and attention to one's assembled data. Induction helps make the familiar strange by purposely helping the researcher shake free from the shackles of preconceived notions, variables, hypotheses, and "scientific" standards.[8]

Induction alone, however, would not suffice, nor is it fully tenable. That is, as much as I, as a researcher, have tried to bracket out my own feelings about Fenway Park and Boston, I could not entirely bracket out my familiarity with relevant literature (primarily from urban sociology, cultural sociology, the sociology of religion); previous studies I have conducted in Boston; my experiences at Fenway Park, Shea Stadium (my home team's playing grounds), and other ballparks prior to this study; or my personal predispositions. Nor should I dismiss such acquired knowledge and experience. This prior knowledge provided me with a foundation on which to build the categories that emerged from the necessary acts of simultaneous data collecting and analysis. Sociologist Robert Wuthnow argues that "cultural analysis, like any other branch of sociology, not only *should* be but *inevitably is*, whether we like or not, essentially an act of interpretation."[9] The goal, then, is to combine prior knowledge, from scholarly literature and personal experience, with an, at least, ideally inductive approach to foster stronger theoretically significant and empirically grounded interpretations.

The *urban culturalist perspective* is a result of my application of grounded theory, whereby the categories used for interpretation and analysis emerged from my field research.[10] Such an inductive approach allowed me to open myself up to the richness of the ballpark or, more to the point, the richness of the ways that Fenway Park has become an important part of Boston's physical and symbolic landscape. One of the goals of grounded theory is to generate new hypotheses. One hypothesis that emerged from this study is the notion that cities rely on places that can be appropriated by individuals for both communal and private interests. Although many people fear the increasing privatization of public spaces, many public spaces can still be used and reappropriated by individuals and communities in unofficial or unsanctioned ways. Such practices at Fenway ranged from marriage proposals and ceremonies at the ballpark to the spreading of a loved one's ashes in seats and on the lush green grass.

As a means for recognizing both the expected and the unexpected, a primary goal throughout my research, and throughout the writing process, was to, in the end, provide a "thick description" of Fenway

Park. Borrowing the term from the philosopher Gilbert Ryle, Geertz introduced "thick description" as the necessary objective for the study of culture and, specifically, for the study of meanings.[11] The researcher must provide rich, detailed descriptions of the events, situations, and places that he or she is investigating in order to untangle the multiple layers of meaning associated with and constructed by people in their particular social worlds. Meaningful actions are different from mere physical responses to an external stimulus. They are actions that are purposeful and can be read as such by an audience or knowledgeable community.[12] Granted, often we say things through and with our actions that are unintended and unexpected. This is the difference between what the actor "gives" and "gives off."[13] But the point to remember is that part of the cultural sociologist's task is to delineate between "natural" behaviors (like eating) and learned or socially constructed behaviors (like eating a hamburger with pickles and ketchup or noodles with chopsticks).

Cultural analysts must be able to differentiate between the blinks and the winks. Although the movements are similar, the contracting of one's eyelids, blinks and winks are very different phenomena. As Geertz observed,

> In one, this is an involuntary twitch; in the other, a conspiratorial signal to a friend. The two movements are, as movements, identical; from an I-am-a-camera, "phenomenalistic" observation of them alone, one could not tell which was twitch and which was wink. Yet the difference, however unphotographable, between a twitch and a wink is vast; as anyone who has had the first taken for the second knows. Contracting your eyelids on purpose when there exists a public code in which so doing counts as a conspiratorial signal *is* winking. That's all there is to it: a speck of behavior, a fleck of culture, and— *voila!*—a gesture.[14]

A person can use this supposedly objective sign for a diverse array of purposes that, in turn, affect the meaning of the action. Any given wink can be a sign of acknowledgment, salutation, sensuality or sex appeal, sarcasm, or a parody of another's wink.

Geertz's example has been important for the development of cultural analyses because it "shows that the cultural materials we deal in are often especially important for the shades of meanings and nuances they take on in concrete situations."[15] It is not only the action but also the context of the action that makes it meaningful, and "thick descriptions" of both the actions (what happens at Fenway Park, like baseball games, charity events, and high fives) and the context (Fenway Park, in Boston, during the early years of the twenty-first century) help convey those meanings.

Although sociologists generally agree with the idea of "thick description," many have questioned whether it is enough. Is a "thick description" all that the field researcher is supposed to achieve? I agree with sociologist Howard Becker, who writes that "a better goal than 'thickness'—one that fieldworkers usually aim for—is 'breadth': trying to find something about every topic the research touches on, even tangentially."[16] So with the goal of breadth in mind, I aimed to pay attention to all the incidental information that the persons I observed, interviewed, and read about "gave off" during their discussions of the ballpark. For example, it may be significant that most of the local Boston sportswriters are from New England and are lifelong Red Sox fans. It may be significant that the overwhelming majority of my interviewees did not know many facts about the origin of Fenway Park's name or location. And it also may be significant that the Red Sox's lamentable racial history and the lack of nonwhite faces at the ballpark was hardly ever discussed by my interviewees. The messages that are "given" and "given off" are both significant.[17]

THE LOGIC OF METHODOLOGICAL PLURALISM: PARTICIPANT OBSERVATION, INTENSIVE INTERVIEWING, ARCHIVAL RESEARCH, AND VISUAL SOCIOLOGY

In order to fully grasp the multiple meanings bestowed on Fenway Park by multiple groups with varying interests and beliefs, I needed to employ multiple methods, albeit all with the intent to grasp those meaning from the persons' who hold them. I set out to learn as much as I could about the ballpark, its history and its patrons, its architecture and its owners, its supporters and its dissenters. Moreover, I set out to understand how and why the reverence of Fenway Park does not secure its survival.

The research design follows sociologist Joshua Gamson's "tripartite model" for studying any type of cultural object. As Gamson writes,

In order to get a strong grasp of a cultural phenomenon, it is necessary to simultaneously study its production (the activities through which it is created), its thematic, narrative, visual, or textual content (what is being said in and through it), and its reception (how those encountering it use and interpret it).[18]

Put a bit differently, I wanted to track the circulation of the meaning, how the meaning of Fenway Park was and is produced and constructed, transmitted and disseminated, and received and interpreted. None of these activities is confined to one group. It would be a mistake to assume that the Red Sox ownership is the only producer of the ballpark, that only sportswriters disseminate ideas and information about Fenway Park, or that fans are the only persons who make up Fenway's audience. The three-pronged practices of cultural production, transmission, and reception cross group boundaries. These issues and idiosyncrasies were explored throughout the data collection, the analysis, and the writing of this text.

In order to take notice and account of these practices, my approach for data collection had to be "triangulated," to use a term popularized by sociologist Norman Denzin. Simply put, triangulation is the use of a combination of two or more research methods for gathering data about the same empirical case. "Because each method reveals different aspects of empirical reality," writes Denzin, "multiple methods of observation must be employed."[19] Although the term has been used to denote a technique that ensures validation by verifying common findings, my claims are far more modest. Methodological pluralism will lead us closer to the truth about our subject of inquiry because we are able to offer, in good faith, perspectives other than our own, but we will nevertheless remain trapped in Zeno's Paradox, cutting our distance to the truth in pieces *ad infinitum*. Even so, methodological pluralism leads to a greater breadth of knowledge than any single method, qualitative or quantitative, would permit.

In order to paint the clearest picture of the ol' ballpark, I employed separate but related methods: participant observation, intensive interviewing, archival research, and visual analysis. These four methods provided more than enough information to grant me at least some semblance of an authoritative voice to speak about Fenway Park and the roles it plays in and outside the city. Moreover, such methods allowed me to describe the "what," document the "how," and interpret the "why" of Fenway Park's status as a revered and valued place.[20]

PARTICIPANT OBSERVATION:
BEING THERE WITHOUT BEING THEM

Participant observation is the easiest type of sociological research to do poorly. This is in part due to the expected differences and unexpected similarities between supposedly disconnected or disparate situations and individuals. As sociologist and veteran ethnographer Gary Alan Fine writes, "Every setting has quirks, tricks, and surprises. That is the challenge—and the fun—of participant observation."[21] Many colleagues and friends have assumed that researching Fenway Park had to be fun. One colleague even claimed that an ethnographic study of Fenway is the ultimate male fantasy. Admittedly, getting free passes to sold-out Red Sox games and chatting it up with celebrity ballplayers, sportswriters, and executives isn't a bad way to spend one's time. But the study presented a number of challenges, and fun was certainly one of them. My levels of fun, however, were gauged by how much I was enjoying myself participating in the situation, events, and practices of those whom I was studying, as well as by my personal enjoyment of being in the field as a professional sociologist. The relationship between myself the researcher and myself the participant, which was sometimes a source of tension brought on by the amount of fun I was having, remained a challenge throughout both the researching and writing of the text.

Participant observation is at the heart of the ethnographer's craft. The researcher is expected to immerse him- or herself in the subjects' culture. How much immersion is too much or too little is a constant subject of debate in both the anthropological and sociological literatures, as is the question about whether a researcher should study his or her own group, however defined. This second question revolves around an important epistemological/philosophy-of-social-science query: Does it take one to know one?[22] The answer to such a question is never either/or. And the goal when doing participant observation is to maintain a foot in both worlds: one foot in the culture of one's subject and the other in the academic sphere of the "professional stranger."

Getting close to one's subject can be both rewarding and risky. Sociologist Daniel Monti offers a fair warning to future ethnographers about the risks of field research in his review of three urban/community ethnographies published in the early 1990s:

> Among the most serious of these risks is that of "going native," of identifying so closely with one's subjects that one inadvertently skews his [or her] description and analysis of the world being portrayed or totally compromises the work and standards of appropriate research. There is a great tension built into the process of doing field research and, ultimately, in the published findings based on such work. The problem of "going native" captures nicely the various strands that create this tension. Any fair assessment of the contributions made by a particular piece of field research necessarily entails a judgment on how the researcher dealt with this tension.[23]

Accordingly, the field researcher should avoid "going native" in order to maintain enough distance to recognize consciously the elements of culture that would allow or help someone go native or, more importantly, *be* native.

Trying simultaneously to be both physically near and analytically remote is the way that I dealt with this tension. I've found Fine's discussion about the necessary analytic distance between the researcher and the researched particularly informative and instructive:

> The goal of ethnography is not to meet people, but to depict action and talk of sets of participants. . . . I do not imagine my subjects as heroic or oppressed, as romantic or malign figures. My writing does not involve the enshrinement or abasement of subjects, but in treating them as morally neutral, as a good ethnologist might treat observed primates. Behaviors matter more than soul. As I compose, I strive to be marginal, to maintain an *ironic detachment* from informants. In some regards, ethnography is a sociological comedy of manners.[24]

Keeping an ironic distance between oneself and those being studied, especially while engaging in the same behaviors, is a necessary element of participant observation. Ironic distance provides a cognitive space for immersion without going native, for being there without being them. I brought this lesson with me to games and events I attend at, inside, outside, and near Fenway Park. I held on to it tightly as I traveled to spring training and when I stood behind the Green Monster during the first game of the 2004 World Series. And I kept it even closer when I would engage in conversations with Red Sox fans about the future of Fenway Park.

Ironic distance also allowed me to act sometimes like a Red Sox fan without actually being one. For the sake of trying to take the role of the Red Sox fan, for two years I tried to act as if I were one. That is, I tried to do what I thought, and was told, Red Sox fans, from the causal observer to the most ardent fanatic, do on a daily basis. And this involved more than simply putting on my Sox cap and going to the local bar to watch the game.

I became a daily devotee of WEEI 850 AM, the sports sections of the *Boston Globe* and *Boston Herald*, and fan websites and forums like those found on redsox.com, BostonDirtDogs.com, and the self-proclaimed elitist branch of Red Sox Nation, the Sons of Sam Horn (sonsofsamhorn.com). I also attended showings of *Still, We Believe: The Boston Red Sox Movie*, which chronicles the trials and tribulations of a few devoted Red Sox fans during the heartbreaking 2003 season; Brendan Bates's play *The Savior of Fenway*, a tale of local Red Sox fans and their woes, which was performed at the YMCA in Cambridge throughout May 2004; and *Fever Pitch*, a movie that included scenes that were filmed during actual games at Fenway Park. I used my conscious "acting as if" as a means of acquiring a wealth of local knowledge about the meanings of Fenway Park.

INTENSIVE INTERVIEWS: HEARING THE STORIES FROM THOSE WHO WROTE THEM, TOLD THEM, AND STARRED IN THEM

Perhaps the most enlightening information came out of the more than one hundred interviews I conducted with people in and outside Boston. I wanted to hear their stories about Fenway Park firsthand. I spoke with Red Sox fans, baseball enthusiasts, Boston residents that are not "into" baseball, local business owners and employees, sportswriters, architects, historic preservationists, and members of the Red Sox organization including former and current players and personnel.

For the most part, my interviews took two forms. First, I conducted semistructured, flexible interviews that lasted from thirty minutes to two hours. There was no correlation between the duration and interviewees' feelings or opinions about the ballpark or any of the related subjects that were broached. These interviews were conducted in my office in the Sociology Department at Boston University, the workplaces of interviewees, the homes of interviewees, the Red Sox spring-training facility and the press box at City of Palms Park in Ft. Myers, Florida, the Red Sox Clubhouse, the Red Sox executive offices, and inside and outside Fenway before, during, and after games. Many of these interviewees were located through snowball sampling.

I also conducted impromptu interviews, which mostly took place during games at Fenway Park, though they also occurred in other public and private places, inside and outside Boston. Regardless of whether the interviews were scheduled or unplanned, I always made my intentions known and always let people say whatever they wanted about the ballpark. I tried to keep the interviews as uniform and structured as possible, but I abandoned unnecessary rigidity when I felt it was necessary for the sake of establishing rapport and providing a forum for the interviewee to feel comfortable and open to speak their minds, and hearts.

A sample interview schedule and a sample list of the people I interviewed follow.

SAMPLE INTERVIEW SCHEDULE

- Why is Fenway Park so important to Boston? Is there anyone for whom the park isn't important?
- If Fenway Park is replaced, should the new stadium have any of the old stadium's features? Why or why not?
- What's the most memorable (best/worst) thing you've seen happen there?
- Have the fans changed over the years? For the better? For worse? How about their behavior?
- How has the team changed?
- Other than ballgames, does anything important happen at Fenway Park?
- What kinds of community activities does the Red Sox organization contribute to or participate in? How many involve Fenway Park?
- What other businesses do they work with in order to do these community activities?
- How often do you see "Save Fenway Park" or "I Love Fenway Park" stickers? Where?

- Do you have any Red Sox souvenirs at home, or do you ever wear Boston Red Sox clothing?
- When was the last time you visited Fenway Park?
- How often do you attend games at Fenway Park?

SAMPLE OF INTERVIEW SUBJECTS

The following list contains the full names of public figures who hold important occupational and/or social positions with power to affect the public debate about Fenway Park's past, present, future. The last names of "everyday" persons have been abbreviated for the sake of both anonymity and generalizability.

- Mike Andrews, Red Sox player (1966–70) and chairman of the Jimmy Fund, the official charity of the Boston Red Sox
- Carl B., Red Sox fan, season-ticket holder since 1978
- Dick Beradino, Red Sox player consultant and coach
- Ed Berliner, host of *Sports Pulse* and managing editor of CN8 Sports, Comcast Network
- Ian Browne, sports reporter (redsox.com, mlb.com)
- Ellis Burks, Red Sox player (1987–92, 2004)
- Jon C., Red Sox fan, Peabody, Massachusetts
- Nick Cafardo, sports columnist (*Boston Globe*)
- Larry Cancro, Red Sox vice president of Fenway affairs
- Joe Cochran, equipment manager for the Red Sox, member of Red Sox organization since 1984
- Jeff Connors, worked in ticket office at Fenway Park (seven seasons), worked on "New Ballpark Project," manager of corporate development for the New England Patriots
- Patton D., "converted" Red Sox fan, Colorado native
- Johnny Damon, Red Sox player (2002–5)
- Alan Embree, Red Sox player (2003–5)
- Donna G., Red Sox fan, Houston, Texas
- Lou Gorman, Red Sox general manager (1984–94)
- Paul Grogan, president and CEO of the Boston Foundation, coauthor (with Tony Proscio) of *Comeback Cities: A Blueprint for Urban Neighborhood Revival*

- Jim Healey, vice president of programs and administration for the Yawkey Foundation; former Red Sox vice president of broadcasting and special projects
- Jethro Heiko, former director of Community Organizing at Fenway Community Development Corporation
- Richard Johnson, curator of the Sports Museum of New England in Boston, coauthor of *Ted Williams: A Portrait in Words and Pictures* and *Red Sox Century* (both with Glenn Stout)
- Gabe Kapler, Red Sox player (2002–4)
- Kasey L., Fenway Ambassador, ball girl, and tour guide
- Paul L., Red Sox fan, Nashua, New Hampshire
- Jim Lonborg, Red Sox player (1965–71), 1967 Cy Young Award winner
- Larry Lucchino, Red Sox president and CEO
- Frank Malzone, Red Sox player (1955–65)
- Len Martin, engineer, author of *Fenway Park: Build It Yourself*
- Sam Mele, Red Sox player (1946–52), Twins manager (1961–67)
- Bob Montgomery, Red Sox player (1970–79)
- Joe Morgan, Red Sox manager (1988–91) and major-league player (1959–61, 1964, Braves, A's, Phillies, Indians, Cardinals)
- Arthur Moscato, worked for the Red Sox for forty years, Red Sox box office manager (1968–87)
- Trot Nixon, Red Sox player (1996–2006)
- Bill P., usher at City of Palms Park, Ft. Myers, Florida, from Woburn, Massachusetts
- Johnny Pesky, Red Sox player (1942–52), also a manager, coach, announcer, and assistant general manager; the namesake of Pesky's Pole
- Donald R., Red Sox fan, Bangor, Maine
- Jim Rice, Red Sox player (1974–89)
- Bill S., Red Sox fan and occasional Fenway Park program vendor
- Sarah S., Red Sox fan, Boston; season-ticket holder since 1982
- Tom S., New York Yankees fan, Braintree, Massachusetts, native
- Dan Shaughnessy, sports columnist (*Boston Globe*); author of *The Curse of the Bambino*, *At Fenway: Dispatches from Red Sox Nation*, and *Reversing the Curse*
- Janet Marie Smith, Red Sox vice president of planning and development

- Tom T., Red Sox fan, Providence, Rhode Island, native
- Erika Tarlin, member on the board of directors for Save Fenway Park!
- Dana Van Fleet, owner and general manager of Cask 'n' Flagon
- Jason Varitek, Red Sox player (1997–current)
- Charlie Wagner, Red Sox player (1935–43, 1946); threw out the first pitch of the 2004 World Series at Fenway Park
- Dan Wilson, founding member of Save Fenway Park!
- Carl Yastrzemski, Red Sox player (1967–83), last player to win the Triple Crown

In their "how-to" text about qualitative methodology, sociologists John and Lyn Lofland "emphasize the *mutuality* of participant observation and intensive interviewing as the central techniques of naturalistic investigation."[25] Even though there is a good deal of overlap between the two techniques, especially when interviewing fans during Red Sox games at the ballpark, I have separated them because I often used each technique for different purposes. I conducted some interviews during which I was observing the interviewee and not the social setting and was only participating in my own research. Conversely, there were times that I tried to participate in full and not be distracted by making observations in order to account for some of the experiential aspects of both Fenway Park and city life.

As a hybrid method that mixes participant observation and interviewing, I employed sociologist Margarethe Kusenbach's "go-along" technique. It provided a useful method for empirically investigating how the meanings of places become a part of persons' cultural repertoires.[26] For the go-along, the researcher accompanies "informants into their familiar environments and track outings they would go on anyway as closely as possible, for instance with respect to the particular day, the time of day, and the routes of the regular trip."[27]

Describing a few different ways to conduct go-alongs, Kusenbach suggests that this technique can shed light on social actors' environmental perceptions, everyday routines, the presence and substance of personal landmarks, place-based social networks, and social patterns and practices in public settings. By employing this technique, we can posit good interpretations of the emotional attachments to and meanings of places from the persons who use, care for, care about, and visit them. To this end, on occasion, I would bring an "assistant" with me to the ballpark. A few times, I was accompanied by someone who had been there before, and I would let that person point out the objects, persons, and events at the ballpark that meant something to him or her. Other times, I would purposely take someone who had not been to Fenway Park before and try to see what he or she saw with unfettered eyes. Although I would not recommend the go-along as the sole method of one's study of a place, I certainly found it to be helpful and informative.

ARCHIVAL RESEARCH: DATA COLLECTION FROM AFAR

Before entering the field, as well as during and after my exit, I dug through "the civic diary we call newspapers."[28] Although I tend not to be overly cautious of media bias and misrepresentations in newspaper reportage, I do not accept the media as totally neutral either. Still, newspapers are important sources of information, especially about large communities like those in and of cities and about celebrities like the Red Sox and the ballpark. Furthermore, the way that local reporters describe a local event or population is as sociologically valuable as what they say.

Interested in the meaning of Fenway Park, I was aware that the media helps construct those meanings. But, again, unlike "mass culture/mass hegemony" theorists who tend to assume that media messages are passively absorbed by readers and viewers, I readily acknowledge that the audience is not a homogeneous population. Moreover, audience members have the creative potential and ability to resist media messages and appropriate their own meanings. I also recognize that the "media" is not a suprahuman, reified entity but is made up of individuals who are affected by the same or at least a similar cultural milieu as their audience members.

Archival research involves more than analyzing media reportage. I looked at official press releases by the Red Sox about the "New Fenway Park" plan, the reconstruction of the ol' ballpark, and events that were held either at Fenway Park or by the Red Sox at another location. I read fan-based websites, message boards, and blogs. I also read fan letters that were sent to Fenway Park. Joe Cochran, the Red Sox's equipment manager, told me, "You can simply write 'Fenway Park' on the front of an envelope and it will get there. And someone will probably read it." Indeed, I saw a letter that simply read, "Yaz, Fenway Park."

VISUAL SOCIOLOGY:
PHOTOGRAPHY BEYOND THE TOURIST GAZE

Visual sociology is an organized attempt to study and use images as part of the sociologist's analytic tool kit. It is motivated by two assumptions. First, images contain data about values, norms, beliefs, and practices that are often inaccessible to other forms of collecting and reporting information. Second, communicating research findings by using visual media can vastly expand and strengthen the rhetoric of sociological expression.

Visual sociology provided me with a way to produce my own archives whereby my photographs of the ballpark, and the people in and around it, became useful bits of data. I was able to reanalyze certain images after they were collected and pinpoint some of the key identifying features of Fenway Park, as well as the patterned behaviors of its patrons. Keeping a visual record of fieldwork helped me capture details that otherwise may have been missed. Even though thinking of photography as an unadulterated reflection of reality is a bit presumptuous, photographs can certainly show us the visual attributes of places that add, for better or for worse, to the tone and texture of the material urban landscape. The assumption, then, is that these visual cues can tell us something, though not everything, about the way of life of and in those places. This is an assumption on which much anthropological fieldwork is based. That is, photography has been used by anthropologists to record and document places and people that are new and strange to the fieldworker. In such situations, photographs become useful tools for structuring information from the new and strange environs, providing data to help the researcher make both the people and place more recognizable and familiar.[29]

The sociologist conducting fieldwork in a setting that is already known from his or her everyday life can use photography as a means for making the familiar strange. Again, whereas the anthropologist has traditionally sought to make the other known, the sociologist seeks to make the known unfamiliar in order to create a degree of cognitive distance between the researcher and the researched. While trying visually to make Fenway Park strange, I felt the need to prevent myself from making it too strange or, for that matter, too extraordinary. The goal was not to create images that would exoticize familiar scenes and persons at

Fenway, nor was it to create images that would appear as if they were taken merely to highlight my "vacation" to the ol' ballpark. So, in the first sense, I didn't want to take photographs that made the ballpark so unfamiliar that it couldn't be recognized, nor did I want to make Fenway Park appear wholly unique. And, as for the second sense, my photographs were of the people and the place and not of me with the people or at the place, despite my inevitable presence behind the camera. But my presence behind the camera, just like my presence while holding my pad and furiously scribbling notes between innings and my presence at the computer writing these words that you're reading, shouldn't be an obstacle for recognizing that the goal of this research was not to document my experience at Fenway Park but to elucidate the Fenway Park experience of those who revere it, are near it, or who hope one day to nestle into one of Fenway's old wooden seats.

NOTES

NOTES TO THE INTRODUCTION

1. During a "celebration" a week earlier, after the Red Sox beat the Yankees in the seventh game of the American League Championship Series, that included relatively minor forms of public vandalism, an Emerson College student was killed by a projectile fired by riot police. "Emerson College Student Dies after Postgame Melee," Denise Lavoie, *Boston Globe*, 21 October 2004; "Fan Anxiety Turns to Delirium, Rowdiness," Brian MacQuarrie, *Boston Globe*, 21 October 2004; "Postgame Police Projectile Kills an Emerson Student: O'-Toole Accepts Responsibility but Condemns 'Punks,'" Thomas Farragher and David Able, *Boston Globe*, 22 October 2004; "Man Says Police Pellets Hit Him, 2 Others," Donovan Slack, *Boston Globe*, 25 October 2004.

2. See Glenn Stout and Richard A. Johnson, *Red Sox Century: One Hundred Years of Red Sox Baseball* (Boston: Houghton Mifflin, 2004).

3. Quoted in Dan Shaughnessy, *The Curse of the Bambino* (New York: Penguin Books, 1990), 19.

4. The case of Bill Buckner is a poignant example of the construction of melodramatic narratives in American sport and popular culture. For any social problem, assuming that we could call the Red Sox's collapse in the 1986 World Series a social problem, different groups and individuals are designated as victims, villains, or heroes. Buckner was immediately labeled the villain, taking his seat in Red Sox history next to Babe Ruth and Bucky Dent. Buckner is even on the cover of Shaughnessy's *The Curse of the Bambino*. After the Red Sox victory in 2004, there was a public outpouring of forgiveness for Buckner. Viewers could see fans, anticipating a win, holding a sign in Busch Stadium during Game 4 that read "We Forgive Bill Buckner." But Buckner was

admittedly less than relieved to see the banner hanging or to hear about an informal campaign for his absolution. "I feel like the guy who got put away for a crime he didn't commit," Buckner explained. "And then the DNA evidence comes back 30 years later and the guy gets out of jail. What do you say for the thirty years he spent suffering? I don't feel like I've committed a crime." Quoted in "Demons Haunt Buckner the Scapegoat," Nick Jezierny, *Idaho Statesman*, 31 October 2004. Buckner, of course, did not commit a "crime." But that didn't stop many fans from believing that he did. Buckner's error did, however, give the New York Mets their opportunity to win, which brought the series to a 3–3 tie. It was in the seventh game of that series that Boston lost the championship to the Mets, in an 8–5 defeat. For eighteen years, Buckner was the villain, a scapegoat for another generation's angst.

5. S. Elizabeth Bird, "It Makes Sense to Us: Cultural Identity in Local Legends of Place," *Journal of Contemporary Ethnography* (31:5, 2002): 526.

6. Theorists who have adopted a postmodernist standpoint—which can look a lot like Marxism without the revolution—often approach culture as a commodity for sale, manipulated by the "visible" hands of self-interested capitalists. As such, for postmodernists, rampant consumption and instant gratification are the leitmotif of cities. Indicative writings include Jean Baudrillard, *America* (New York: Verso, 1989); Fredric Jameson, *Postmodernism; or, The Cultural Logic of Late Capitalism* (Durham, NC: Duke University Press, 1991); Sharon Zukin, *Landscapes of Power: From Detroit to Disney World* (Berkeley: University of California Press, 1991); Michael Sorkin, *Variations on a Theme Park: The New American City and the End of Public Space* (New York: Hill and Wang, 1992); Mark Gottdiener, *The Theming of America: Dreams, Visions, and Commercial Spaces* (Boulder, CO: Westview, 1997); John Hannigan, *Fantasy City: Pleasure and Profit in the Postmodern Metropolis* (New York: Routledge, 1998); Michael J. Dear, *The Postmodern Urban Condition* (Malden, MA: Blackwell, 2000); and Michael J. Dear, "Los Angeles and the Chicago School: Invitation to a Debate," *City & Community* (1:1, 2002): 5–32. For a few critiques of postmodernism and alternative approaches to studying urban culture, see Lyn H. Lofland, *The Public Realm: Exploring the City's Quintessential Social Territory* (Hawthorne, NY: Aldine de Gruyter, 1998); Daniel J. Monti, *The American City: A Social and Cultural History* (Malden, MA: Blackwell, 1999); Kevin Fox Gotham, "Urban Sociology and the Postmodern Challenge," *Humboldt Journal of Social Relations* (26:1–2, 2001): 57–79; Edward M. Bruner, *Culture on Tour: Ethnographies of Travel* (Chicago: University of Chicago Press, 2005); and Michael Ian Borer, "The Location of Culture: The Urban Culturalist Perspective," *City & Community* (5:2, 2006): 173–98.

7. For a full explanation and description of this approach and how it differs from other urban sociological schools of thought, see Borer, "The Location of Culture."

8. Gerald D. Suttles, "The Cumulative Texture of Local Urban Culture," *American Journal of Sociology* (90:2, 1984): 283–304; Ray Oldenburg, *The Great Good Place: Cafés, Coffee Shops, Community Centers, Beauty Parlors, General Stores, Bars, Hangouts and How They Get You through the Day* (New York: Paragon House, 1989); David M. Hummon, *Commonplaces: Community Ideology and Identity in American Culture* (Albany: State University of New York Press, 1990); Lofland, *The Public Realm*; Bird, "It Makes Sense to Us."

9. Monti, *The American City*, 10; Lynn Hollen Lees, "Urban Public Space and Imagined Communities in the 1980s and 1990s," *Journal of Urban History* (20:4, 1994): 442–58.

10. Clifford Geertz, *The Interpretation of Cultures* (New York: Basic Books, 1973).

NOTES TO CHAPTER 1

1. Dan Shaughnessy, *At Fenway: Dispatches from Red Sox Nation* (New York: Crown, 1996), 18.

2. "Hub Fans Bid Kid Adieu," John Updike, *New Yorker*, 22 October 1960.

3. The term "social fact" is not used here in a positivistic sense as if to assume that the meaning of Fenway Park is somehow a static and autonomous entity. Instead, I am using the term to indicate that common beliefs and meanings are often perceived as permanent by social actors and can thereby exert a certain amount of power over their experiences and behaviors. So, whereas Durkheim told us to "treat social facts as things," it might be more fruitful to investigate how people treat things as social facts. For Durkheim's original discussion of social facts, see Émile Durkheim, *The Rules of Sociological Method* (New York: Free Press, 1982), 50–59.

4. For a few good examples, see Edward M. Bruner, "Abraham Lincoln as Authentic Reproduction: A Critique of Postmodernism," *American Anthropologist* (96:2, 1994): 397–415; Chris C. Park, *Sacred Worlds: An Introduction to Geography and Religion* (New York: Routledge, 1994); Philip Smith, "The Elementary Forms of Place and Their Transformations: A Durkheimian Model," *Qualitative Sociology* (22:1, 1999): 13–36; Timothy A. Simpson, "Streets, Sidewalks, Stores, and Stories: Narrative and Uses of Urban Space," *Journal of Contemporary Ethnography* (29:6, 2000): 684–716; Krista E. Paulsen, "Saving a Place for the County Fair: Institutional Space and the Maintenance of Community," *Research in Community Sociology* (10, 2000): 387–406; S. Elizabeth Bird, "It Makes Sense to Us: Cultural Identity in Local Legends of Place," *Journal of Contemporary Ethnography* (31:5, 2002): 519–47; and Richard D. Hecht, "Private Devotions and the Sacred Heart of Elvis: The Durkheimians and the (Re)Turn of the Sacred," in Roger Friedland and John Mohr, eds., *Matters of Culture: Cultural Sociology in Practice* (Cambridge: Cambridge University Press, 2004).

5. Quoted in "Red Sox Fans Are Not Content with Patriotism," Peter De-Marco, *Boston Globe*, 7 February 2004.

6. "A Nation Unlike Any Other," Mike Barnicle, *Boston Globe*, 9 April 2004.

7. "Season Nearly a Sell-Out," Michael Silverman, *Boston Herald*, 1 February 2004; "Ticket Sales Red-Hot, Sox Already Past 2 Million Mark," Nick Cafardo, *Boston Globe*, 10 February 2004.

8. "Boston's Fenway Park to Get 400 More Seats," Meg Vaillancourt, *Boston Globe*, 27 March 2002.

9. R. Richard Wohl and Anselm L. Strauss, "Symbolic Representation and the Urban Milieu," *American Journal of Sociology* (63:5, 1958): 526.

10. "Red Sox' New Lineup Steps Up," Gordon Edes, *Boston Globe*, 22 December 2001.

11. "N.H. Says 'Farewell, Old Man,'" *Boston Globe*, 4 May 2003.

12. See Charles C. Euchner, *Playing the Field: Why Sports Teams Move and Cities Fight to Keep Them* (Baltimore: Johns Hopkins University Press, 1993); Paul M. Anderson, "Playing the Stadium Game," *Journal of Sport and Social Issues* (21:1, 1997): 103–11; William Beaver, "Building Sports Stadiums in Pittsburgh: A Case Study in Urban Power Structures," *Sociological Focus* (34:1, 2001): 21–32; Anouk Belanger, "Sport Venues and the Spectacularization of Urban Spaces in North America: The Case of the Molson Centre in Montreal," *International Review for the Sociology of Sport* (35:3, 2000): 378–97; Clyde Brown and David M. Paul, "The Political Scorecard of Professional Sports Facility Referendums in the United States, 1984–2000," *Journal of Sport and Social Issues* (26:3, 2002): 248–67; Michael N. Danielson, *Home Team: Professional Sports and the American Metropolis* (Princeton, NJ: Princeton University Press, 1997); Kevin J. Delaney and Rick Eckstein, *Public Dollars, Private Stadiums: The Battle over Building Sports Stadiums* (New Brunswick, NJ: Rutgers University Press, 2003); Costas Spirou and Larry Bennett, "Revamped Stadium . . . New Neighborhood?" *Urban Affairs Review* (37:5, 2002): 675–702; Costas Spirou and Larry Bennett, *It's Hardly Sportin': Stadiums, Neighborhoods, and the New Chicago* (DeKalb: Northern Illinois University Press, 2003); Ralph C. Wilcox, *Sporting Dystopias: The Making and Meaning of Urban Sport Cultures* (Albany: State University of New York Press, 2003).

13. I am using "cultural capital" here to refer to noneconomic attachments and not necessarily as an indicator of hierarchical class status the way that Bourdieu and others do. See Pierre Bourdieu, *Distinction: A Social Critique of the Judgement of Taste* (Cambridge, MA: Harvard University Press, 1984).

14. In 1938, George Herbert Mead wrote, "History serves the community in the same way as the memory does the individual. A person has to bring up a certain portion of the past to determine what his present situation is, and in the same way the community wants to bring up the past so it can state the

present situation and bring out what the actual issues themselves are. I think that is what history uniformly is. It is always prejudiced in one sense, that is, determined by the problem before the community." Quoted in Fred Davis, *Yearning for Yesterday: A Sociology of Nostalgia* (New York: Free Press, 1979), 96.

15. "Red Sox Are Open to Domed Stadium," Matthew Rezendes, *Boston Globe*, 31 October 1991; "Hubdome vs. Fenway," *Boston Globe*, 4 November 1991.

16. Red Sox official press release, 15 May 1999.

17. Quoted in Dan Shaughnessy, *Fenway: A Biography in Words and Picture* (Boston: Houghton Mifflin, 1999), 31.

18. John Demos, "A Fan's Homage to Fenway (Or, Why We Love It When They Always Break Our Hearts," in William E. Leuchtenberg, ed., *American Places: Encounters with History* (Oxford: Oxford University Press, 2000), 106.

19. David Grazian, *Blue Chicago: The Search for Authenticity in Urban Blues Clubs* (Chicago: University of Chicago Press, 2003), 13, emphasis in the original.

20. Charles Taylor, *The Ethics of Authenticity* (Cambridge, MA: Harvard University Press, 1991), 21.

21. Much of this work stems from the early critical theories of the Frankfurt School. See Stephen Eric Bronner and Douglas M. Kellner, eds., *Critical Theory and Society: A Reader* (New York: Routledge, 1989); and Douglas M. Kellner, *Media Culture: Cultural Studies, Identity, and Politics between the Modern and the Postmodern* (New York: Routledge, 1995).

22. Lionel Trilling, *Sincerity and Authenticity* (Cambridge, MA: Harvard University Press, 1972).

23. Edward M. Bruner, *Culture on Tour: Ethnographies of Travel* (Chicago: University of Chicago Press, 2005), 161.

24. Grazian, *Blue Chicago*, 11.

25. Richard A. Peterson, *Creating Country Music: Fabricating Authenticity* (Chicago: University of Chicago Press, 1997).

26. Dean MacCannell, *The Tourist: A New Theory for the Leisure Class* (New York: Schocken, 1976); Richard Handler, "Authenticity," *Anthropology Today* (2:1, 1986): 2–4; and Richard Handler and William Saxton, "Dyssimmulation: Reflexivity, Narrative, and the Quest for Authenticity in 'Living,'" *Cultural Anthropology* (3:3, 1988): 242–60.

27. Bruner, *Culture on Tour*, 163.

28. See George Ritzer and Todd Stillman, "The Postmodern Ballpark as a Leisure Setting: Enchantment and Simulated De-McDonaldization," *Leisure Sciences* (23, 2001): 99–113.

29. Ruth Behar, "Ethnography and the Book That Was Lost," *Ethnography* (4:1, 2003): 16.

30. See Michael A. Messner, *Power at Play: Sports and the Problem of Masculinity* (Boston: Beacon, 1992).

31. Originally called Bank One Ballpark (a.k.a. the "Bob") when it opened in 1998, the name of Arizona's ballpark was changed to Chase Field on September 23, 2005. Bank One Corporation, which owned the naming rights to the stadium, merged with J. P. Morgan Chase & Company in 2004. San Francisco's ballpark has had three different names since it opened in 2000. Pacific Telesis Group paid $53 million in 1996 to name the ballpark Pacific Bell Park during the years 2000 through 2019. SBC Communications, Inc., then known as Southwestern Bell Corp., bought Pacific Telesis Corp. in 1997 and changed the name of the ballpark to SBC Park on January 1, 2004. SBC Communications, Inc., merged with AT&T Corp. in 2005. The new company, known as AT&T, Inc., announced on February 3, 2006, that the name of the ballpark would be changed to AT&T Park on March 1, 2006.

32. The term "public sociology" was first introduced by Herbert Gans in his presidential address to the American Sociological Association, Atlanta, Georgia, August 24–28, 1988. The address was entitled "Sociology in America: The Discipline and the Public."

NOTES TO CHAPTER 2

1. While doing research on the origins of baseball, historian John Thorn stumbled on a document revealing a 1791 bylaw that prohibited anyone from playing baseball within eighty yards of Pittsfield's new town meeting house. According to Thorn, "It's clear that not only was baseball played here in 1791, but it was rampant. . . . It was rampant enough to have an ordinance against it." Quoted in "Pittsfield Stakes Its Claim to Baseball History," Adam Gorlick, *Boston Globe*, 11 May 2004.

2. Red Sox CEO Larry Lucchino publicly anointed the Yankees the "Evil Empire" during the off-season prior to the 2003 season. Lucchino and Co. were upset that the Yankees successfully outbid them and signed pitching ace and Cuban defector Jose Contreras.

3. Game 7 of the 2003 American League Championship Series ended in another gut-wrenching loss to the Yankees for Red Sox fans, old and young. Five outs away from their first trip to the World Series since 1986, Red Sox manager Grady Little chose not to pull his ace, Red Sox starting pitcher Pedro Martinez, with the Red Sox up 5–2. Shortly after Little's decision, a decision that would lead to his eventual firing, Martinez gave up three runs, and the game was tied 5–5. The score remained the same until Aaron Boone crushed a Tim Wakefield pitch in the eleventh inning for a home run to left field, sending the Yankees to the World Series and plunging a dagger into the heart of Red Sox Nation. I watched Game 7 in an apartment in Boston's South End with four lifelong Red Sox fans. These men cried. And they surely were not the only men who shed tears that night. As I drove home to my apartment in Brighton, which brought

me near Fenway Park and through Kenmore Square, I saw men, women, and children wandering aimlessly out of the bars and through the streets as if they were collectively reenacting a scene from *Night of the Living Dead*. Talk of curses and ghosts filled the air over the course of the next few weeks as the city mourned. Even more present was the idea that the Red Sox's dramatic loss served as an initiation rite for the youngest generation of Red Sox fans. The year 2003 was going to be a defining moment for young fans the way the heartbreaks of 1986, 1978, 1975, 1967, and 1946 were for previous generations. Of course, some, though not all, of those sentiments changed a year later.

4. For good historical accounts of the connections between urbanization and the rise of consumerism, see Gunther Barth, *City People: The Rise of Modern City Culture in Nineteenth-Century America* (New York: Oxford University Press, 1980); Steven A. Riess, *City Games: The Evolution of American Urban Society and the Rise of Sports* (Urbana: University of Illinois Press, 1989); David Nasaw, *Going Out: The Rise and Fall of Public Amusements* (New York: Basic Books, 1993); Michael G. Kammen, *American Culture, American Tastes: Social Change and the 20th Century* (New York: Knopf, 1999); Daniel J. Monti, *The American City: A Social and Cultural History* (Malden, MA: Blackwell, 1999); and Howard P. Chudacoff and Judith E. Smith, *The Evolution of American Urban Society* (Englewood Cliffs, NJ: Prentice-Hall, 2000)

5. Robert F. Bluthardt, "Fenway Park and the Golden Age of the Baseball Park, 1909–1915," *Journal of Popular Culture* (21:1, 1987): 43–52; Riess, *City Games*; Karl B. Raitz, ed., *The Theater of Sport* (Baltimore: Johns Hopkins University Press, 1995); and Michael N. Danielson, *Home Team: Professional Sports and the American Metropolis* (Princeton, NJ: Princeton University Press, 1997).

6. Michael Schudson, "How Culture Works: Perspectives from Media Studies on the Efficacy of Symbols," *Theory and Society* (18:2, 1989): 170.

7. See Theodor W. Adorno, "Valery Proust Museum," in *Prisms (Cambridge, MA: MIT Press, 1981)*.

8. Barbara Johnstone, *Stories, Community, and Place: Narratives from Middle America* (Bloomington: Indiana University Press, 1990), 90.

9. See David R. Maines and Jeffrey C. Bridger, "Narratives, Community and Land Use Decisions," *Social Science Journal* (29:4, 1992): 363–80; and John Walton, *Storied Land: Community and Memory in Monterey* (Berkeley: University of California Press, 2001).

10. Barry Schwartz, *Abraham Lincoln and the Forge of National Memory* (Chicago: University of Chicago Press, 2000), 9.

11. Monti, *The American City*, 18.

12. Thomas L. Altherr, "A Swing and a Myth: The Persistence of Baseball in the American Imagination," in Alvin L. Hall, ed., *Cooperstown Symposium on Baseball and the American Culture* (Oneonta: State University of New York at Oneonta, 1991), 62.

13. Riess, *City Games*, 219.

14. Johnstone, *Stories, Community, and Place*, 26.

15. For good discussions of Olmsted's projects, see Thomas Bender, *Toward an Urban Vision: Ideas and Institutions in Nineteenth-Century America* (Lexington: University Press of Kentucky, 1975); Cynthia Zaitzevsky, *Frederick Law Olmsted and the Boston Park System* (Cambridge, MA: Harvard University Press, 1982); Lawrence W. Kennedy, *Planning the City upon a Hill: Boston since 1630* (Amherst: University of Massachusetts Press, 1992); and Roy Rosenzweig and Elizabeth Blackmar, *The Park and the People: A History of Central Park* (Ithaca, NY: Cornell University Press, 1992).

16. Quoted in Michael Gershman, *Diamonds: The Evolution of Ballparks* (Boston: Houghton Mifflin, 1993), 107.

17. Bluthardt, "Fenway Park and the Golden Age," 44.

18. "Major League Baseball," *Sports Facility Reports* (National Sports Law Institute of Marquette University Law School, Milwaukee, WI) (4:1, 6 June 2003): appendix 1.

19. According to Marcita Thompson, director of Fenway Park Enterprises, approximately eighty-five thousand people took the guided tour at Fenway Park in 2003. The Red Sox began offering tours year-round, rather than only during the summer, in 2002. This is one of the many changes the Henry-Werner ownership group has made to make the ballpark more available for both residents and tourists.

20. Anselm L. Strauss, *Mirrors and Masks: The Search for Identity* (San Francisco: Sociology Press, 1969), 67.

21. Glenn Stout and Richard A. Johnson, *Red Sox Century: One Hundred Years of Red Sox Baseball* (Boston: Houghton Mifflin, 2004), 72–73.

22. Dan Shaughnessy, *At Fenway: Dispatches from Red Sox Nation* (New York: Crown, 1996), 31.

23. Quoted in Stout and Johnson, *Red Sox Century*, 186.

24. "Fenway Park Is Formally Opened with Red Sox Win," Paul Shannon, *Boston Post*, 21 April 1912, reprinted in Glenn Stout, ed., *Impossible Dreams: A Red Sox Collection* (Boston: Houghton Mifflin, 2003), 48.

25. Stout and Johnson, *Red Sox Century*, 78.

26. Quoted in ibid., 77.

27. "Fenway Park Is Formally Opened."

28. Riess, *City Games*.

29. About sixty-five thousand people a year visit Dyersville, Iowa, between April and November to see the site where *Field of Dreams* was filmed, lending support to the film's adage: "If you build it, they will come."

30. Riess, *City Games*, 213; Bluthardt, "Fenway Park and the Golden Age," 43–52.

31. Stephen Hardy, "Sport in Urbanizing America: A Historical Review," *Journal of Urban History* (23:6, 1997): 676.

32. See Richard Slotkin, *Gunfighter Nation: The Myth of the Frontier in Twentieth-Century America* (New York: Atheneum, 1992), 1–26.

33. David Block, *Baseball Before We Knew It: A Search for the Roots of the Game* (Lincoln: University of Nebraska Press, 2005), 299.

34. George B. Kirsch, *The Creation of American Team Sports: Baseball and Cricket, 1838–72* (Urbana: University of Illinois Press, 1989), 50.

35. Quoted in ibid., 51.

36. See Block, *Baseball Before We Knew It*, chap. 3.

37. Ibid., 16–21.

38. Kirsch, *The Creation of American Team Sports*, 52.

39. See Block, *Baseball Before We Knew It*.

40. See Chudacoff and Smith, *The Evolution of American Urban Society*, chaps. 5, 8.

41. G. Edward White, *Creating the National Pastime: Baseball Transforms Itself, 1903–1953* (Princeton, NJ: Princeton University Press, 1996), 23.

42. George Kirsch notes that "references to the 'national game of baseball' appeared frequently in the daily and sporting press throughout the late 1850s, even before the modern form actually achieved a truly national scope." Kirsch, *The Creation of American Team Sports*, 92.

43. Ibid., 55.

44. David Quentin Voigt, *American Baseball* (University Park: Pennsylvania State University Press, 1983), vii.

45. Claude S. Fischer, "Change in Leisure Activities, 1890–1940," *Journal of Social History* (28:1, 1994): 469.

46. See Warren Jay Goldstein, *Playing for Keeps: A History of Early Baseball* (Ithaca, NY: Cornell University Press, 1989).

47. On the mass media's role in the production of nostalgia, see Fred Davis, *Yearning for Yesterday: A Sociology of Nostalgia* (New York: Free Press, 1979), 125–42. For the media's influence on the rise and fall of players' fame, see David L. Andrews and Steven J. Jackson, eds., *Sport Stars: The Cultural Politics of Sporting Celebrity* (New York: Routledge, 2001).

48. Georg Simmel, *On Individuality and Social Forms* (Chicago: University of Chicago Press, 1971), 136.

49. Quoted in Voigt, *American Baseball*, 49.

50. Steven A. Riess, *Touching Base: Professional Baseball and American Culture in the Progressive Era* (Westport, CT: Greenwood, 1980), 222.

51. Extending Richard Hofstader's argument about an overarching American "covenant of comity," Monti details the ways that Americans have negotiated "the promise of *prosperity* and the accomplishment of *order*." Monti, *The American City*, 40, emphasis in the original.

52. For a detailed history of sports in Boston, see Stephen Hardy, *How Boston Played: Sport, Recreation, and Community, 1865–1915* (Boston: Northeastern University Press, 1982).

53. John R. Betts, "Mind and Body in Early American Thought," *Journal of American History* (54:2, 1968): 27–42.

54. Quoted in Kirsch, *The Creation of American Team Sports*, 15.

55. See Claude S. Fischer, *The Urban Experience* (New York: Harcourt Brace Jovanovich, 1976).

56. Riess, *City Games*, 14–15.

57. Ibid., 15.

58. Ibid., 16.

59. Melvin L. Adelman, *A Sporting Time: New York City and the Rise of Modern Athletics, 1820–70* (Urbana: University of Illinois Press, 1986).

60. See Roy Rosenzweig, *Eight Hours for What We Will: Workers and Leisure in an Industrial City, 1870–1920* (New York: Cambridge University Press, 1983).

61. Benjamin G. Rader, *In Its Own Image: How Television Has Transformed Sports* (New York: Free Press, 1984), 2.

62. Riess, *Touching Base*, 25; see Linda A. Kittel, "From Dreams to Diamonds to Dictionaries: Baseball as Acculturating Force," in Hall, ed., *Cooperstown Symposium*.

63. Steven M. Gelber, "Working at Playing: The Culture of the Work Place and the Rise of Baseball," *Journal of Social History* (16, 1983): 3–22; Goldstein, *Playing for Keeps*. Melvin Adelman challenges Gelber's "congruence" theory, which argues that people seek to replicate their work situations, attitudes, and behaviors in their leisure time. Adelman acknowledges the oversimplification of a strict unidirectional work-leisure dichotomy and instead rightly favors a more dialectical approach whereby actors' intentions are given equal weight to structural conditions. Thus, "the *a priori* assumption that work determined leisure" is nonsensical from a dialectical standpoint. Melvin L. Adelman, "Baseball, Business, and the Work Place: Gelber's Thesis Reexamined," *Journal of Social History* (23:2, 1989): 285–301.

64. Henry S. Curtis, *The Practical Conduct of Play* (New York: Macmillan, 1915), 212.

65. Riess, *Touching Base*, 13–14, emphasis added.

66. Danielson, *Home Team*, 22.

67. See Riess, *Touching Base*, 23–28.

68. Quoted in ibid., 24.

69. Riess, *City Games*, 67.

70. For a good collection on "hooliganism" as global social problem, see Eric Dunning, Patrick Murphy, Ivan Waddington, and Antonios Astrinakis, eds., *Fighting Fans: Football Hooliganism as a World Phenomenon* (Dublin, Ireland: University College Dublin Press, 2002).

71. Quoted in Riess, *Touching Base*, 27–28.

72. Barth, *City People*, 154.

73. For a good review of the competing historical literature about baseball's inclusive/exclusive qualities, see Hardy, "Sport in Urbanizing America."

74. Riess, *City Games*, 101–3; also see Robin Faith Bachin, *Building the South Side: Urban Space and Civic Culture in Chicago, 1890–1919* (Chicago: University of Chicago Press, 2004).

75. Nasaw, *Going Out*, 99.

76. For a detailed history of race relations within the Red Sox organization and the city, see Howard Bryant, *Shut Out: A Story of Race and Baseball in Boston* (New York: Routledge, 2002).

77. See Catherine Cocks, *Doing the Town: The Rise of Urban Tourism in the United States, 1850–1915* (Berkeley: University of California Press, 2001).

78. The argument that cities use ballparks to enhance their "major league" status can be found in Paul M. Anderson, "Playing the Stadium Game," *Journal of Sport and Social Issues* (21:1, 1997): 103–11; Danielson, *Home Team*; and Timothy J. Curry, Kent P. Schwirian, and Rachel A. Woldoff, *High Stakes: Big Time Sports and Downtown Redevelopment* (Columbus: Ohio State University Press, 2004).

79. Gerald D. Suttles, "The Cumulative Texture of Local Urban Culture," *American Journal of Sociology* (90:2, 1984): 283–304.

80. Monti, *The American City*, 105.

81. Danielson, *Home Team*, 104.

82. Quoted in "Friendly and Familiar Confines," William Gildea, *Washington Post*, 12 April 1992. For a detailed discussion that places the construction of Camden Yards within the context of the entire redevelopment of Baltimore's Inner Harbor, see Donald F. Norris, "If We Build It, They Will Come! Tourism-Based Economic Development in Baltimore," in Dennis R. Judd, ed., *The Infrastructure of Play: Building the Tourist City* (Armonk, NY: M. E. Sharpe, 2003).

83. "No Hits, No Runs, One Error: The Dome," Ronald Smothers, *New York Times*, 15 June 1991.

84. For an exploration of the collective emotional loss suffered by Brooklyn's urban community as a result of the Dodgers' move to Los Angeles, see Carl E. Prince, *Brooklyn's Dodgers: The Bums, the Borough, and the Best of Baseball* (New York: Oxford University Press, 1996).

85. Quoted in Brad Schultz, "A Geographical Study of the American Ballpark," *International Journal of the History of Sport* (20:1, 2003): 140.

86. For extended discussions that link American sports and religion, see George Gmelch, "Baseball Magic," *Transaction* (8:8, 1971): 39–43; Michael Novak, *The Joy of Sports: End Zones, Bases, Baskets, Balls, and the Consecration of the American Spirit* (New York: Basic Books, 1976); Charles S. Prebish, ed., *Reli-*

gion and Sport: The Meeting of Sacred and Profane (Westport, CT: Greenwood, 1993); Joseph L. Price, ed., *From Season to Season: Sports as American Religion* (Macon, GA: Mercer University Press, 2001); and Christopher H. Evans and William R. Herzog II, eds., *The Faith of 50 Million: Baseball, Religion, and American Culture* (Louisville, KY: Westminster John Knox Press, 2002).

NOTES TO CHAPTER 3

1. Philip J. Lowry, *Green Cathedrals: The Ultimate Celebration of All 271 Major League and Negro League Ballparks Past and Present* (Reading, MA: Addison-Wesley, 1992), 11.

2. For a detailed discussion of "identity continuity," as well as "identity discontinuity," see Fred Davis, *Yearning for Yesterday: A Sociology of Nostalgia* (New York: Free Press, 1979), and for a recent ethnographic test of Davis's ideas and a critique of his understanding of the role of place for identity construction and maintenance, see Melinda J. Milligan, "Displacement and Identity Discontinuity: The Role of Nostalgia in Establishing New Identity Categories," *Symbolic Interaction* (26:3, 2003): 381–403.

3. R. Richard Wohl and Anselm L. Strauss, "Symbolic Representation and the Urban Milieu," *American Journal of Sociology* (63:5, 1958): 523–32.

4. Lyn H. Lofland, *The Public Realm: Exploring the City's Quintessential Social Territory* (Hawthorne, NY: Aldine de Gruyter, 1998), 65–66. Lofland discusses these two types of locales as distinct categories. But in the case of Fenway Park, the two are intertwined. One could easily assume that when a place becomes familiar it loses its special or unique significance and becomes simply mundane. This is far from true at Fenway. Even the people who work there, from the vendors to the executive assistants to the players, still get a bit giddy when they talk about the ballpark.

5. Mihaly Csikszentmihalyi and Eugene Rochberg-Halton, *The Meaning of Things: Domestic Symbols and the Self* (New York: Cambridge University Press, 1981), 122.

6. Ray Oldenburg, *The Great Good Place: Cafés, Coffee Shops, Community Centers, Beauty Parlors, General Stores, Bars, Hangouts and How They Get You through the Day* (New York: Paragon House, 1989), 16.

7. Daniel J. Monti, *The American City: A Social and Cultural History* (Malden, MA: Blackwell, 1999), 10; also see Lynn Hollen Lees, "Urban Public Space and Imagined Communities in the 1980s and 1990s," *Journal of Urban History* (20:4, 1994): 442–58.

8. Lofland, *The Public Realm*, 74.

9. Stanley Milgram, *The Individual in a Social World: Essays and Experiments* (New York: McGraw-Hill, 1977), 68–71.

10. "A public character is anyone who is in frequent contact with a wide circle of people and who is sufficiently interested to make himself a public character. A public character need have no special talents or wisdom to fulfill his function—although he often does. He just needs to be present, and there need to be enough of his counterparts. His main qualification is that he is public, that he talks to a lot of different people." Jane Jacobs, *The Death and Life of Great American Cities* (New York: Vintage, 1961), 68.

11. For an ethnographic description of the lives of book vendors who "tame" the sidewalks of New York, see Mitchell Duneier, *Sidewalk* (New York: Farrar, Straus and Giroux, 1999).

12. Lofland, *The Public Realm*.

13. "Absence of 'George the Peanut Guy,' a Fixture for Three Decades, Leaves Void in Fenway Lineup," Peter DeMarco, *Boston Globe*, 16 April 2004.

14. Quoted in ibid.

15. "Romney Campaign Get a Hit at Fenway," Joanna Wiess, *Boston Globe*, 11 June 2002.

16. Rites of inversions and rites of reversal often involve the switching of roles between high- and low-status persons. See Michael Ian Borer, "Rites of Inversion," in Frank A. Salamone, ed., *Encyclopedia of Religious Rites, Rituals, and Festivals* (New York: Routledge, 2004).

17. For the multiple functions of coffee shops, see Oldenburg, *The Great Good Place*, chap. 10; Melinda J. Milligan, "Interactional Past and Potential: The Social Construction of Place Attachment," *Symbolic Interaction* (21:1, 1998): 1–33; and Milligan, "Displacement and Identity Discontinuity". For bars and taverns, see Oldenburg, *The Great Good Place*; Roy Rosenzweig, *Eight Hours for What We Will: Workers and Leisure in an Industrial City, 1870–1920* (New York: Cambridge University Press, 1983); and Michael A. Katovich and William A. Reese II, "The Regular: Full-Time Identities and Memberships in an Urban Bar," *Journal of Contemporary Ethnography* (16:3, 1987): 308–43. The idea that businesses play many different roles in the communities they serve and, in effect, function as "civic associations" can be found in Michael Ian Borer and Daniel J. Monti Jr., "Community, Commerce, and Consumption: Businesses as Civic Associations," in Michael Ian Borer, ed., *Varieties of Urban Experience: The American City and the Practice of Culture* (Lanham, MD: University Press of America, 2006).

18. Warren Jay Goldstein, *Playing for Keeps: A History of Early Baseball* (Ithaca, NY: Cornell University Press, 1989), 2–3.

19. Monti, *The American City*, 321.

20. Ibid., 322.

21. Paul M. Anderson, "Playing the Stadium Game," *Journal of Sport and Social Issues* (21:1, 1997): 103.

22. Benjamin G. Rader, *In Its Own Image: How Television Has Transformed Sports* (New York: Free Press, 1984), 197.

23. See "Rallying Cry Spurs Sox to Finish Ride," Joseph P. Kahn, *Boston Globe*, 24 September 2003.

24. "Red Sox Hit Jackpot, Land Shilling," Bob Hohler, *Boston Globe*, 29 November 2003.

25. "Schilling Talked a Good Game—and Was a Man of His Word," Jackie MacMullan, *Boston Globe*, 31 October 2004.

26. Soon after Schilling arrived in Boston, he set up a chapter of his organization there, to which he donates $100 a strikeout and $100 a win three times over, which he also does for the chapters in his two former baseball homes, Arizona and Philadelphia.

27. Details of this story were reported in "Superfan Now Rests at Fenway," Gayle Fee and Laura Raposa, *Boston Herald*, 7 October 2002.

28. At the time, no one knew about the public debacle that would ensue regarding Williams's postmortem head and body, which were separated and frozen in liquid nitrogen at the Arizona-based Alcor Life Extension Foundation later that summer. The decision to cryogenically freeze Williams was made by his son, John Henry, and has been disputed by his daughter, Bobby Jo William Ferrell, who declared that her father's remains should be cremated and then sprinkled off the coast of the Florida Keys, as the Red Sox legend's will dictates. See "Williams Daughter: Body Being Frozen," Beth Daley, *Boston Globe*, 7 June 2002.

29. For a discussion of both cemetery and crematorium placement, see the section "Landscapes of Death," in Chris C. Park, *Sacred Worlds: An Introduction to Geography and Religion* (New York: Routledge, 1994), 213–26.

30. Stephen Prothero, "Cremation American Style: Consumer's Last Rites," in Marjorie B. Garber and Rebecca L. Walkowitz, eds., *One Nation under God? Religion and American Culture* (New York: Routledge, 1999), 204.

31. "Taking the Grim Out of Reaper: Baby Boomers Are Putting a New, Often Merrier, Spin on Last Rites," Joseph P. Kahn, *Boston Globe Magazine*, 29 September 2002.

32. This story was posted by Sarah (under the name BoSox33) on a message board on modernbride.com. The post contained a link to a website that included pictures of the tour and the proposal.

33. Cochran told me that, in retrospect, it reminded him of an old photograph of the "Gas House Gang," the 1934 St. Louis Cardinals.

34. "The Only Tie Ever Recorded at Fenway?" Beth Carney and Jim Sullivan, *Boston Globe*, 23 May 2000.

35. At the start of the 2004 season the Red Sox began offering three "Wedding Packages." Each package included a wedding ceremony on the Right Field Roof Deck overlooking the ballpark, and the cost ranged from $3,000 to $10,000.

36. Quoted in "Field of Dreams: This Is the Year for Fenway Couple," Dana Bisbee, *Boston Herald*, 7 December 2003.

37. "Parade of Champs: Series Bliss Turns Serious for This Couple," *Boston Herald*, 30 October 2004.

38. Lowry, *Green Cathedrals*, 1.

39. Ibid., 2.

40. "Hitting It Off at Fenway," Dan Shaughnessy, *Boston Globe*, 16 May 2001.

41. Sex and Fenway Park, however, have been connected in other ways. The surrounding area, known as the Fens, which is composed of fifteen-foot-high weeds and other strange-looking vegetation, has a longstanding tradition as a place where men go to seek out sex with other men.

42. John E. Bodnar, *Remaking America: Public Memory, Commemoration, and Patriotism in the Twentieth Century* (Princeton, NJ: Princeton University Press, 1992), 14.

43. Ibid., 14–15.

44. "Red Sox Owners Fielding More Non-Game Revenue," Naomi Aoki, *Boston Globe*, 16 October 2004.

45. See Monti, *The American City*, chap. 8.

46. According to Monti, "The essential feature of subscription campaigns was that persons volunteered their own labor or game money to a project that was deemed good but probably would not have been initiated otherwise. . . . The money or help sometimes was viewed as an "investment" when contributors thought that a profit might be realized or they wanted to make the point that the cause being supported someday would yield a social and economic dividend for the whole community." Ibid., 248–49.

47. Quoted in "Fenway Conversion: Springsteen Turns Ballpark into House Party," Michael Rosenwald and Peter DeMarco, *Boston Globe*, 7 September 2003.

48. "Margaritaville II: Tavern Bracing to Refill Parrotheads," *Boston Herald*, 12 September 2004.

49. "Still Not Fading Away," Eileen McNamara, *Boston Globe*, 16 March 2005.

50. "Hub's Heavy Hitters Go Deep for ABCD," Scott Van Voorhis, *Boston Herald*, 14 July 2002; "ABCD Makes Fenway Real Field of Dreams," Bob Ryan, *Boston Globe*, 6 June 2002; "This Giving of Their Ballpark Is as Good as It Gets," Bob Ryan, *Boston Globe*, 12 May 2004.

51. "Auditioning for Parents," David Abel, *Boston Globe*, 29 August 2001; "Fenway Plays Host to Adoption Party," David Abel, *Boston Globe*, 9 September 2001; "Party Fosters Family Hope," Jules Crittenden, *Boston Herald*, 9 September 2001.

52. Glenn Stout and Richard A. Johnson, *Red Sox Century: One Hundred Years of Red Sox Baseball* (Boston: Houghton Mifflin, 2004), 76.

53. See "Falsehood Marks Republican Pleas, President Asserts," C. P. Trussell, *New York Times*, 5 November 1944; "Text of Roosevelt's Final Campaign Address in Boston," *New York Times*, 5 November 1944.

54. For a good discussion of the turbulent race relations in the Red Sox organization's past, see Howard Bryant, *Shut Out: A Story of Race and Baseball in Boston* (New York: Routledge, 2002).

55. "Young Catholics Gather Today at Fenway," Eric Convey, *Boston Herald*, 29 April 2000; "Cardinal Leads Thousands in Pilgrimage," Doug Hanchett, *Boston Herald*, 30 April 2000.

56. Robert N. Bellah, *Beyond Belief: Essays on Religion in a Post-traditional World* (New York: Harper & Row, 1970).

57. Barry Schwartz, *George Washington: The Making of an American Symbol* (New York: Free Press, 1987); Barry Schwartz, *Abraham Lincoln and the Forge of National Memory* (Chicago: University of Chicago Press, 2000); and Bodnar, *Remaking America*.

58. Christopher H. Evans and William R. Herzog II, eds., *The Faith of 50 Million: Baseball, Religion, and American Culture* (Louisville, KY: Westminster John Knox Press, 2002).

59. Quoted in "For Father's Day, Catch This: Red Sox Offer Parents the Gift of a Romp across Fenway's Greens," Scott S. Greenberger, *Boston Globe*, 6 June 2002.

60. Boston Red Sox press release, 16 June 2004.

61. Émile Durkheim, *The Elementary Forms of the Religious Life* (New York: Free Press, 1965), 400, 466.

62. "Fenway Is the Essence of Spring in New England," Scott MacKay, *Providence Journal*, 10 April 2004.

63. Quoted in "Banner Day at Fenway: World Champions Ring in New Year," Rich Thompson, *Boston Herald*, 11 April 2005.

64. The notion of competitive religious firms comes from the "religious economies" paradigm that sees religions as "firms," beliefs as "products," and believers as rational "consumers." Sociologists who work from this paradigm have yet to analyze the competition between conventional and civic religious organizations. For the "religious economies" paradigm, see Roger Finke and Rodney Stark, "Religious Economies and Sacred Canopies," *American Sociological Review* (53, 1988): 41–49; R. Stephen Warner, "Work in Progress toward a New Paradigm for the Sociological Study of Religion in the United States," *American Journal of Sociology* (98:5, 1993): 1044–93; and Rodney Stark, *One True God: Historical Consequences of Monotheism* (Princeton, NJ: Princeton University Press, 2001).

65. Quoted in "Cheers, Boos for Opening Day Beer Ban," Anthony Flint and Stephanie Ebbert, *Boston Globe*, 4 April 1998; "Opening Day at Fenway Always Sacred for Fans," Jack Sullivan, *Boston Herald*, 10 April 1998.

66. Peter L. Berger, *The Sacred Canopy: Elements of a Sociological Theory of Religion* (Garden City, NY: Doubleday, 1967).

67. Gunther Barth, *City People: The Rise of Modern City Culture in Nineteenth-Century America* (New York: Oxford University Press, 1980), 4.

68. Alan Klein studied the Pedromania/"embracing the ace" phenomena, seeking to compare and find a disjuncture between the media's reportage of Latinos' increased presence at Fenway Park and the actual sentiments of both the Latinos and Anglos who attended the games. He "tried to show that what might appear as unity on one level, is in fact very different, that is, fractious at another." Alan Klein, "Latinizing Fenway Park: A Cultural Critique of the Boston Red Sox," *Sociology of Sport Journal* (17, 2000): 420. Klein, however, fails to note that in spite of some of the negative sentiments he reports between Latinos and Anglos, they still managed to get along well enough together at the ballpark to escape without incident or provocation. Of course, this does not mean that everyone has to be pleased with everyone else; the urban community is never a matter of pure consensus.

69. Quoted in "At Fenway, It's Fiesta Time," Cindy Rodriguez, *Boston Globe*, 6 June 2001.

70. Quoted in ibid.

71. John A. Hall and Charles Lindholm, *Is America Breaking Apart?* (Princeton, NJ: Princeton University Press, 1999), 27. Even though Tocqueville, a French aristocrat, came to the United States with his co-researcher Gustave de Beaumont to study the penitentiary system, he sailed away with the seeds of a "grounded" theoretical treatise on the social life of the newly budding democracy. See Alexis de Tocqueville, *Democracy in America* (New York: Vintage Books, 1945). For a discussion of Tocqueville's legacy as a sociologist, see the introductory essay in John Stone and Stephen Mennell, eds., *Alexis de Tocqueville: On Democracy, Revolution, and Society* (Chicago: University of Chicago Press, 1980).

72. Hall and Lindholm, *Is America Breaking Apart?* 128, emphasis in the original.

NOTES TO CHAPTER 4

1. Émile Durkheim, *The Elementary Forms of the Religious Life* (New York: Free Press, 1965), 52.

2. Ibid., 217.

3. Yi-Fu Tuan, "Sacred Space: Exploration of an Idea," in Karl W. Butzer, ed., *Dimensions of Human Geography: Essays on Some Familiar and Neglected Themes* (Chicago: University of Chicago Press, 1978).

4. Durkheim, *The Elementary Forms of the Religious Life*, 55.

5. Colleen McDannell, *Material Christianity: Religion and Popular Culture in America* (New Haven, CT: Yale University Press, 1995), 6.

6. Ibid., 25.

7. Ibid., 45.

8. "At Festivals, Faith, Rock, and T-Shirts Take Center Stage," John Leland, *New York Times*, 5 July 2003.

9. Chris C. Park, *Sacred Worlds: An Introduction to Geography and Religion* (New York: Routledge, 1994), 263, 265.

10. David E. Sopher, *Geography of Religions* (Englewood Cliffs, NJ: Prentice-Hall, 1967), 52.

11. For good, detailed discussions of the relationship between pilgrimages and tourism, see Victor Turner and Edith L. B. Turner, *Image and Pilgrimage in Christian Culture: Anthropological Perspectives* (Oxford, UK: Blackwell, 1978); and Jaakko Suvantola, *Tourists' Experience of Place* (Burlington, VT: Ashgate, 2002).

12. See Leigh Eric Schmidt, *Consumer Rites: The Buying and Selling of American Holidays* (Princeton, NJ: Princeton University Press, 1995).

13. For a sincere and nonironic use of the term "pilgrimage" to describe going to Fenway Park and major- and minor-league ballparks, see www.baseballpilgrimages.com.

14. In order to detect the multiple facets of local urban culture, Gerald Suttles argues that sociologists should be looking "not just [at] what people put in museums, but what they put on their car bumpers and T-shirts." Gerald D. Suttles, "The Cumulative Texture of Local Urban Culture," *American Journal of Sociology* (90:2, 1984): 284. In Boston and throughout the New England region, it is easy to find cars with bumper stickers like "I Love Fenway Park," "Fenway Faithful," and "Save Fenway Park!" and to find people wearing T-shirts that honor the ballpark.

15. "Cannoncockers Build Miniature Version of Fenway Park in Iraq," Cpl. Veronika R. Tuskowski, United States Marine Corps official press release, 31 August 2004.

16. Even though I am focusing on consumption before and after the point of purchase, I acknowledge the act of purchasing as an important means of cultural exchange as well. Marcel Mauss's classic analysis of gift-giving remains a seminal text for studies of material culture. Marcel Mauss, *The Gift: The Form and Reason for Exchange in Archaic Societies* (London: Routledge, 1950).

17. In his discussion of the role of the "generalized other" (or culture "out there") in the development of the individual self, George Herbert Mead addressed, though very briefly, the social significance of individuals' interactions with material objects. A Meadian theory of consumption, then, could begin with the following quotation from :

It is possible for inanimate objects, no less than other human organisms, to form parts of the generalized and organized—the completely socialized—other for any given human individual, in so far that he responds to such objects socially or in a social fashion (by means of the mechanism of thought, the internalized conversation of gestures). Any thing—any object or set of objects, whether animate or inanimate, human or animal, or merely physical—toward which he acts, or to which he responds, socially, is an element in what for him is the generalized other; by taking the attitudes of which toward himself he becomes conscious of himself as an object or individual, and thus develops a self or personality.

George Herbert Mead, *Mind, Self, and Society: From the Standpoint of a Social Behaviorist* (Chicago: University of Chicago Press, 1934), 154n. Following Mead's line of thought, consumption is akin to having a conversation with a material object in the sense that it involves interpretation and assessment of the group's relationship to it and its relationship to the individual.

18. Pierre Bourdieu, *Distinction: A Social Critique of the Judgement of Taste* (Cambridge, MA: Harvard University Press, 1984), 2.

19. For a narrower though complementary take on the sacred acts of consumption in cities, see Ira G. Zepp Jr., *The New Religious Image of Urban America: The Shopping Mall as Ceremonial Center* (Niwot: University Press of Colorado, 1997).

20. Kalle Lasn, *Culture Jam: How to Reverse America's Suicidal Consumer Binge—and Why We Must* (New York: HarperCollins, 1999).

21. See Henry Jenkins, *Textual Poachers: Television Fans and Participatory Culture* (New York: Routledge, 1992).

22. See M. G. Lord, *Forever Barbie: The Unauthorized Biography of a Real Doll* (New York: Walker & Co., 2004).

23. Bourdieu, *Distinction*; David Halle, *Inside Culture: Class, Culture, and Everyday Life in Modern America* (Chicago: University of Chicago Press, 1994).

24. Daniel J. Monti, *The American City: A Social and Cultural History* (Malden, MA: Blackwell, 1999), 340; for "conspicuous consumption," see Thorstein Veblen, *The Theory of the Leisure Class* (New York: Macmillan, 1899).

25. At the beginning of the 2005 season, a high-end retailer started selling "classy" Red Sox jewelry for people to show their Red Sox allegiance at black-tie affairs and other formal events. Shreve, Crump & Low donate a percentage of its earnings from Red Sox jewelry to the Red Sox Foundation. The items for sale include a twelve-karat-gold Red Sox pin ($225), a sterling-silver Red Sox charm ($225), a fourteen-karat Fenway Park pin ($325), and sterling-silver Red Sox cuff links ($85). See "Flash on the Fan: Upscale Red Sox 'Bling' Shows Off Team Spirit in Stylish Fashion," Meredith Goldstein, *Boston Globe*, 7 April 2005.

26. Monti, *The American City*, 341.

27. "On Foot or by Phone, Fans Chase Few Tickets," Bruce Mohl and Mac Daniel, *Boston Globe*, 22 October 2004.

28. Quoted in "Winning Tickets: For Fans, Drizzle, Long Lines Worth the Soggy Wait," Tracy Jan, *Boston Globe*, 12 December 2004.

29. A sacred place provides an orientation point from which the world can be understood. Mircea Eliade calls this place the *axis mundi*, "the navel of the world," that connects the transcendent and the imminent, the sacred and the profane. Mircea Eliade, *The Sacred and the Profane: The Nature of Religion* (New York: Harcourt Brace, 1959). On the importance of the "center" for the way we experience spaces and places, see Yi-Fu Tuan, *Space and Place: The Perspective of Experience* (Minneapolis: University of Minnesota Press, 1977), 126, 149–50.

30. Quoted in "Clashing with Pinstripes: Red Sox Fans Recoil in Yankees' Backyard," Davie Koeppel, *New York Times*, 21 May 2003.

31. Quoted in "Red Sox Nation Really Does Cover the Nation—and Beyond," Mark Pratt, *Boston Globe*, 25 October 2005.

32. "Pennant Fever: Sox Fans Find Safe Haven in NYC," Lauren J. Sweet, *Boston Herald*, 14 October 2004. The Riviera eventually began charging admission to the bar on game days.

33. Quoted in "Red Sox Nation Thrives in California," Peter DeMarco, *Boston Globe*, 6 October 2004.

34. Quoted in "Lights! Camera! Fenway! Beloved Ballpark a Hollywood Hit," Sean L. McCarthy, *Boston Herald*, 9 April 2005.

35. "Down with a Bad 'Fever,'" Bill Simmons, ESPN.com, http://sports.espn.go.com/espn/page2/story?page=simmons/050420 emphasis in the original.

36. Here is how three Boston reporters explain the "Tessie" phenomenon: Back in the Good Old Days, when Boston's ball club won a string of World Series victories, there was a group of fans called the Royal Rooters. The boisterous—some might say drunken—group of Boston lads, were the original Red Sox Nation and they were out in force when their team, led by the immortal Cy Young, took on Honus Wagner's Pittsburgh Pirates in the very first World Series. Things started out rather poorly for the Olde Town Team and they fell behind Pittsburgh four games to one in the best-of-nine series. At Game Six, with Young on the mound and the game tied 0–0 in the seventh, the Rooters began singing what Pittsburgh outfielder Tommy Leach would later call "that damn Tessie song." . . . To the Rooters' delight, Boston went on to win the next five games—and the World Series. Pittsburgh players gave credit to the "Tessie"-singing fans for the amazing comeback.

"'Tessie' Remake May Dropkick the Sox Curse," Gayle Fee and Laura Raposa with Nichole Gleisner, *Boston Herald*, 26 May 2004.

37. See Michel de Certeau, *The Practice of Everyday Life* (Berkeley: University of California Press, 1984).

38. Quoted in "Fenway Model a Mini-Masterpiece of Love," Chris Fusco, *Chicago Sun-Times*, 12 April 2002.

39. Edward M. Bruner, "Abraham Lincoln as Authentic Reproduction: A Critique of Postmodernism," *American Anthropologist* (96:2, 1994): 397–415.

40. Steven M. Schnell, "The Ambiguities of Authenticity in Little Sweden, U.S.A.," *Journal of Cultural Geography* (20:2, 2003): 43–68.

41. See Jean Baudrillard, *Simulations* (New York: Semiotext(e), 1983); David B. Clarke, "Consumption and the City, Modern and Postmodern," *International Journal of Urban and Regional Research* (21:2, 1997): 218–37; and Michael J. Dear, *The Postmodern Urban Condition* (Malden, MA: Blackwell, 2000).

42. On the use of places as "mnemonic" devices, see Eviatar Zerubavel, "Social Memories: Steps to a Sociology of the Past," *Qualitative Sociology* (19:3, 1996): 283–99.

43. "Annual Opening Day at Pupque Park Draws Big Crows of Wiffle Ball Fans," Marvin Payne, *Boston Globe*, 3 June 2001.

44. Quoted in "Walls of Fame," James Whitters, *Boston Globe*, 24 July 2004.

45. Ibid.

46. The Red Sox blew their shot at Jackie Robinson before the Brooklyn Dodgers even had a chance to give him a tryout and eventually a contract. Instead of becoming the first racially integrated team in major-league baseball, the Red Sox ended up being the last. The Red Sox signed Pumpsie Green, their first black player, in 1959, twelve years after Robinson began hitting doubles and stealing bases for the Dodgers in 1947. For details on both Robinson's and Green's experiences with the Red Sox, see Howard Bryant, *Shut Out: A Story of Race and Baseball in Boston* (New York: Routledge, 2002), 1–12, 31–33, 52–64.

47. Laura Chester, *Holy Personal: Looking for Small Private Places of Worship* (Bloomington: Indiana University Press, 2000).

48. Ibid., xix, emphasis added.

49. Quoted in "Annual Opening Day at Pupque Park Draws Big Crowds of Wiffle Ball Fans," Marvin Payne, *Boston Globe*, 3 June 2001.

50. "Little League: Even the Lowly Red Sox Could Go Yard in This Tiny Replica of Fenway Park," *Maxim*, April 2003.

51. Quoted in "Making a Dream Come True: Mini Fenway Park Feels Like Playing in the Real Stadium," Matt DiFilippo, *Kennebec Journal*, 13 July 2003.

52. Quoted in "Sox Player Touts Replica of Fenway for Quincy Site," Tina Cassidy, *Boston Globe*, 15 May 1998.

53. Quoted in "Walls of Fame," James Whitters, *Boston Globe*, 24 July 2004.

54. Gregory P. Stone, "Sport as a Community Representation," in Gunther R. F. Luschen and George H. Sage, eds., *Handbook of Social Science of Sport* (Champaign, IL: Stipes, 1981), 221.

NOTES TO CHAPTER 5

1. Quoted in "Sox to Stay, "No Strings Attached," Sarah Talcott, *Boston Globe*, 24 March 2005.

2. Quoted in ibid.

3. Edward M. Bruner, "Abraham Lincoln as Authentic Reproduction: A Critique of Postmodernism," *American Anthropologist* (96:2, 1994): 399. On constructing and searching for authenticity, see, respectively, Richard A. Peterson, *Creating Country Music: Fabricating Authenticity* (Chicago: University of Chicago Press, 1997); and David Grazian, *Blue Chicago: The Search for Authenticity in Urban Blues Clubs* (Chicago: University of Chicago Press, 2003).

4. Ann Swidler, "Culture in Action: Symbols and Strategies," *American Sociological Review* (51:2, 1986): 273–86.

5. Ibid., 277.

6. Daniel J. Monti, *The American City: A Social and Cultural History* (Malden, MA: Blackwell, 1999), 33–40.

7. Erving Goffman, *Frame Analysis: An Essay on the Organization of Experience* (Cambridge, MA: Harvard University Press, 1974), 21.

8. "Kicking the Connection: U.S., Philip Morris Dispute Marlboro Sign at Fenway Park," Mitchell Zuckoff, *Boston Globe*, 2 July 1995.

9. Quoted in "Fenway Snuffs Out Marlboro Man Ad," Michael Gee, *Boston Herald*, 7 June 1995.

10. Brian J. Neilson, "Baseball," in Karl B. Raitz, ed., *The Theater of Sport* (Baltimore: Johns Hopkins University Press, 1995), 51.

11. Monti, *The American City*, 40–3.

12. See Howard Bryant, *Shut Out: A Story of Race and Baseball in Boston* (New York: Routledge, 2002).

13. "Sign Healed, Deliver," Sam Allis, *Boston Globe*, 7 September 2003.

14. Quoted in "Citgo Sign Repair Won't Leave Fenway Park in the Dark," Heather Allen, *Boston Globe*, 28 September 2004.

15. See Victor Turner and Edward M. Bruner, eds., *The Anthropology of Experience* (Urbana: University of Illinois Press, 1986); Lyn H. Lofland, *The Public Realm: Exploring the City's Quintessential Social Territory* (Hawthorne, NY: Aldine de Gruyter, 1998); Terry Eagleton, *The Idea of Culture* (Malden, MA: Blackwell, 2000); and Edward M. Bruner, *Culture on Tour: Ethnographies of Travel* (Chicago: University of Chicago Press, 2005).

16. Red Sox official press release, 15 May 1999.

17. Rick Eckstein and Kevin Delaney, "New Sports Stadiums, Community Self-Esteem, and Community Collective Conscience," *Journal of Sport and Social Issues* (26:3, 2002): 235–47.

18. For the "economic insignificance" of building new sports facilities, see Charles C. Euchner, *Playing the Field: Why Sports Teams Move and Cities Fight to Keep Them* (Baltimore: Johns Hopkins University Press, 1993); Joanne Cagan and Neil DeMause, *Field of Schemes: How the Great Stadium Swindle Turns Public Money into Private Profit* (Monroe, ME: Common Courage Press, 1998); Mark S. Rosentraub, *Major League Losers: The Real Cost of Sports and Who's Paying for It* (New York: Basic Books, 1999); Peter Eisinger, "The Politics of Bread and Circuses: Building the City for the Visitor Class," *Urban Affairs Review* (35:3, 2000): 316–33; and Kevin J. Delaney and Rick Eckstein, *Public Dollars, Private Stadiums: The Battle over Building Sports Stadiums* (New Brunswick, NJ: Rutgers University Press, 2003). And for a positive case where the construction of a sports arena helped support urban redevelopment in Columbus, Ohio, see Timothy J. Curry, Kent P. Schwirian, and Rachel A. Woldoff, *High Stakes: Big Time Sports and Downtown Redevelopment* (Columbus: Ohio State University Press, 2004).

19. John Kiley, the organist at Fenway Park during the 1975 season, added to the transcendent feel of Fisk's homerun by playing Handel's "Hallelujah Chorus" as Fisk rounded the bases. This is a good example of the often blurred line between "high" and "low" culture.

20. Author Doug Horning may not be the first person to claim that the 1975 World Series was socially important, restoring the childlike imagination of a nation suffering from a "Vietnam hangover," but his retrospective account of those seven games between the Cincinnati Reds and the Boston Red Sox may be the most eloquent and thorough. Horning's rendering of the serendipitous events that were necessary for the future preservation of Fisk's monumental blast is worth quoting at length:

> When Carlton Fisk connected off Pat Darcy and sent that long, looping fly ball at the left-field foul pole, one of the cameras providing coverage was in the room behind the Wall, shooting through the little opening in the scoreboard that the announcers had referred to hours earlier. The camera was on-line after Fisk hit the ball, although the center-field camera was the one that caught the swing. A third camera tracked the flight of the ball from the first-base side. The director called for a cut, asking that the feed from the left-field camera be killed and taping of its signal halted. But at that instant—and this is according to official Red Sox history of Fenway Park—the baseball gods themselves intervened. The left-field cameraman was supposed

to switch his camera off. He didn't. So the image he was relaying continued to be recorded. And why did this happen? Because a rat ran across his foot and he jumped back.

Doug Horning, *The Boys of October: How the 1975 Boston Red Sox Embodied Baseball's Ideals and Restored Our Spirits* (Chicago: Contemporary Books, 2003), 190.

21. "Red Sox Are Fit for Fisk: He's Named Special Assistant," Gordon Edes, *Boston Globe*, 8 March 1999.

22. Fred Davis, *Yearning for Yesterday: A Sociology of Nostalgia* (New York: Free Press, 1979), 111–15.

23. Eviatar Zerubavel, "Social Memories: Steps to a Sociology of the Past," *Qualitative Sociology* (19:3, 1996): 292.

24. Bruce Kuklick, *To Every Thing a Season: Shibe Park and Urban Philadelphia, 1909–1976* (Princeton, NJ: Princeton University Press, 1991), 193.

25. Quoted in "In Philly, the Vet Is Now Just a Memory," *Washington Post*, 22 March 2004.

26. Quoted in "Park's Design Impresses Many," Lynnley Browning and Steven Wilmsen, *Boston Globe*, 16 May 1999.

27. Diane L. Barthel, *Historic Preservation: Collective Memory and Historical Identity* (New Brunswick, NJ: Rutgers University Press, 1996).

28. "Group Lists Ballpark as Endangered," Meg Vaillancourt, *Boston Globe*, 24 September 1999.

29. The "Ortiz Has a Posse" stickers are a group of Red Sox fans' play on the stickers that began appearing across the country in 1997 that spread the message "Andre the Giant Has a Posse." Instead of featuring the former World Wrestling Federation star, the Boston-based stickers feature a picture of Boston's own giant, 6'4", 230-pound designated hitter David "Big Papi" Ortiz.

30. Monti, *The American City*, 165.

31. Davis, *Yearning for Yesterday*, 34.

32. Dan Shaughnessy, *Fenway: A Biography in Words and Picture* (Boston: Houghton Mifflin, 1999), 27.

33. Ibid.

34. Japonica Brown-Saracino, "Social Preservationists and the Quest for Authentic Community," *City & Community* (3:2, 2004): 135–36.

35. Richard Florida, *The Rise of the Creative Class: And How It's Transforming Work, Leisure, Community and Everyday Life* (New York: Basic Books, 2002).

36. Ibid., 182.

37. Ray Oldenburg, *The Great Good Place: Cafés, Coffee Shops, Community Centers, Beauty Parlors, General Stores, Bars, Hangouts and How They Get You through the Day* (New York: Paragon House, 1989).

38. Brown-Saracino, "Social Preservationists and the Quest for Authentic Community," 136.

39. Quoted in "Fenway Groups and Elected Officials Call for Review of Renovation Alternative—Design Symposium Planned for August," Dan Wilson, *Save Fenway Park! Newsletter*, June/July 2000.

40. During both the 2003 and 2004 seasons, the Red Sox prided themselves on the way they wore the hair on their heads and faces. Corn rows, dreadlocks, jerry curls, unkempt facial hair, bushy goatees, and fu-manchus were found across the Red Sox roster. Symbolically, the Red Sox were trying to present themselves as the anti-Yankees, who are known for their policy of no facial hair and no long hair.

41. "One of Our Own Should Own Sox," Joan Vennochi, *Boston Globe*, 6 December 2001.

42. Quoted in "Red Sox' New Lineup Steps Up," Gordon Edes, *Boston Globe*, 22 December 2001.

43. Quoted in ibid.

44. Glenn Stout and Richard A. Johnson, *Red Sox Century: One Hundred Years of Red Sox Baseball* (Boston: Houghton Mifflin, 2004), 468.

45. Writing from outside both Boston and Chicago, journalist Mark Kiszla offered his interpretation of the "cursed" histories of the Red Sox and the Cubs while both were in the playoffs making a run at the World Series. Comparing the two clubs and their ballparks, Kiszla writes:

> In Chicago, who cares about that silly curse of the goat? A philosophical discussion involving the Cubs begins and ends with whether your cup of Bud is half empty or half full. . . . In Boston, the curse of the Bambino is not a choice. It's a genetic flaw for grown New Englanders who still awake in cold sweat during the middle of the night, certain there's a green Monster under the bed. . . . If ballparks are green cathedrals, then Wrigley Field is a church of eternal optimism, and Fenway Park is the house of unrelenting cynicism.

"Baseball's True Tale of Two Cities," Mark Kiszla, *Denver Post*, 12 October 2003.

46. In each of the six seasons prior to the Red Sox's 1967 "Impossible Dream" season, the average attendance at Fenway Park was about eight hundred thousand. The Red Sox did not play above .500 in any of those seasons, and actually lost one hundred games in 1965. For the sake of comparison, between 1999 and 2004), an average of about 2.6 million attended Red Sox home games. Each of those seasons the Red Sox were above .500, and they made the playoffs in 1999, 2003, and 2004.

47. Peter Richmond, *Ballpark: Camden Yards and the Building of an American Dream* (New York: Simon & Schuster, 1992), 161.

48. See Rosentraub, *Major League Losers*; and Delaney and Eckstein, *Public Dollars, Private Stadiums*.

49. "If We Build It Right," Robert Campbell, *Boston Globe*, 30 July 2000.

50. "Kelly: Sox Fenway Site Plan Is Dead," Cosmo Macero Jr., *Boston Herald*, 23 December 2000.

51. "Sox in Somerville? To One Man, It's More than a Dream," Daniel Smith, *Boston Globe*, 9 December 2001.

52. Ellison can often be seen wearing a chicken costume in his kayak. The chicken has become a symbol of opposing teams' fear of pitching to Bonds. During the 2004 season, fans lined the right-field wall with rubber chickens, one for each of Bonds's walks. Stories of Bonds's homerun successes, however, have been deeply tainted due to accusations regarding Bonds's alleged use of illegal steroids.

53. Mario Luis Small, "Culture, Cohorts, and Social Organization Theory: Understanding Local Participation in a Latino Housing Project," *American Journal of Sociology* (108:1, 2002): 22.

NOTES TO CHAPTER 6

1. David Chidester, "The Church of Baseball, the Fetish of Coca-Cola, and the Potlatch of Rock 'n' Roll," in Bruce David Forbes and Jeffrey H. Mahan, eds., *Religion and Popular Culture in America* (Berkeley: University of California Press, 2000), 224.

2. "Red Sox Nation, the Diaspora," *Boston Globe*, 14 November 2004.

3. Quoted in ibid.

4. "Don't Despair, There's Plenty of Sox 'Crumbs' for just $5," Scott Van Voorhis, *Boston Herald*, 6 November 2004.

5. "Sox Nation Globalizes with Card," Scott Van Voorhis, *Boston Herald*, 5 January 2005.

6. For people interested in examining the everyday cultural practices of people within cities, the perspectives of the traditional Chicago School, the neo-Marxian Urban Political Economy approach, and the postmodernist Los Angeles School are unsatisfactory. By positioning urbanization over urbanism, proponents of these perspectives approach the subject from the wrong angle for that task. That is, these perspectives view an urban way of life only as derivative of the ways that cities and metropolitan areas are built and populated by different types of people and activities. The city's governance, the way cities grow, and how different people and activities tend to be identified with some areas and not others take precedence over the way people approach and use the city's environment as a means to foster and reconstruct their personal and collective beliefs and practices. For all three of these schools of thought, culture is understood as a byproduct of economic and politically interested decisions and actions. Consequently, urbanism can only be approached as a dependent

variable, as something that is caused by more "important" forces, often from outside the city and usually not amenable to control by everyday people.

7. Gerald D. Suttles, "The Cumulative Texture of Local Urban Culture," *American Journal of Sociology* (90:2, 1984): 284.

8. Ibid., 291.

9. Ibid., 301.

10. See Howard S. Becker, *Art Worlds* (Berkeley: University of California Press, 1982).

11. Barry Schwartz, "Memory as a Cultural System: Abraham Lincoln in World War II," *American Sociological Review* (6:5, 1996): 908–37.

12. For an overview of Chicago School studies, see Louis Wirth, "Urbanism as a Way of Life," *American Journal of Sociology* (44:1, 1938): 1–24.

13. See William Foote Whyte, *Street Corner Society* (Chicago: University of Chicago Press, 1943); Gregory P. Stone, "City Shoppers and Urban Identification: Observations on the Social Psychology of City Life," *American Journal of Sociology* (60:1, 1954): 36–45; R. Richard Wohl and Anselm L. Strauss, "Symbolic Representation and the Urban Milieu," *American Journal of Sociology* (63:5, 1958): 523–32; Anselm L. Strauss, *Images of the American City* (New Brunswick, NJ: Transaction Books, 1976); Herbert J. Gans, *The Urban Villagers: Group and Class in the Life of Italian-Americans* (New York: Free Press, 1962); Gerald D. Suttles, *The Social Order of the Slum* (Chicago: University of Chicago Press, 1968); Gerald D. Suttles, *The Social Construction of Communities* (Chicago: University of Chicago Press, 1972); Albert Hunter, *Symbolic Communities: The Persistence and Change of Chicago's Local Communities* (Chicago: University of Chicago Press, 1974); Lyn H. Lofland, *A World of Strangers: Order and Action in Urban Public Space* (New York: Basic Books, 1973); Claude S. Fischer, *The Urban Experience* (New York: Harcourt Brace Jovanovich, 1976).

14. Daniel J. Monti, *The American City: A Social and Cultural History* (Malden, MA: Blackwell, 1999).

15. Clifford Geertz, *The Interpretation of Cultures* (New York: Basic Books, 1973), 144.

16. Norton Long, "The Local Community as an Ecology of Games," *American Journal of Sociology* (64, 1958): 253.

17. John Walton, *Storied Land: Community and Memory in Monterey* (Berkeley: University of California Press, 2001), 299.

18. Barry Schwartz, *Abraham Lincoln and the Forge of National Memory* (Chicago: University of Chicago Press, 2000), 9.

19. Lyn H. Lofland, *The Public Realm: Exploring the City's Quintessential Social Territory* (Hawthorne, NY: Aldine de Gruyter, 1998), 74–75.

20. See Setha M. Low, "Symbolic Ties That Bind: Place Attachment in the Plaza," and David M. Hummon, "Community Attachment: Local Sentiment

and Sense of Place," in Irwin Altman and Setha M. Low, eds., *Place Attachment* (New York: Plenum, 1992).

21. Michèle Lamont, John Schmalzbauer, Maureen Waller, and Daniel Weber, "Cultural and Moral Boundaries in the United States: Structural Position, Geographic Location, and Lifestyle Explanations," *Poetics* (24, 1996): 31–56.

22. See Elijah Anderson, *Code of the Street: Decency, Violence, and the Moral Life of the Inner City* (New York: Norton, 1999).

23. For a wealth of examples, see Ken Gelder and Sarah Thornton, eds., *The Subcultures Reader* (New York: Routledge, 1997).

24. John Irwin, *Scenes* (Beverly Hills, CA: Sage, 1977); and Long, "The Local Community as an Ecology of Games," 251–61.

25. See Belinda Wheaton and Becky Beal, "Keeping It Real: Subcultural Media and the Discourse of Authenticity in Alternative Sport," *International Review for the Sociology of Sport* (38:2, 2003): 155–76.

26. Terry Eagleton, *The Idea of Culture* (Malden, MA: Blackwell, 2000), 37.

27. See Stone, "City Shoppers and Urban Identification," 36–45; Michael A. Katovich and William A. Reese II, "The Regular: Full-Time Identities and Memberships in an Urban Bar," *Journal of Contemporary Ethnography* (16:3, 1987): 308–43; David Grazian, *Blue Chicago: The Search for Authenticity in Urban Blues Clubs* (Chicago: University of Chicago Press, 2003).

28. Herbert Blumer, "Fashion: From Class Differentiation to Collective Selection," *Sociological Quarterly* (10:2, 1969): 281.

29. Ibid., 282.

30. Marshall McLuhan, *Understanding Media: The Extensions of Man* (Cambridge, MA: MIT Press, 1964), 9.

31. Lofland, *The Public Realm*, chap. 4.

32. "Don't Take a Wrecking Ball to History," Jim Caple, *ESPN.com*, http://espn.go.com/mlb/columns/caple_jim.

33. See Fred Davis, *Yearning for Yesterday: A Sociology of Nostalgia* (New York: Free Press, 1979).

NOTES TO THE APPENDIX

1. Anselm L. Strauss, *Images of the American City* (New Brunswick, NJ: Transaction Books, 1976), 18.

2. Sherri Grasmuck, *Protecting Home: Class, Race, and Masculinity in Boys' Baseball* (New Brunswick, NJ: Rutgers University Press, 2005), 13.

3. Horace Miner, "The Body Rituals among the Nacirema," *American Anthropologist* (58:3, 1956): 504.

4. Ibid., 503.

5. Jaber F. Gubrium and A. James Holstein, "At the Border of Narrative and Ethnography," *Journal of Contemporary Ethnography* (28:5, 1999): 563. Fear-

ful of postmodernism's incessant "navel-gazing" and reckless endangerment of qualitative sociological research, Joel Best writes,

> Today, the postmodernist slogan might be: "out of the streets, into the armchairs." After all, if the analyst inevitably shapes the analysis, the reasoning goes, we should focus our attention, not on the subject of analysis, but on the analytic act. The focus shifts from social life to the self-centered, self-congratulatory, and self-indulgent. Anything— but especially anything personal—is grist for the postmodernist mill. . . . When we adopt the postmodernist fad, we surrender our ability to do what we have always done best, in return for some new jargon. It's a bad trade.

Joel Best, "Lost in the Ozone Again: The Postmodernist Fad and Interactionist Foibles," *Studies in Symbolic Interaction* (17, 1995): 128.

6. Clifford Geertz, *The Interpretation of Cultures* (New York: Basic Books, 1973), 436.

7. See Barney G. Glaser and Anselm L. Strauss, *The Discovery of Grounded Theory: Strategies for Qualitative Research* (New York: Aldine, 1967); and Kathy Charmaz, "Grounded Theory," in Robert M. Emerson, ed., *Contemporary Field Research: Perspectives and Formulations* (Prospect Heights, IL: Waveland, 2001).

8. It is in this sense that I envision the sociological project, especially what I am referring to here as urban cultural analysis, as an art and a craft. For a defense of "the ethnographer's craft" against positivistic-oriented critiques primarily made by quantitative researchers, see David A. Karp, "Social Science, Progress, and the Ethnographer's Craft," *Journal of Contemporary Ethnography* (28:6, 1999): 597–609.

9. Robert Wuthnow, *Meaning and Moral Order: Explorations in Cultural Analysis* (Berkeley: University of California Press, 1987), 17.

10. Michael Ian Borer, "The Location of Culture: The Urban Culturalist Perspective," *City & Community* (5:2, 2006): 173–98.

11. See Geertz, *The Interpretation of Cultures*, 3–30.

12. See George Herbert Mead, *Mind, Self, and Society: From the Standpoint of a Social Behaviorist* (Chicago: University of Chicago Press, 1934).

13. Erving Goffman, *The Presentation of Self in Everyday Life* (Garden City, NY: Doubleday, 1959), 2.

14. Geertz, *The Interpretation of Cultures*, 6.

15. John R. Hall, Mary Jo Neitz, and Marshall Battani, *Sociology on Culture* (New York: Routledge, 2003), 12.

16. Howard S. Becker, "The Epistemology of Qualitative Research," in Robert M. Emerson, ed., *Contemporary Field Research: Perspectives and Formulations* (Prospect Heights, IL: Waveland, 2001).

17. See Goffman, *The Presentation of Self in Everyday Life*.

18. Joshua Gamson, *Freaks Talk Back: Tabloid Talk Shows and Sexual Nonconformity* (Chicago: University of Chicago Press, 1998), 227. For a similar use and discussion of these methods, also see Joshua Gamson, *Claims to Fame: Celebrity in Contemporary America* (Berkeley: University of California Press, 1994).

19. Norman K. Denzin, *The Research Act: A Theoretical Introduction to Sociological Methods* (New York: McGraw-Hill, 1978), 28.

20. See Jack Katz, "From How to Why: On Luminous Description and Causal Inference in Ethnography (Part I)," *Ethnography* (2:4, 2001): 443–73.

21. Gary Alan Fine, *Kitchens: The Culture of Restaurant Work* (Berkeley: University of California Press, 1996), 233.

22. For a useful discussion of this issue, see Brian Fay, *Contemporary Philosophy of Social Science: A Multicultural Approach* (Cambridge, MA: Blackwell, 1996).

23. Daniel J. Monti, "On the Risks and Rewards of 'Going Native,'" *Qualitative Sociology* (15:3, 1992): 326.

24. Gary Alan Fine, "Toward a Peopled Ethnography: Developing Theory from Group Life," *Ethnography* (4:1, 2003): 54, emphasis in the original.

25. John Lofland and Lyn H. Lofland, *Analyzing Social Settings: A Guide to Qualitative Observation and Analysis* (Belmont, CA: Wadsworth, 1995), 19, emphasis in the original.

26. Margarethe Kusenbach, "Street Phenomenology: The Go-Along as Ethnographic Research Tool," *Ethnography* (4:3, 2003): 455–85. For detailed discussions of the construction and usage of "cultural repertoires," see Ulf Hannerz, *Soulside: Inquiries into Ghetto Culture and Community* (New York: Columbia University Press, 1969); and Ann Swidler, *Talk of Love: How Culture Matters* (Chicago: University of Chicago Press, 2001).

27. Kusenbach, "Street Phenomenology," 464.

28. Daniel J. Monti, *The American City: A Social and Cultural History* (Malden, MA: Blackwell, 1999), 5.

29. See Elizabeth Chaplin, *Sociology and Visual Representation* (London: Routledge, 1994); and Sarah Pink, *Doing Visual Ethnography: Images, Media, and Representations in Research* (London: Sage, 2001).

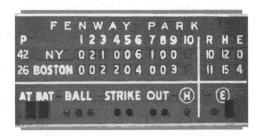

BIBLIOGRAPHY

Adelman, Melvin L. 1986. *A Sporting Time: New York City and the Rise of Modern Athletics, 1820–70*. Urbana: University of Illinois Press.

———. 1989. "Baseball, Business, and the Work Place: Gelber's Thesis Reexamined." *Journal of Social History* 23: 285–301.

Adorno, Theodor W. 1981. *Prisms*. Cambridge, MA: MIT Press.

Altherr, Thomas L. 1991. "A Swing and a Myth: The Persistence of Baseball in the American Imagination." In Alvin L. Hall, ed., *Cooperstown Symposium on Baseball and the American Culture*. Oneonta: State University of New York at Oneonta.

Altman, Irwin, and Setha M. Low, eds. 1992. *Place Attachment*. New York: Plenum.

Anderson, Elijah. 1999. *Code of the Street: Decency, Violence, and the Moral Life of the Inner City*. New York: Norton.

Anderson, Paul M. 1997. "Playing the Stadium Game." *Journal of Sport and Social Issues* 21: 103–11.

Andrews, David L., and Steven J. Jackson, eds. 2001. *Sport Stars: The Cultural Politics of Sporting Celebrity*. New York: Routledge.

Bachin, Robin Faith. 2004. *Building the South Side: Urban Space and Civic Culture in Chicago, 1890–1919*. Chicago: University of Chicago Press.

Barth, Gunther. 1980. *City People: The Rise of Modern City Culture in Nineteenth-Century America*. New York: Oxford University Press.

Barthel, Diane L. 1996. *Historic Preservation: Collective Memory and Historical Identity*. New Brunswick, NJ: Rutgers University Press.

Baudrillard, Jean. 1983. *Simulations*. New York: Semiotext(e).

———. 1989. *America*. New York: Verso.

Beaver, William. 2001. "Building Sports Stadiums in Pittsburgh: A Case Study in Urban Power Structures." *Sociological Focus* 34: 21–32.

Becker, Howard S. 1982. *Art Worlds*. Berkeley: University of California Press.

———. 2001. "The Epistemology of Qualitative Research." In Robert M. Emerson, ed., *Contemporary Field Research: Perspectives and Formulations*. Prospect Heights, IL: Waveland.

Behar, Ruth. 2003. "Ethnography and the Book That Was Lost." *Ethnography* 4: 15–39.

Belanger, Anouk. 2000. "Sport Venues and the Spectacularization of Urban Spaces in North America: The Case of the Molson Centre in Montreal." *International Review for the Sociology of Sport* 35: 378–97.

Bellah, Robert N. 1970. *Beyond Belief: Essays on Religion in a Post-traditional World*. New York: Harper & Row.

Bender, Thomas. 1975. *Toward an Urban Vision: Ideas and Institutions in Nineteenth-Century America*. Lexington: University Press of Kentucky.

Berger, Peter L. 1967. *The Sacred Canopy: Elements of a Sociological Theory of Religion*. Garden City, NY: Doubleday.

Best, Joel. 1995. "Lost in the Ozone Again: The Postmodernist Fad and Interactionist Foibles." *Studies in Symbolic Interaction* 17: 125–30.

Betts, John R. 1968. "Mind and Body in Early American Thought." *Journal of American History* 54: 27–42.

Bird, S. Elizabeth. 2002. "It Makes Sense to Us: Cultural Identity in Local Legends of Place." *Journal of Contemporary Ethnography* 31: 519–47.

Block, David. 2005. *Baseball Before We Knew It: A Search for the Roots of the Game*. Lincoln: University of Nebraska Press.

Blumer, Herbert. 1969. "Fashion: From Class Differentiation to Collective Selection." *Sociological Quarterly* 10: 275–91.

Bluthardt, Robert F. 1987. "Fenway Park and the Golden Age of the Baseball Park, 1909–1915." *Journal of Popular Culture* 21: 43–52.

Bodnar, John E. 1992. *Remaking America: Public Memory, Commemoration, and Patriotism in the Twentieth Century*. Princeton, NJ: Princeton University Press.

Borer, Michael Ian. 2004. "Rites of Inversion." In Frank A. Salamone, ed., *Encyclopedia of Religious Rites, Rituals, and Festivals*. New York: Routledge.

———. 2006. "The Location of Culture: The Urban Culturalist Perspective." *City & Community* 5: 173–98.

———, ed. 2006. *Varieties of Urban Experience: The American City and the Practice of Culture*. Lanham, MD: University Press of America.

Borer, Michael Ian, and Daniel J. Monti Jr. 2006. "Community, Commerce, and Consumption: Businesses as Civic Associations." In Michael Ian Borer, ed., *Varieties of Urban Experience: The American City and the Practice of Culture*. Lanham, MD: University Press of America.

Bourdieu, Pierre. 1984. *Distinction: A Social Critique of the Judgement of Taste*. Cambridge, MA: Harvard University Press.

Bronner, Stephen Eric, and Douglas M. Kellner, eds. 1989. *Critical Theory and Society: A Reader.* New York: Routledge.

Brown, Clyde, and David M. Paul. 2002. "The Political Scorecard of Professional Sports Facility Referendums in the United States, 1984–2000." *Journal of Sport and Social Issues* 26: 248–67.

Brown-Saracino, Japonica. 2004. "Social Preservationists and the Quest for Authentic Community." *City & Community* 3: 135–56.

Bruner, Edward M. 1994. "Abraham Lincoln as Authentic Reproduction: A Critique of Postmodernism." *American Anthropologist* 96: 397–415.

———. 2005. *Culture on Tour: Ethnographies of Travel.* Chicago: University of Chicago Press.

Bryant, Howard. 2002. *Shut Out: A Story of Race and Baseball in Boston.* New York: Routledge.

Butzer, Karl W., ed. 1978. *Dimensions of Human Geography: Essays on Some Familiar and Neglected Themes.* Chicago: University of Chicago Press.

Cagan, Joanne, and Neil DeMause. 1998. *Field of Schemes: How the Great Stadium Swindle Turns Public Money into Private Profit.* Monroe, ME: Common Courage Press.

Certeau, Michel de. 1984. *The Practice of Everyday Life.* Berkeley: University of California Press.

Chaplin, Elizabeth. 1994. *Sociology and Visual Representation.* London: Routledge.

Charmaz, Kathy. 2001. "Grounded Theory." In Robert M. Emerson, ed., *Contemporary Field Research: Perspectives and Formulations.* Prospect Heights, IL: Waveland.

Chester, Laura. 2000. *Holy Personal: Looking for Small Private Places of Worship.* Bloomington: Indiana University Press.

Chidester, David. 2000. "The Church of Baseball, the Fetish of Coca-Cola, and the Potlatch of Rock 'n' Roll." In Bruce David Forbes and Jeffrey H. Mahan, eds., *Religion and Popular Culture in America.* Berkeley: University of California Press.

Chudacoff, Howard P., and Judith E. Smith. 2000. *The Evolution of American Urban Society.* Englewood Cliffs, NJ: Prentice-Hall.

Clarke, David B. 1997. "Consumption and the City, Modern and Postmodern." *International Journal of Urban and Regional Research* 21: 218–37.

Cocks, Catherine. 2001. *Doing the Town: The Rise of Urban Tourism in the United States, 1850–1915.* Berkeley: University of California Press.

Csikszentmihalyi, Mihaly, and Eugene Rochberg-Halton. 1981. *The Meaning of Things: Domestic Symbols and the Self.* New York: Cambridge University Press.

Curry, Timothy J., Kent P. Schwirian, and Rachel A. Woldoff. 2004. *High Stakes: Big Time Sports and Downtown Redevelopment.* Columbus: Ohio State University Press.

Curtis, Henry S. 1915. *The Practical Conduct of Play*. New York: Macmillan.

Danielson, Michael N. 1997. *Home Team: Professional Sports and the American Metropolis*. Princeton, NJ: Princeton University Press.

Davis, Fred. 1979. *Yearning for Yesterday: A Sociology of Nostalgia*. New York: Free Press.

Dear, Michael J. 2000. *The Postmodern Urban Condition*. Malden, MA: Blackwell.

———. 2002. "Los Angeles and the Chicago School: Invitation to a Debate." *City & Community* 1: 5–32.

Delaney, Kevin J., and Rick Eckstein. 2003. *Public Dollars, Private Stadiums: The Battle over Building Sports Stadiums*. New Brunswick, NJ: Rutgers University Press.

Demos, John. 2000. "A Fan's Homage to Fenway (Or, Why We Love It When They Always Break Our Hearts." In William E. Leuchtenberg, ed., *American Places: Encounters with History*. Oxford: Oxford University Press.

Denzin, Norman K. 1978. *The Research Act: A Theoretical Introduction to Sociological Methods*. New York: McGraw-Hill.

Duneier, Mitchell. 1999. *Sidewalk*. New York: Farrar, Straus and Giroux.

Dunning, Eric, Patrick Murphy, Ivan Waddington, and Antonios Astrinakis, eds. 2002. *Fighting Fans: Football Hooliganism as a World Phenomenon*. Dublin, Ireland: University College Dublin Press.

Durkheim, Émile. 1965. *The Elementary Forms of the Religious Life*. New York: Free Press.

———. 1982. *The Rules of Sociological Method*. New York: Free Press.

Eagleton, Terry. 2000. *The Idea of Culture*. Malden, MA: Blackwell.

Eckstein, Rick, and Kevin Delaney. 2002. "New Sports Stadiums, Community Self-Esteem, and Community Collective Conscience." *Journal of Sport and Social Issues* 26: 235–47.

Eisinger, Peter. 2000. "The Politics of Bread and Circuses: Building the City for the Visitor Class." *Urban Affairs Review* 35: 316–33.

Eliade, Mircea. 1959. *The Sacred and the Profane: The Nature of Religion*. New York: Harcourt Brace.

Emerson, Robert M., ed. 2001. *Contemporary Field Research: Perspectives and Formulations*. Prospect Heights, IL: Waveland.

Euchner, Charles C. 1993. *Playing the Field: Why Sports Teams Move and Cities Fight to Keep Them*. Baltimore: Johns Hopkins University Press.

Evans, Christopher H., and William R. Herzog II, eds. 2002. *The Faith of 50 Million: Baseball, Religion, and American Culture*. Louisville, KY: Westminster John Knox Press.

Fay, Brian. 1996. *Contemporary Philosophy of Social Science: A Multicultural Approach*. Cambridge, MA: Blackwell.

Fine, Gary Alan. 1996. *Kitchens: The Culture of Restaurant Work*. Berkeley: University of California Press.

———. 2003. "Toward a Peopled Ethnography: Developing Theory from Group Life." *Ethnography* 4: 41–60.

Finke, Roger, and Rodney Stark. 1988. "Religious Economies and Sacred Canopies." *American Sociological Review* 53: 41–49.

Fischer, Claude S. 1976. *The Urban Experience*. New York: Harcourt Brace Jovanovich.

———. 1994. "Change in Leisure Activities, 1890–1940." *Journal of Social History* 28: 453–75.

Florida, Richard. 2002. *The Rise of the Creative Class: And How It's Transforming Work, Leisure, Community and Everyday Life*. New York: Basic Books.

Forbes, Bruce David, and Jeffrey H. Mahan, eds. 2000. *Religion and Popular Culture in America*. Berkeley: University of California Press.

Friedland, Roger, and John Mohr, eds. 2004. *Matters of Culture: Cultural Sociology in Practice*. Cambridge: Cambridge University Press.

Gamson, Joshua. 1994. *Claims to Fame: Celebrity in Contemporary America*. Berkeley: University of California Press.

———. 1998. *Freaks Talk Back: Tabloid Talk Shows and Sexual Nonconformity*. Chicago: University of Chicago Press.

Gans, Herbert J. 1962. *The Urban Villagers: Group and Class in the Life of Italian-Americans*. New York: Free Press.

Garber, Marjorie B., and Rebecca L. Walkowitz, eds. 1999. *One Nation under God? Religion and American Culture*. New York: Routledge.

Geertz, Clifford. 1973. *The Interpretation of Cultures*. New York: Basic Books.

Gelber, Steven M. 1983. "Working at Playing: The Culture of the Work Place and the Rise of Baseball." *Journal of Social History* 16: 3–20.

Gelder, Ken, and Sarah Thornton, eds. 1997. *The Subcultures Reader*. New York: Routledge.

Gershman, Michael. 1993. *Diamonds: The Evolution of Ballparks*. Boston: Houghton Mifflin.

Glaser, Barney G., and Anselm L. Strauss. 1967. *The Discovery of Grounded Theory: Strategies for Qualitative Research*. New York: Aldine.

Gmelch, George. 1971. "Baseball Magic." *Transaction* 8: 39–43.

Goffman, Erving. 1959. *The Presentation of Self in Everyday Life*. Garden City, NY: Doubleday.

———. 1974. *Frame Analysis: An Essay on the Organization of Experience*. Cambridge, MA: Harvard University Press.

Goldstein, Warren Jay. 1989. *Playing for Keeps: A History of Early Baseball*. Ithaca, NY: Cornell University Press.

Gotham, Kevin Fox. 2001. "Urban Sociology and the Postmodern Challenge." *Humboldt Journal of Social Relations* 26: 57–79.

Gottdiener, Mark. 1997. *The Theming of America: Dreams, Visions, and Commercial Spaces*. Boulder, CO: Westview.

Grasmuck, Sherri. 2005. *Protecting Home: Class, Race, and Masculinity in Boys' Baseball*. New Brunswick, NJ: Rutgers University Press.

Grazian, David. 2003. *Blue Chicago: The Search for Authenticity in Urban Blues Clubs*. Chicago: University of Chicago Press.

Gubrium, Jaber F., and A. James Holstein. 1999. "At the Border of Narrative and Ethnography." *Journal of Contemporary Ethnography* 28: 561–73.

Hall, Alvin L., ed. 1991. *Cooperstown Symposium on Baseball and the American Culture*. Oneonta: State University of New York at Oneonta.

Hall, John A., and Charles Lindholm. 1999. *Is America Breaking Apart?* Princeton, NJ: Princeton University Press.

Hall, John R., Mary Jo Neitz, and Marshall Battani. 2003. *Sociology on Culture*. New York: Routledge.

Halle, David. 1994. *Inside Culture: Class, Culture, and Everyday Life in Modern America*. Chicago: University of Chicago Press.

Handler, Richard. 1986. "Authenticity." *Anthropology Today* 2: 2–4.

Handler, Richard, and William Saxton. 1988. "Dyssimmulation: Reflexivity, Narrative, and the Quest for Authenticity in 'Living.'" *Cultural Anthropology* 3: 242–60.

Hannerz, Ulf. 1969. *Soulside: Inquiries into Ghetto Culture and Community*. New York: Columbia University Press.

Hannigan, John. 1998. *Fantasy City: Pleasure and Profit in the Postmodern Metropolis*. New York: Routledge.

Hardy, Stephen. 1982. *How Boston Played: Sport, Recreation, and Community, 1865–1915*. Boston: Northeastern University Press.

———. 1997. "Sport in Urbanizing America: A Historical Review." *Journal of Urban History* 23: 675–708.

Hecht, Richard D. 2004. "Private Devotions and the Sacred Heart of Elvis: The Durkheimians and the (Re)Turn of the Sacred." In Roger Friedland and John Mohr, eds., *Matters of Culture: Cultural Sociology in Practice*. Cambridge: Cambridge University Press.

Horning, Doug. 2003. *The Boys of October: How the 1975 Boston Red Sox Embodied Baseball's Ideals and Restored Our Spirits*. Chicago: Contemporary Books.

Hummon, David M. 1990. *Commonplaces: Community Ideology and Identity in American Culture*. Albany: State University of New York Press.

———. 1992. "Community Attachment: Local Sentiment and Sense of Place." In Irwin Altman and Setha M. Low, eds., *Place Attachment*. New York: Plenum.

Hunter, Albert. 1974. *Symbolic Communities: The Persistence and Change of Chicago's Local Communities*. Chicago: University of Chicago Press.

Irwin, John. 1977. *Scenes*. Beverly Hills, CA: Sage.

Jacobs, Jane. 1961. *The Death and Life of Great American Cities*. New York: Vintage.

Jameson, Fredric. 1991. *Postmodernism; or, The Cultural Logic of Late Capitalism.* Durham, NC: Duke University Press.

Jenkins, Henry. 1992. *Textual Poachers: Television Fans and Participatory Culture.* New York: Routledge.

Johnstone, Barbara. 1990. *Stories, Community, and Place: Narratives from Middle America.* Bloomington: Indiana University Press.

Judd, Dennis R., ed. 2003. *The Infrastructure of Play: Building the Tourist City.* Armonk, NY: M. E. Sharpe.

Kammen, Michael G. 1999. *American Culture, American Tastes: Social Change and the 20th Century.* New York: Knopf.

Karp, David A. 1999. "Social Science, Progress, and the Ethnographer's Craft." *Journal of Contemporary Ethnography* 28: 597–609.

Katovich, Michael A., and William A. Reese II. 1987. "The Regular: Full-Time Identities and Memberships in an Urban Bar." *Journal of Contemporary Ethnography* 16: 308–43.

Katz, Jack. 2001. "From How to Why: On Luminous Description and Causal Inference in Ethnography (Part I)." *Ethnography* 2: 443–73.

Kellner, Douglas M. 1995. *Media Culture: Cultural Studies, Identity, and Politics between the Modern and the Postmodern.* New York: Routledge.

Kennedy, Lawrence W. 1992. *Planning the City upon a Hill: Boston since 1630.* Amherst: University of Massachusetts Press.

Kirsch, George B. 1989. *The Creation of American Team Sports: Baseball and Cricket, 1838–72.* Urbana: University of Illinois Press.

Kittel, Linda A. 1991. "From Dreams to Diamonds to Dictionaries: Baseball as Acculturating Force." In Alvin L. Hall, ed., *Cooperstown Symposium on Baseball and the American Culture.* Oneonta: State University of New York at Oneonta.

Klein, Alan. 2000. "Latinizing Fenway Park: A Cultural Critique of the Boston Red Sox." *Sociology of Sport Journal* 17: 403–22.

Kuklick, Bruce. 1991. *To Every Thing a Season: Shibe Park and Urban Philadelphia, 1909–1976.* Princeton, NJ: Princeton University Press.

Kusenbach, Margarethe. 2003. "Street Phenomenology: The Go-Along as Ethnographic Research Tool." *Ethnography* 4: 455–85.

Lamont, Michèle, John Schmalzbauer, Maureen Waller, and Daniel Weber. 1996. "Cultural and Moral Boundaries in the United States: Structural Position, Geographic Location, and Lifestyle Explanations." *Poetics* 24: 31–56.

Lasn, Kalle. 1999. *Culture Jam: How to Reverse America's Suicidal Consumer Binge —and Why We Must.* New York: HarperCollins.

Lees, Lynn Hollen. 1994. "Urban Public Space and Imagined Communities in the 1980s and 1990s." *Journal of Urban History* 20: 442–58.

Leuchtenberg, William E., ed. 2000. *American Places: Encounters with History.* Oxford: Oxford University Press.

Lofland, John, and Lyn H. Lofland. 1995. *Analyzing Social Settings: A Guide to Qualitative Observation and Analysis*. Belmont, CA: Wadsworth.

Lofland, Lyn H. 1973. *A World of Strangers: Order and Action in Urban Public Space*. New York: Basic Books.

———. 1998. *The Public Realm: Exploring the City's Quintessential Social Territory*. Hawthorne, NY: Aldine de Gruyter.

Long, Norton. 1958. "The Local Community as an Ecology of Games." *American Journal of Sociology* 64: 251–61.

Lord, M. G. 2004. *Forever Barbie: The Unauthorized Biography of a Real Doll*. New York: Walker & Co.

Low, Setha M. 1992. "Symbolic Ties That Bind: Place Attachment in the Plaza." In Irwin Altman and Setha M. Low, eds., *Place Attachment*. New York: Plenum.

Lowry, Philip J. 1992. *Green Cathedrals: The Ultimate Celebration of All 271 Major League and Negro League Ballparks Past and Present*. Reading, MA: Addison-Wesley.

Luschen, Gunther R. F., and George H. Sage, eds. 1981. *Handbook of Social Science of Sport*. Champaign, IL: Stipes.

MacCannell, Dean. 1976. *The Tourist: A New Theory for the Leisure Class*. New York: Schocken.

Maines, David R., and Jeffrey C. Bridger. 1992. "Narratives, Community and Land Use Decisions." *Social Science Journal* 29: 363–80.

Mauss, Marcel. 1950. *The Gift: The Form and Reason for Exchange in Archaic Societies*. London: Routledge.

McDannell, Colleen. 1995. *Material Christianity: Religion and Popular Culture in America*. New Haven, CT: Yale University Press.

McLuhan, Marshall. 1964. *Understanding Media: The Extensions of Man*. Cambridge, MA: MIT Press.

Mead, George Herbert. 1934. *Mind, Self, and Society: From the Standpoint of a Social Behaviorist*. Chicago: University of Chicago Press.

Messner, Michael A. 1992. *Power at Play: Sports and the Problem of Masculinity*. Boston: Beacon.

Milgram, Stanley. 1977. *The Individual in a Social World: Essays and Experiments*. New York: McGraw-Hill.

Milligan, Melinda J. 1998. "Interactional Past and Potential: The Social Construction of Place Attachment." *Symbolic Interaction* 21: 1–33.

———. 2003. "Displacement and Identity Discontinuity: The Role of Nostalgia in Establishing New Identity Categories." *Symbolic Interaction* 26: 381–403.

Miner, Horace. 1956. "The Body Rituals among the Nacirema." *American Anthropologist* 58: 503–7.

Monti, Daniel J. 1992. "On the Risks and Rewards of 'Going Native.'" *Qualitative Sociology* 15: 325–32.

———. 1999. *The American City: A Social and Cultural History.* Malden, MA: Blackwell.

Nasaw, David. 1993. *Going Out: The Rise and Fall of Public Amusements.* New York: Basic Books.

Neilson, Brian J. 1995. "Baseball." In Karl B. Raitz, ed., *The Theater of Sport.* Baltimore: Johns Hopkins University Press.

Norris, Donald F. 2003. "If We Build It, They Will Come! Tourism-Based Economic Development in Baltimore." In Dennis R. Judd, ed., *The Infrastructure of Play: Building the Tourist City.* Armonk, NY: M. E. Sharpe.

Novak, Michael. 1976. *The Joy of Sports: End Zones, Bases, Baskets, Balls, and the Consecration of the American Spirit.* New York: Basic Books.

Oldenburg, Ray. 1989. *The Great Good Place: Cafés, Coffee Shops, Community Centers, Beauty Parlors, General Stores, Bars, Hangouts and How They Get You through the Day.* New York: Paragon House.

Park, Chris C. 1994. *Sacred Worlds: An Introduction to Geography and Religion.* New York: Routledge.

Paulsen, Krista E. 2000. "Saving a Place for the County Fair: Institutional Space and the Maintenance of Community." *Research in Community Sociology* 10: 387–406.

Peterson, Richard A. 1997. *Creating Country Music: Fabricating Authenticity.* Chicago: University of Chicago Press.

Pink, Sarah. 2001. *Doing Visual Ethnography: Images, Media, and Representations in Research.* London: Sage.

Prebish, Charles S., ed. 1993. *Religion and Sport: The Meeting of Sacred and Profane.* Westport, CT: Greenwood.

Price, Joseph L., ed. 2001. *From Season to Season: Sports as American Religion.* Macon, GA: Mercer University Press.

Prince, Carl E. 1996. *Brooklyn's Dodgers: The Bums, the Borough, and the Best of Baseball.* New York: Oxford University Press.

Prothero, Stephen. 1999. "Cremation American Style: Consumer's Last Rites." In Marjorie B. Garber and Rebecca L. Walkowitz, eds., *One Nation under God? Religion and American Culture.* New York: Routledge.

Rader, Benjamin G. 1984. *In Its Own Image: How Television Has Transformed Sports.* New York: Free Press.

Raitz, Karl B., ed. 1995. *The Theater of Sport.* Baltimore: Johns Hopkins University Press.

Richmond, Peter. 1992. *Ballpark: Camden Yards and the Building of an American Dream.* New York: Simon & Schuster.

Riess, Steven A. 1980. *Touching Base: Professional Baseball and American Culture in the Progressive Era.* Westport, CT: Greenwood.

———. 1989. *City Games: The Evolution of American Urban Society and the Rise of Sports.* Urbana: University of Illinois Press.

Ritzer, George, and Todd Stillman. 2001. "The Postmodern Ballpark as a Leisure Setting: Enchantment and Simulated De-McDonaldization." *Leisure Sciences* 23: 99–113.

Rosentraub, Mark S. 1999. *Major League Losers: The Real Cost of Sports and Who's Paying for It*. New York: Basic Books.

Rosenzweig, Roy. 1983. *Eight Hours for What We Will: Workers and Leisure in an Industrial City, 1870–1920*. New York: Cambridge University Press.

Rosenzweig, Roy, and Elizabeth Blackmar. 1992. *The Park and the People: A History of Central Park*. Ithaca, NY: Cornell University Press.

Salamone, Frank A., ed. 2004. *Encyclopedia of Religious Rites, Rituals, and Festivals*. New York: Routledge.

Schmidt, Leigh Eric. 1995. *Consumer Rites: The Buying and Selling of American Holidays*. Princeton, NJ: Princeton University Press.

Schnell, Steven M. 2003. "The Ambiguities of Authenticity in Little Sweden, U.S.A." *Journal of Cultural Geography* 20: 43–68.

Schudson, Michael. 1989. "How Culture Works: Perspectives from Media Studies on the Efficacy of Symbols." *Theory and Society* 18: 153–80.

Schultz, Brad. 2003. "A Geographical Study of the American Ballpark." *International Journal of the History of Sport* 20: 126–42.

Schwartz, Barry. 1987. *George Washington: The Making of an American Symbol*. New York: Free Press.

———. 1996. "Memory as a Cultural System: Abraham Lincoln in World War II." *American Sociological Review* 6: 908–37.

———. 2000. *Abraham Lincoln and the Forge of National Memory*. Chicago: University of Chicago Press.

Shaughnessy, Dan. 1990. *The Curse of the Bambino*. New York: Penguin Books.

———. 1996. *At Fenway: Dispatches from Red Sox Nation*. New York: Crown.

———. 1999. *Fenway: A Biography in Words and Picture*. Boston: Houghton Mifflin.

Simmel, Georg. 1971. *On Individuality and Social Forms*. Chicago: University of Chicago Press.

Simpson, Timothy A. 2000. "Streets, Sidewalks, Stores, and Stories: Narrative and Uses of Urban Space." *Journal of Contemporary Ethnography* 29: 684–716.

Slotkin, Richard. 1992. *Gunfighter Nation: The Myth of the Frontier in Twentieth-Century America*. New York: Atheneum.

Small, Mario Luis. 2002. "Culture, Cohorts, and Social Organization Theory: Understanding Local Participation in a Latino Housing Project." *American Journal of Sociology* 108: 1–54.

Smith, Philip. 1999. "The Elementary Forms of Place and Their Transformations: A Durkheimian Model." *Qualitative Sociology* 22: 13–36.

Sopher, David E. 1967. *Geography of Religions*. Englewood Cliffs, NJ: Prentice-Hall.

Sorkin, Michael. 1992. *Variations on a Theme Park: The New American City and the End of Public Space*. New York: Hill and Wang.

Spirou, Costas, and Larry Bennett. 2002. "Revamped Stadium . . . New Neighborhood?" *Urban Affairs Review* 37: 675–702.

———. 2003. *It's Hardly Sportin': Stadiums, Neighborhoods, and the New Chicago*. DeKalb: Northern Illinois University Press.

Stark, Rodney. 2001. *One True God: Historical Consequences of Monotheism*. Princeton, NJ: Princeton University Press.

Stone, Gregory P. 1954. "City Shoppers and Urban Identification: Observations on the Social Psychology of City Life." *American Journal of Sociology* 60: 36–45.

———. 1981. "Sport as a Community Representation." In Gunther R. F. Luschen and George H. Sage, eds., *Handbook of Social Science of Sport*. Champaign, IL: Stipes.

Stone, John, and Stephen Mennell, eds. 1980. *Alexis de Tocqueville: On Democracy, Revolution, and Society*. Chicago: University of Chicago Press.

Stout, Glenn, ed. 2003. *Impossible Dreams: A Red Sox Collection*. Boston: Houghton Mifflin.

Stout, Glenn, and Richard A. Johnson. 2004. *Red Sox Century: One Hundred Years of Red Sox Baseball*. Boston: Houghton Mifflin.

Strauss, Anselm L. 1969. *Mirrors and Masks: The Search for Identity*. San Francisco: Sociology Press.

———. 1976. *Images of the American City*. New Brunswick, NJ: Transaction Books.

Suttles, Gerald D. 1968. *The Social Order of the Slum*. Chicago: University of Chicago Press.

———. 1972. *The Social Construction of Communities*. Chicago: University of Chicago Press.

———. 1984. "The Cumulative Texture of Local Urban Culture." *American Journal of Sociology* 90: 283–304.

Suvantola, Jaakko. 2002. *Tourists' Experience of Place*. Burlington, VT: Ashgate.

Swidler, Ann. 1986. "Culture in Action: Symbols and Strategies." *American Sociological Review* 51: 273–86.

———. 2001. *Talk of Love: How Culture Matters*. Chicago: University of Chicago Press.

Taylor, Charles. 1991. *The Ethics of Authenticity*. Cambridge, MA: Harvard University Press.

Tocqueville, Alexis de. 1945. *Democracy in America*. New York: Vintage Books.

Trilling, Lionel. 1972. *Sincerity and Authenticity*. Cambridge, MA: Harvard University Press.

Tuan, Yi-Fu. 1977. *Space and Place: The Perspective of Experience*. Minneapolis: University of Minnesota Press.

———. 1978. "Sacred Space: Exploration of an Idea." In Karl W. Butzer, ed., *Dimensions of Human Geography: Essays on Some Familiar and Neglected Themes*. Chicago: University of Chicago Press.

Turner, Victor, and Edward M. Bruner, eds. 1986. *The Anthropology of Experience*. Urbana: University of Illinois Press.

Turner, Victor, and Edith L. B. Turner. 1978. *Image and Pilgrimage in Christian Culture: Anthropological Perspectives*. Oxford, UK: Blackwell.

Veblen, Thorstein. 1899. *The Theory of the Leisure Class*. New York: Macmillan.

Voigt, David Quentin. 1983. *American Baseball*. University Park: Pennsylvania State University Press.

Walton, John. 2001. *Storied Land: Community and Memory in Monterey*. Berkeley: University of California Press.

Warner, R. Stephen. 1993. "Work in Progress toward a New Paradigm for the Sociological Study of Religion in the United States." *American Journal of Sociology* 98: 1044–93.

Wheaton, Belinda, and Becky Beal. 2003. "Keeping It Real: Subcultural Media and the Discourse of Authenticity in Alternative Sport." *International Review for the Sociology of Sport* 38: 155–76.

White, G. Edward. 1996. *Creating the National Pastime: Baseball Transforms Itself, 1903–1953*. Princeton, NJ: Princeton University Press.

Whyte, William Foote. 1943. *Street Corner Society*. Chicago: University of Chicago Press.

Wilcox, Ralph C. 2003. *Sporting Dystopias: The Making and Meaning of Urban Sport Cultures*. Albany: State University of New York Press.

Wirth, Louis. 1938. "Urbanism as a Way of Life." *American Journal of Sociology* 44: 1–24.

Wohl, R. Richard, and Anselm L. Strauss. 1958. "Symbolic Representation and the Urban Milieu." *American Journal of Sociology* 63: 523–32.

Wuthnow, Robert. 1987. *Meaning and Moral Order: Explorations in Cultural Analysis*. Berkeley: University of California Press.

Zaitzevsky, Cynthia. 1982. *Frederick Law Olmsted and the Boston Park System*. Cambridge, MA: Harvard University Press.

Zepp, Ira G., Jr. 1997. *The New Religious Image of Urban America: The Shopping Mall as Ceremonial Center*. Niwot: University Press of Colorado.

Zerubavel, Eviatar. 1996. "Social Memories: Steps to a Sociology of the Past." *Qualitative Sociology* 19: 283–99.

Zukin, Sharon. 1991. *Landscapes of Power: From Detroit to Disney World*. Berkeley: University of California Press.

INDEX

ABOUT THE AUTHOR

Michael Ian Borer is Assistant Professor of Sociology and Urban Studies at Furman University, where he teaches courses on urban communities, religion, and sociological theory.

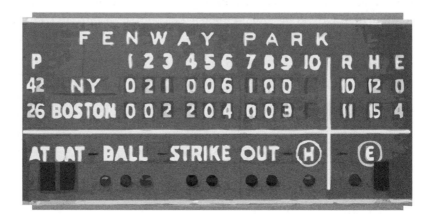